TER   Y

Implementing Total Quality Management

To Amelia Emma

Implementing Total Quality Management

LESLEY & MALCOLM MUNRO-FAURE

FINANCIAL TIMES
PITMAN PUBLISHING

Pitman Publishing
128 Long Acre, London WC2E 9AN

A Division of Longman Group UK Limited

First published in 1992
Reprinted 1992 (three times), 1993 (three times)

© Longman Group UK Limited 1992

British Library Cataloguing in Publication Data
A CIP catalogue record for this book can be obtained
from the British Library

ISBN 0 273 03848 6 ✓

Phototypeset in Linotron Times Roman by
Northern Phototypesetting Co. Ltd, Bolton
Printed and bound in Great Britain by
Biddles Ltd, Guildford and King's Lynn

CONTENTS

FOREWORD

Quality Management was first developed in the manufacturing industry. Managers sought to provide customers with products conforming to pre-defined specifications. A growing realisation that applying Quality Management disciplines to all activities would result in considerably improved efficiency led to the development of Total Quality Management (TQM). TQM is fast becoming the business philosophy of the 1990s. It is not just about cost cutting; it is about improving company performance. TQM requires a radical rethink of how every operation within any business is performed. The principle of TQM is to ensure all activities contribute towards achieving the corporate objectives and are completed 'right first time'.

Many managers in service and manufacturing businesses recognise the profitable impact Quality Management methods have on competitiveness and customer satisfaction. This has fuelled a rapidly growing interest in the subject.

This book explains how to implement TQM using a powerful six step approach and describes the results achieved by organisations which have already implemented a TQM programme. A case study is used as a means of reinforcing significant points.

The practical guidance in this book is an invaluable aid to managers. It will enable them to understand the benefits available from TQM, and how to implement a TQM programme.

Roger Young
Director General of the British Institute of Management

PREFACE

TQM can seem confusing because of all the jargon and the apparent difficulty of finding hard evidence to demonstrate the benefits of implementing a programme of continuous quality improvement. In fact the broad concepts are quite straightforward and logical.

The objective of Total Quality Management is to satisfy customer requirements as efficiently and profitably as possible. This means that there is a requirement to continuously improve performance as fast as developments allow. This is why the commitment to TQM must be both absolute, and ongoing.

In a total quality environment all employees must strive to:

 (i) do the right things. This means that only activities that help a business to satisfy the requirements of their customers are acceptable. Other activities should be analysed and, if they are unnecessary, discontinued.

 (ii) do things right. This means that all activities should be performed correctly, so that the output from the activity conforms to the requirements of the customer.

(iii) do things right first time, every time. If this can be achieved, then no more money should be wasted on checking and scrapping output or correcting errors. This type of environment is based on the concept of preventing errors arising in the first place.

These three requirements are captured in the expression:

'Do the right things right, first time, every time.'

How can you introduce a TQM environment?

Many, but not all, organisations operate procedures to ensure that the quality of their output will be acceptable to their customers. This is the starting point for a Total Quality environment.

The next steps involve ensuring that errors are prevented and the business focuses only on activities that satisfy the requirements of their customers.

Introducing a TQM environment is hard work and it takes the absolute commitment of everyone – especially senior management – to achieve. It also takes a considerable amount of planning.

We have written this book to help managers to understand the concepts underlying TQM and the significant benefits it can bring; and to enable them to implement continuous quality improvement in any organisation that is determined to succeed.

We are very grateful to the many friends and colleagues who have helped us to make this book come to life. In particular, we would like to thank the following for enthusiastically contributing time and effort to explain their experiences in implementing TQM: Joe Goasdoué of ICL; Karen Evans and Neil Clackett of the Doncaster Royal Infirmary and Montagu Hospital National Health Service Trust; David Owen and Roger Cliffe of the TSB Bank plc; Raj Nadarajah and Lance Arrington of Philip Crosby Associates, Inc.

Above all, we would like to thank Ted Bones for his patience, commitment, enthusiasm and support over many years.

INTRODUCTION

'Total Quality Management' (TQM) is a proven, systematic approach to the planning and management of activities. It can be successfully applied to any type of organisation.

The fundamental concepts behind TQM are very simple:

(i) A successful business relies on making profitable sales to its customers. A business will only retain the support of its existing customer base and attract new customers if it produces output (whether products or services) which conforms to the requirements of its customers.

(ii) A business will only be able to satisfy the requirements of its customers if it:

(a) identifies the requirements of its customers; and

(b) produces output which conforms to those requirements.

(iii) A business will be able to maximise profits only if it produces its output efficiently. In order to do this, a business must direct all its activities towards producing the necessary output at minimum cost. This may be achieved by:

(a) ensuring the design process results in output which conforms to customer requirements; and can be produced cost effectively.

(b) minimising inefficiencies when producing services or products, such as waste and rework.

(c) reviewing all activities to ensure they are directed at satisfying the requirements of external customers. If they are not, then consideration should be given to ceasing those activities.

Most managers are shocked by the cost of the errors and waste which they have previously accepted as 'normal'. By focusing on eliminating this burden, an organisation can significantly improve its performance.

Three companies which have made significant steps towards implementing TQM demonstrate the magnitude of the problem:

Company	*Quality costs*
● ICL	£160 million in 1987
● Otis Elevator European Transcontinental Operations	29 per cent of sales prior to 1987
● National Westminster Bank PLC	25 per cent of operating costs in 1988

This level of cost burden is typical of much of industry today; similar results can be found in almost any organisation.

It is only possible to develop a TQM environment with the absolute commitment of management and all employees; but it can yield significant competitive advantage to any business which is prepared to invest the necessary time and effort to succeed.

The organisation needs to be flexible and adaptable, continuously seeking to improve. This can only be achieved within a strong framework which responds to change whilst retaining effective control over operations. As a consequence there are a number of key elements which help management to produce a TQM environment:

(i)   a strong framework to retain order and control;
(ii) the continuous striving for improvement; and
(iii) the adaptability to change to ensure the organisation responds to customer requirements.

Fig i illustrates the components which help to produce a successful TQM environment.

This book explains how management can introduce a TQM environment based on a wealth of practical experience. By following a logical progression, readers are introduced to:

1 Total Quality Management – A Quality Revolution
This explains the significance of TQM as a business management tool.

2 Know Your Customers
The key to implementing TQM is to understand the needs of the customers, and the way the organisation meets those needs.

3 Quality Costs
The costs incurred through not meeting the real requirements of customers first time can be enormous. It is only by understanding how these

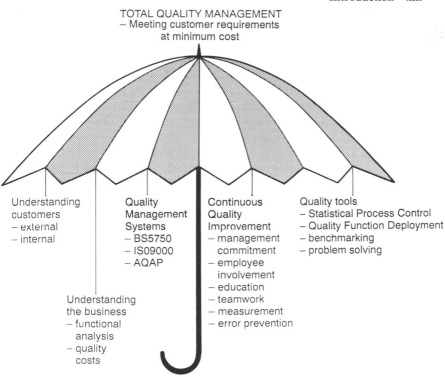

TOTAL QUALITY MANAGEMENT
– Meeting customer requirements
at minimum cost

Understanding
customers
– external
– internal

Quality
Management
Systems
– BS5750
– ISO9000
– AQAP

Continuous
Quality
Improvement
– management
  commitment
– employee
  involvement
– education
– teamwork
– measurement
– error prevention

Quality tools
– Statistical Process Control
– Quality Function Deployment
– benchmarking
– problem solving

Understanding
the business
– functional
  analysis
– quality
  costs

Figure (i) Components of Total Quality Management

costs are calculated that a business can focus attention on the most significant areas for action.

4 Functional Analysis
The tremendous opportunities for improving efficiency which may be available from organising the business so that it is really customer-oriented.

5 A Quality Management System
The first step involves developing a strong management framework to ensure customer requirements are fully defined, understood, and met by the organisation. This Quality Management System forms the essential foundation on which a programme of continuous quality improvement can be built.

6 A story of continuous quality improvement
It is then necessary to harness the skills of the whole work-force to

examine every activity carried out by the organisation and identify opportunities for improvement, by following a six step approach:

1. Planning
2. Understanding customers
3. Understanding quality costs
4. Quality awareness
5. Measurement of performance
6. Prevention of errors

7 Quality Tools

A wide range of tools and techniques are available to assist management in the implementation of TQM. These help organisations to improve performance in the following key areas:

- Statistical Process Control – manage processes.
- Benchmarking – achieve world class performance.
- Quality Function Deployment – apply customer requirements to product design.
- Quality Awards – understand current best practice.
- Teamwork for quality – resolve problems.

8 Problem solving

A fundamental requirement for continuous quality improvement is a commitment to eliminate all problems which prevent individuals from performing activities right first time.

9 Success stories

By analysing the application of TQM across a broad range of organisations it is possible to identify:

(i)   the significant benefits from TQM;
(ii) successful approaches and pitfalls; and
(iii) how TQM can be applied to specific industries.

10 What can we learn from the Quality gurus?

Much can be learnt from studying the philosophies and methods of the 'Quality gurus', but it is important to adopt an approach which suits each individual organisation, and to thoroughly research and plan the implementation to ensure the organisation takes 'ownership' of the process.

Total Quality Management is fundamental to the continued success of any organisation. By following the approach outlined in this book, management will be able to understand the concepts underlying TQM and the significant benefits it can bring. The comprehensive practical advice will enable management to implement the process of continuous quality improvement successfully in any organisation which is determined to succeed.

1 TOTAL QUALITY MANAGEMENT – A QUALITY REVOLUTION

THE QUALITY CONCEPT

Quality is one of the most misunderstood issues in business today, and yet it is central to the survival of even the largest organisation. Quality is defined by customers. First of all, you agree what the customer wants (the customer's requirements). Then you produce exactly what is wanted within the agreed timeframe, at minimum cost. The perspective of the customer is not always effectively addressed by western companies. In many cases, Japanese competitors have gained an edge over their western counterparts because they understand the need to satisfy the requirements of their customers. The markets for home audio and video are two cases in point: car and microchip manufacturing are examples where western businesses are coming under increasing pressure.

There is only one key focal point for businesses in the world today: *the customer*.

Only businesses which focus on the requirements of their customers will survive into the future. This has been the driving force behind the leading elements in Japanese industry since the Second World War. Industry in the USA, Germany, and latterly the UK are rapidly recognising the importance of this shift in focus and are responding. In some cases the response has been too little and too late. Adopting a strict customer focus may well emerge as the most successful strategy for remaining competitive in the face of the opening of the Single European Market.

Quality is probably the best way of assuring customer loyalty, the best defence against foreign competition and the only way to secure continuous growth and profits in difficult market conditions.

The Quality concept is not difficult to understand, but it does require a new focus of attention from everyone involved in business.

The evolution of Quality

The concept has grown a long way since the early disciples defined Quality as 'producing output in conformance to customer requirements'. The evolutionary path has passed through two generations already, and leading edge industries are pioneering third and fourth generations.

This evolution demonstrates how businesses are increasingly understanding and responding to the requirements of their customers. The building blocks of a Total Quality environment are illustrated in Fig. 1.1.

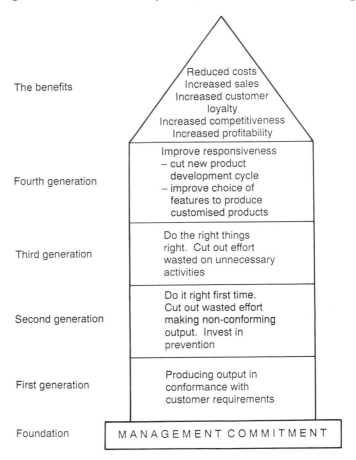

The benefits

Reduced costs
Increased sales
Increased customer
loyalty
Increased competitiveness
Increased profitability

Fourth generation

Improve responsiveness
– cut new product
development cycle
– improve choice of
features to produce
customised products

Third generation

Do the right things
right. Cut out effort
wasted on unnecessary
activities

Second generation

Do it right first time.
Cut out wasted effort
making non-conforming
output. Invest in
prevention

First generation

Producing output in
conformance with
customer requirements

Foundation

MANAGEMENT COMMITMENT

Figure 1.1 The quality building blocks

(i)   The first generation is to ensure the requirements of every customer are understood and are met. This marks the realisation that customers will only accept output (whether a product or service) that meets their requirements. Any output that does not conform will be rejected. This leads to dissatisfied customers and additional costs for the organisation. This stage is reached by ensuring a management system exists to identify customer requirements and ensure those requirements are consistently met. Ensuring conformance to requirements may initially be achieved by checking and reworking/ replacing any non-conforming output before releasing it to a customer.

In order to reach this level, many organisations implement a Quality Management System based on the guidelines in BS5750/ ISO9000. Having initially been of particular interest to manufacturing organisations, this standard is now being adopted in such service industries as accountancy and legal firms.

(ii) The next generation aims to 'do it right first time, every time'. The act of producing defective output is immensely wasteful in terms of time and money. By implementing preventive measures, companies are able to monitor processes and prevent errors arising in the first place.

(iii) The third generation recognises that some activities are unnecessary. By analysing the functions undertaken by an organisation (functional analysis), it is possible to identify these operations. Internal meetings and many of the internal reports which are produced may be discontinued, so freeing up valuable time and money.

(iv) The second and third generations of quality awareness have focused on producing conforming output more efficiently. The fourth generation focuses on the twin objectives of improving product responsiveness; and improving the efficiency of the product development process.

The objective of the fourth generation is to shorten the time taken, and costs incurred in bringing new products to the market. Being the first to the market with a new product frequently yields a significant competitive advantage. An example of the techniques being developed to achieve this objective is Quality Function Deployment (QFD). This methodology was developed originally at the Mitsubishi Kobe shipyard. QFD brings marketing, design and manufacturing personnel together to determine customer needs and translate them into design specifications and manufacturing processes efficiently and effectively.

Each of these evolutionary steps marks a closer link between the producer and the customer. By developing this link the producer is able to strengthen its foundations. Ignoring the importance of the link will lead to extinction.

Do management recognise Quality as one of the key competitive issues of the 1990s?

The 1990 International Manufacturing Futures Survey conducted jointly by Boston University, INSEAD (the European Institute for Business Administration), and Waseda University in Japan produced an intriguing insight into current management thinking. This survey of manufacturing executives from over 500 large manufacturing businesses drawn from Europe, the USA and Japan sheds some light on how factories may develop in the future.

Earlier reports by the same institutes have described the spread of the quality revolution from Japan (in the 1970s) to the USA in the 1980s and more recently to Europe. Improving product quality remains a key priority for management, but is increasingly becoming a qualification for entry into a market rather than a means to separate competitors.

The five key competitive priorities in the next five years have been identified as:

Europe	*Japan*	*United States*
Conformance quality	Reliable products	Conformance quality
Dependable delivery	Dependable delivery	Dependable delivery
Reliable products	Rapid design changes	Reliable products
High performance	Conformance quality	High performance
Fast delivery	Product customisation	Price competition

Respondents identified these categories having been asked to rank fifteen possible competitive priorities.

Although each of the regions is trying to develop more integrated factories producing improved quality goods, they differ in their focus. US manufacturers are focusing on producing high quality output at a reasonable price; Japanese manufacturers are developing systems allowing a continuing stream of new customised designs; and European manufacturers are streamlining operations to take advantage of the single European market and elsewhere.

The same respondents were asked to identify the five activities which provided the highest pay off in the past two years, see below.

Europe	Japan	United States
Training of supervisors, management and workers	Developing new processes for old products	Inter-functional work teams
Manufacturing reorganisation	Developing new processes for new products	Manufacturing reorganisation
Linking manufacturing to business strategy	Quality circles	Statistical process control
Quality function deployment	Computer-aided design	Linking manufacturing to business strategy
Developing new processes for new products	Quality function deployment	Just in time

Table 1.1 Effectiveness of activities 1988–89: The five activities yielding the highest pay off.
Source: Miller, J. G., de Meyer, A., Nakane, J., Kim, J. S., Kurosa, S., and Ferdows, K., 1992, *Factories for the Future*, in Miller, J. G., de Meyer, A. and Nakane, J., Benchmarking Global Operations, Business One, Irwin, Illinois.

To develop a Quality strategy and ensure this is a key part of the overall business strategy, it is important to understand Quality, what it means, how it developed and possible future developments.

WHAT IS QUALITY?

The term 'Quality' has suffered over the years by being used to describe attributes such as beauty, goodness, expensiveness, freshness and, above all, luxury. So, a car might be described as a 'Quality car' when, in reality, it is an expensive or luxurious car. Cloth might be described as a 'Quality cloth' when it is really an 'all wool' cloth, or a cloth that has a high density of threads.

All this makes Quality appear a very difficult concept to understand and almost impossible to manage. How can you manage something which is so imprecise and means so many things!

Before Quality can be planned and managed it must be defined more precisely and meaningfully.

Quality is now defined by many companies as total conformance to requirements; these requirements are the total customer requirement, not just a product or service specification.

This broad, far-reaching application of Quality to every activity has taken many years to develop and is a long way from where Quality first began . . .

THE DEVELOPMENT OF QUALITY – AN OBJECTIVE STANDARD

Following the Second World War, manufacturing industry began to develop a specific meaning for Quality. Driven by the need to meet customer demands for products which did what they claimed, Quality began to mean the design and manufacture of a product which met customer specifications and expectations. This was driven in Japan by the need to rebuild its manufacturing industry and in Europe and the USA primarily by the armed forces with their need for conforming equipment which allowed them to fulfil their military role.

The manufacturing industries adopted the term Quality to mean 'conformance to product requirements', whether these requirements were a stated specification or a perceived customer need. Industry was moving towards a philosophy that a product should unfailingly do what the customer needed and wanted it to do.

By adopting this definition of Quality, management could measure, assess and improve their Quality performance. Quality became an objective concept. It was something that the whole workforce could understand and measure, and for which they could accept responsibility. To achieve this product conformance companies introduced the concepts of:

(i)   Quality assurance; and
(ii) Quality control.

Quality control and Quality assurance

Quality control is a system of activities designed to assess the quality of product or service supplied to a customer. If a product does not conform to requirements, it is reworked, scrapped or downgraded. Quality control typically employs test inspection and repair techniques. Quality control is designed to answer the question: 'Have we done the job in accordance with the requirements?'

Quality assurance is a management system designed to control the activities at all stages (product design; production; delivery and service), to prevent quality problems and ensure only conforming products reach the customer. The key features of an effective quality assurance system are:

(i) An effective quality management system (QMS);
(ii) Periodic audit of the operation of the system to ensure it is effective; and
(iii) Periodic review of the system to ensure it continually meets the changing requirements imposed on it.

QUALITY SYSTEM STANDARDS

A number of Quality Management System standards have been developed in the UK and overseas to provide an objective basis for assessing a company's ability to ensure the conformance of goods and services to specification. The first standards used in the UK were the Defence Standard 05–21 series. These were developed by the Ministry of Defence and introduced in the 1960s to improve the quality of equipment supplied to the armed forces and reduce the risk of equipment failure in the field. The Ministry of Defence required its suppliers to conform to this series of standards and employed auditors to assess compliance with the standard. During the 1980s these standards were replaced by the North Atlantic Treaty Organisation Allied Quality Assurance Publication (NATO AQAP) equivalents.

The use of formal Quality System standards then spread to other industries where the risks of equipment failure were high, particularly where safety was an issue. The nuclear industry, where BS5882 defines the Quality System standard, and the process plant industries are two early examples.

As the benefits associated with formal Quality Systems became apparent, the need arose for a Quality System standard to apply throughout industry. This requirement was met with the introduction of BS5750 in 1979. At the start, only a relatively small number of companies sought approval under this standard. These were mainly manufacturing companies.

In order to gain wider adoption of Quality management techniques, the Government introduced an initiative to publicise the importance of Quality, and provided grants to companies to help implement Quality systems. This initiative, together with a greater awareness of the benefits arising from Quality Management systems, led to an increase in the number of approved organisations both within the manufacturing and service sectors. In 1987 a number of key nations ratified an agreement recognising an International Quality System standard, the ISO9000 series. This is a direct equivalent of BS5750 (1987) and is widely recognised throughout the world. The ISO9000 series is the leading international quality system standard today.

The benefits of an effective Quality Management System

A Quality Management System (QMS) is the formal management system which defines the Quality environment within a business. A QMS can be developed for every type of business, whether service or manufacturing, high technology or traditional. Increasingly customers are seeking assurance from their suppliers that they operate a Quality Management System to provide product assurance. The independent approval of a company's QMS to an internationally recognised standard, such as ISO9000, demonstrates that a company takes its customers' requirements seriously and has implemented a system which can recognise and ensure conformance to those requirements.

TOTAL QUALITY MANAGEMENT – A QUALITY REVOLUTION

'Quality' is not just concerned with whether or not a product or service meets the claims made for it. Today's Quality is much more than this. The modern concept of Quality embraces how the company meets all its customer's requirements including how they are greeted on the telephone; the speed with which sales staff respond to a request for a quotation; having new products and services when required and even ensuring the invoice is correct!

Every contact with the customer, on every occasion, at every level builds a picture of the sort of company with which a customer is doing business. Of course any product or service supplied has to meet its requirements; but this is the beginning – not the end – of the quest for a Total Quality Organisation!

A Quality Management System designed to conform to the Quality system standards is the starting point for Total Quality Management. Quality System standards define the control measures required to help ensure the finished product or service conforms to the customer's requirements. However, the standards are not primarily concerned with achieving conformance to requirements in the most efficient or cost effective manner. Nor do they focus on non-product related activities.

The realisation that applying Quality disciplines to all activities would result in a more efficient and competitive company led to the evolution of Total Quality Management (TQM). The aim of TQM is to ensure that each activity contributes to achieving the key objectives of the business, and is carried out efficiently. The basic philosophy of Total Quality is ' do the right things right first time'.

To succeed in today's competitive marketplace a company must supply products and services in accordance with the customer's requirements and at minimum cost. To achieve this, the company must understand its role in the marketplace, organise itself to fulfil that role and ensure all employees understand, and are committed to fulfilling, the customer's requirements first time every time, whatever task is being performed.

TQM generally requires a change in how a company operates. It requires quality to be the first priority of every employee and for their efforts to be focused on the prevention of errors. It is no longer sufficient to rely on the detection and correction of errors. These are a costly, wasteful approach to assuring quality, and are now largely redundant. Every department, every activity, every person at every level, starting at the top of the organisation, must be wholly committed to the TQM philosophy.

Why does everyone need to be involved?

TQM requires a change in the basic philosophy of everyone in the company, especially management. In the past we have generally followed the principles of management proposed by Taylor. Under this regime, the manager's role is to plan, organise, direct and solve problems. The worker's role is to carry out tasks as directed by the managers.

TQM requires us to recognise the contributions which every employee can make and to harness the skills and enthusiasm of everyone in the business. To achieve this individuals must be provided with the skills, tools and authority to investigate problems and introduce improvements. Managers must demonstrate that they believe their employees can make an important contribution to managing the business and must create an open atmosphere to allow this to happen. Teamwork will be the key to the successful businesses of the 1990s and beyond. This is a radical change. It will only happen if it is actively and passionately led from the top and involves everyone. This radical change cannot happen overnight and it is unlikely to be painless, unless it is carefully managed.

Customer requirements

The customer's perception of his supplier is formed partly on the basis of the product or service which he receives and partly on the day-to-day contact he has with the company. The receptionist who answers telephone calls, the security people who control access to the site, and the accounts person who sends out the invoice can all have a direct and important influence on customers. All these people must be involved in Total Quality; in meeting the customer requirements; in creating a world-class company.

The ability to meet these external customer requirements relies on a series of often complex internal supplier-customer links. The sales office which sends out a quotation is the customer of the salesperson who provides the input for the quote. The person who packs the goods is the customer of the person who provides the goods, the person who provides the delivery note and the person who provides the packaging material. A breakdown in any one of these internal chains may result in an error which will affect the service received by the external customer.

TQM must therefore involve all the internal customer-supplier chains to ensure external customers only receive conforming goods or services. No one is exempt from Total Quality.

Eliminating errors

We have already stated that the role of TQM is to satisfy the internal and external customers and, through prevention, to eliminate the causes of error. It is estimated that the costs of not getting the right things right first time, the non-conformance costs, can amount to 25 per cent of turnover. Eliminating this unnecessary burden will enable companies to improve profitability in the short term and enhance competitiveness in the longer term.

Non-conformance costs may arise in any department. All departments spend some time doing unnecessary activities, correcting their own mistakes or rectifying other people's errors. Consequently all departments are open to Quality Improvement; no one is exempt.

The objective of TQM is continuously to improve Quality by eliminating non-conformance in every activity throughout the company. Everyone, starting with management, is encouraged to refuse to accept the inevitability of error and to concentrate on preventing errors occurring in the first place. Total Quality leads the company towards new attitudes. Starting with senior management and working down through every layer of the organisation and across every function, Total Quality involves everyone and influences the performance of the whole business.

The benefits which can accrue from the successful implementation of TQM are enormous. Improved customer satisfaction; elimination of errors and waste; reduced operating costs; increased motivation and commitment of employees; improved customer satisfaction; increased profitability and competitiveness: indeed the very survival of the company itself may be at stake.

Adopting a TQM approach to Quality has led companies to use a new set of definitions for Quality; these include:

Continuing pursuit of perfection by the company as a whole
(Sieger Ltd)

Search for excellence and customer satisfaction
(Texas Instruments Ltd)

Quality links everyone in a chain of effort to achieve customer satisfaction
(Ind Coope Burton Brewery Ltd)

Quality means total customer satisfaction
(RHP Bearings)

Quality means products and services which perform exactly to customer requirements
(Cossor Electronics)

Products and services which fully meet the internal and external customer requirements, first time, on time, every time
(ICL)

(Definitions taken from DTI booklet, 'The Case for Quality', published as part of '*The Enterprise Initiative*').

In its initial stages Total Quality often focuses on doing all activities right first time. As TQM progresses the company then begins to recognise that not all the activities it carries out are necessary; and that customer satisfaction could be increased, or the cost of non-conformance reduced, by carrying out different activities. Companies then look critically at the activities they perform to identify those which are either unnecessary, inadequately focused, or inadequately performed. These are then subjected to an improvement programme, or discontinued.

QUALITY COSTS – A DRIVING FORCE

Costs are inevitably incurred ensuring that products or services meet the customer's requirements. These are the Quality related costs. An understanding of Quality costs is essential for any business. The costs associated with the mismanagement of Quality (the costs of non-conformance) are often large; are non-productive; and are avoidable through the implementation of TQM. Quality costs can amount to 25 per cent of company turnover.

In most companies, the majority of Quality related costs are incurred putting things right after they have gone wrong. These are the costs associated with failure to achieve conformance to requirements and are generally known as the costs of non-conformance (CONC). Many companies are already aware of the product related CONC, such as warranty, scrap and rework, but ignore the CONC associated with, for example, administration, activities or excessive debtor days. The collection of CONC across the company often acts as a catalyst to convince management to implement a company wide Total Quality programme.

Companies which suffer a high CONC generally also support extensive appraisal activities. The output from processes is checked at many stages in production. This appraisal activity and its associated cost is only necessary because the system produces so many errors. These have to be found and corrected. Once the CONC is identified and the causes of failure are eliminated by the introduction of prevention activities; then an extensive appraisal activity is no longer required.

Most companies find that a relatively small investment in prevention activities (such as training, calibration, equipment maintenance and planning) results in the reduction of both the failure and the appraisal costs.

Eliminating the CONC can increase profitability and improve the service provided to customers. These are very important driving forces behind TQM.

SUMMARY – AND THE FUTURE

In today's market companies need continually to provide their customers with what they want. They must be innovative and quick to the market with new products, and do all this at minimum cost. Quality has a vital role in achieving all these objectives. It is only through understanding external customer requirements, organising the company and harnessing the skills of every employee to satisfy these requirements that companies will continue to be successful.

Industry in the UK has generally come to recognise the importance of Quality and is starting to implement TQM initiatives by meeting the customer's requirements first time every time. Japanese industry is moving towards another generation of satisfying customer requirements. They see the way forward as:

(i)   reducing the time it takes to bring new products to the market; and
(ii) improving manufacturing flexibility to encompass short run production. This will enable them to provide a rapid response to customer orders.

Both these developments will improve responsiveness to their customers' requirements. Once again they may be able to pull ahead of their western competitors, unless they respond to this threat. The competitive advantage available to companies which can shorten product development cycles is immense, and illustrated by the results of recent work in America by the independent consultant Donald Reinerstein. He reported in a recent book (*Developing Products in Half the Time*, published by Chapman and Hall) that in high growth markets with product life cycles of some five years, a delay in launching a product of only six months would cut its expected lifetime profits by a third. This is a substantial CONC and seems certain to be the next phase of the Total Quality revolution.

How can businesses develop a leading edge Total Quality Culture?

Every organisation should determine whether or not it operates Total Quality Management. In most cases, companies operate some of the elements that make up TQM, but most companies have room for improvement. By instituting a process of Continuous Quality Improvement, businesses may:

Fundamental requirement	Possible actions
1. Know your customers (i) who they are; (ii) their current needs; (iii) their future requirements; and (iv) respond to changing customer needs.	1. Customer surveys 2. Functional analysis 3. Quality cost analysis 4. Quality function deployment
2. Know your competitors	1. Customer surveys 2. Competitor analysis 3. Benchmarking
3. Know your cost of non-conformance	1. Quality cost analysis 2. Functional analysis
4. Measure your performance against key customer driven parameters	1. Customer surveys 2. Competitor analysis 3. Benchmarking
5. Make sure each employee understands and commits himself to the Quality objectives of the business	1. Functional analysis 2. Education and training 3. Communication
6. Management commitment to continuous improvement of Quality within the business	1. Quality cost analysis 2. Functional analysis 3. Education and training 4. Communication
7. Define the purpose of each department and activity in terms of satisfying external or internal customer requirements	1. Functional analysis
8. Enable employees to fulfil their commitment to Quality by influencing the programme of continuous improvement	1. Education and training 2. Communication 3. Corrective Action Task Force, Corrective Action Groups 4. Error Cause Removal schemes 5. Problem solving 6. Statistical Process Control 7. Recognition of performance
9. Replace inspection and correction techniques to control the Quality of output with preventive actions	1. Quality cost analysis 2. Functional analysis 3. Quality management system 4. Corrective action systems
10. Never accept non-conforming output in the form of product or services for external or internal customers	1. Quality cost analysis 2. Functional analysis 3. Education and training 4. Communication
11. Plan effectively before undertaking actions	1. Quality Improvement Team

Figure 1.2   The fundamental requirements of Total Quality Management

- improve competitiveness and profitability;
- increase customer satisfaction;
- reduce the costs of non-conformance; and
- increase employee motivation.

The fundamental requirements of a Total Quality Culture arc illustrated in Fig. 1.2, together with details of methods to help achieve these objectives. This constitutes an outline of the action plan necessary for companies that want to achieve a Total Quality Culture.

KNOW YOUR CUSTOMERS

WHO ARE YOUR CUSTOMERS?

A supplier/customer relationship is forged whenever a business purchases goods or services from another and each time a person asks another to undertake an activity. These examples illustrate the two principal categories of customer, namely:

(i) *external customers*. These are the ones who pay your bills! Businesses only continue to survive because of their ability to meet the requirements of their external customers.

(ii) *internal customers*. Each transaction in a large business is the result of a number of internal supplier/customer relationships. The sales team concludes the sale; it specifies the characteristics required to the production team; the delivery team arranges for it to be delivered; and the finance team renders the invoice for the transaction. Each of these teams relies on inputs from their colleagues to enable them to complete their process right first time. It is only by satisfying the (internal) requirements for each of these processes that the requirements of the external customer can be met.

This chapter describes how external customer requirements can be identified accurately, and how the operation of internal processes can be improved so that external customer requirements are met at the first attempt, every time.

WHO ARE YOUR EXTERNAL CUSTOMERS?

All companies should know the names of their principal customers. Their purchasing departments are likely to be the focal points for component, material and product purchases. But do you know who else within these businesses might assess your performance against their requirements for you as a supplier?

If the business is quality driven then their quality team might be monitoring the quality of the goods you supply to them, or the response times for service call-outs. If they are dissatisfied with your performance, they are likely to look for another supplier. Their goods inwards department may have requirements about when and how goods should be delivered. Their finance department will have requirements concerning the address and content of your invoice. Liaison with their marketing team might even yield an opportunity for the joint development of products to your mutual advantage.

Each of these customers may influence the decision to purchase goods or services from you. It is important to understand the requirements of all the groups within your customer's organisation who influence their purchasing decision. Only then will you be able to try and satisfy their requirements.

WHAT DO YOUR EXTERNAL CUSTOMERS REALLY WANT FROM YOUR BUSINESS?

External customers may have significantly different requirements to the ones you might expect. For example, a professional firm of lawyers or accountants which is asked to advise a client about appropriate locations for a new headquarters might believe that the client only requires a one-off report, provided it is comprehensive, well-written and technically competent. However, the client might really want a continuous flow of advice which responds to the changing demands which surface as its business requirements become fully recognised. The report is only one element in the service the customer really wants; but he will settle for that unless he can find a more responsive service elsewhere.

Meeting the external customer's requirements requires two major steps:

(i) identify the external customer's requirements; and
(ii) ensure internal processes result in meeting external customer requirements at minimum cost.

There are a number of means to obtain the necessary information to enable you to complete these steps. The following table outlines an effective, practical approach:

Objective	Activity
Identify the requirements of your external customers	1. Identify the existing products and services you agree to provide to customers. (a) What services do you provide to your customers? (b) Do you enter into an agreement with all your customers specifying the services you will provide, using standard terms of trade, an engagement letter or contract? (c) If not, how do you know what your customers expect from you?
	2. How do your customers perceive the value of your products and services compared to those available from your competitors? Information to answer this can be obtained from a number of sources: (a) Customer surveys (b) Competitor analysis (c) Complaints log (d) Trade surveys
	3. Can you improve the products or services you provide to customers? Consider using the following techniques: (a) Customer surveys (b) Competitor analysis (c) Benchmarking (d) Quality Function Deployment (e) Marketing activities
Ensure internal processes result in meeting external customer requirements at minimum cost.	The key means for achieving this are: 1. Functional analysis 2. Continuous Quality Improvement 3. Quality cost analysis

Table 2.1 The two step approach to meeting external customer requirements

'Hard' and 'soft' customer requirements

Customer requirements may be divided into two key categories:

(i) 'Hard' requirements: those requirements which must be met by the deliverable product or service. They are often specified in the contract and may include some, or all, of the following:

   (a) Size, weight, colour, texture and taste;
   (b) Functions, reliability and facilities required;
   (c) Packaging, labelling, delivery times and methods;
   (d) Cost and payment arrangements;
   (e) Customer support required; and
   (f) Response times to failures.

   These are the basic requirements for each product or service. They are the minimum customer requirements which must be met if a product is to be considered satisfactory.

(ii) 'Soft' requirements: relate to the perception given to the customer of the sort of company they are doing business with. These factors convey a message to customers about whether they are welcome or just a nuisance. Are they kept waiting? This indicates to a customer that you believe your time is more valuable than theirs; IT IS NOT! It is the little things that show you really care for your customers, and the effort you take will generally be well received. Examples of factors which may influence this impression may include:

   (a) *Telephone answering*: How easy is it to get through to the person you want to speak to? Are calls answered courteously and promptly? Do receptionists know where people are? Are messages taken reliably? If the contact is not available, will someone else take 'ownership' of the problem? Is the switchboard manned at all 'reasonable' times including lunchtimes and after office hours?
   (b) *Security and parking*: What impression is given when people arrive at the site? Are the security people courteous? Are they warned to expect all visitors? Is there somewhere convenient and safe to park? Do all visitors receive a map showing how to get to the location?
   (c) *Reception and lift area*: Does the reception and lift area give the impression you would like to give? Are these areas attractive and comfortable? Remember that for many operations, customers do not have many opportunities for assessing the quality of your service. If they receive a bad impression during a visit to your premises, that could have a considerable influence on future

business. Are customers made to feel welcome? Are they offered coffee and a reasonable selection of reading? Is there a visitors' board?

(d) *Maintenance*: Are buildings and facilities clean and well maintained?

(e) *Correspondence*: Does all correspondence create a professional image? Is there a standard layout? Are letters well written and free from errors and corrections? Are all letters acknowledged and replied to promptly? Are customers kept informed of the reasons for, and the likely duration of, any delay?

(f) *Cars*: Are company cars kept clean and tidy?

(g) *Hospitality*: Are visitors kept waiting for extended periods on arrival whilst their contact arrives? Are they offered refreshments? Are the refreshments served in china or plastic cups?

(h) *Meetings*: Do your employees turn up for meetings on time? Are they adequately prepared for the meeting? Do they have all the equipment and information required? If your people are chairing the meeting, is there an agenda? Do the meetings run to schedule?

These are customer requirements which are often overlooked, but which can make a lasting impression. Every individual within the organisation who makes any contacts with people outside the organisation creates an impression of the company. It is important that a professional impression is given at every level, in every activity. The business has to demonstrate that it is committed to Quality and to customer satisfaction. Everyone is a potential future customer and should be treated as such.

The quality of output depends on the quality of internal processes and the internal supply chain. Understanding the underlying customer requirements is an essential first step towards improving your ability to meet those requirements. But how does a business meet the requirements of its external customers?

External customer requirements can only be met by the correct functioning of internal processes.

WHAT IS A PROCESS?

A process is any activity which takes an input and transforms it into an output. Fig. 2.1 illustrates the basic characteristics of a typical process. Any process can be described in this way.

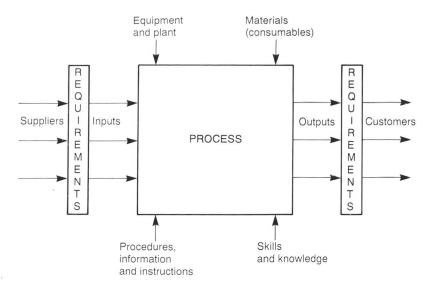

Equipment and plant

Materials (consumables)

Suppliers — REQUIREMENTS — Inputs — PROCESS — Outputs — REQUIREMENTS — Customers

Procedures, information and instructions

Skills and knowledge

Figure 2.1 Process model

A supplier is anyone who supplies the input and a customer is anyone who receives the output from a process. All activities within a business are made up of a series of often complex supplier/customer chains. Each person is a customer of the previous process in the chain and a supplier to the next process. If activities are to be carried out right first time, it is essential that the customer requirements for each process within the chain are identified and met.

Consider the supplier/customer relationships which arise in the case of a meeting between a salesman and a customer to discuss the services a business can provide. Here, the customer requires a formal proposal within 48 hours so that he can award the contract. The activities associated with producing the output (in this case the proposal document) are illustrated in Fig. 2.2.

Even apparently simple processes can require a number of inputs to enable it to produce the correct output. Consider the case of typing the proposal document. The process diagram for this is illustrated in Fig. 2.3. Here, the key process requirements are:

(i)   The proposal dictated by the salesman (these are the direct inputs)
(ii)   Equipment (here, a typewriter/word processor and photocopier)
(iii) Raw materials (paper)
(iv)   Knowledge of how the equipment works

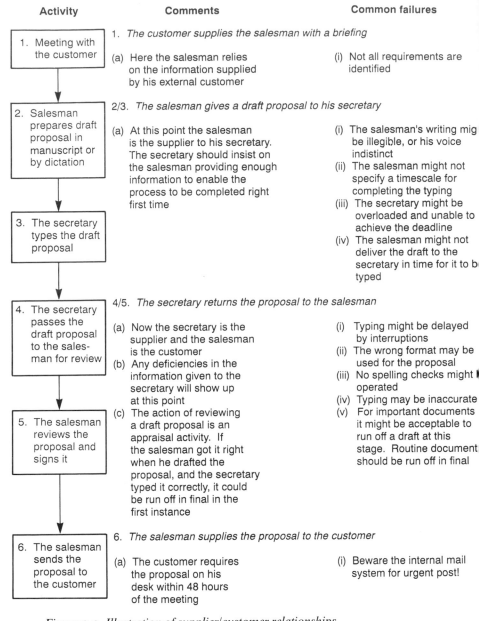

Activity	Comments	Common failures
1. Meeting with the customer	1. *The customer supplies the salesman with a briefing* (a) Here the salesman relies on the information supplied by his external customer	(i) Not all requirements are identified
2. Salesman prepares draft proposal in manuscript or by dictation **3. The secretary types the draft proposal**	2/3. *The salesman gives a draft proposal to his secretary* (a) At this point the salesman is the supplier to his secretary. The secretary should insist on the salesman providing enough information to enable the process to be completed right first time	(i) The salesman's writing might be illegible, or his voice indistinct (ii) The salesman might not specify a timescale for completing the typing (iii) The secretary might be overloaded and unable to achieve the deadline (iv) The salesman might not deliver the draft to the secretary in time for it to be typed
4. The secretary passes the draft proposal to the sales-man for review **5. The salesman reviews the proposal and signs it**	4/5. *The secretary returns the proposal to the salesman* (a) Now the secretary is the supplier and the salesman is the customer (b) Any deficiencies in the information given to the secretary will show up at this point (c) The action of reviewing a draft proposal is an appraisal activity. If the salesman got it right when he drafted the proposal, and the secretary typed it correctly, it could be run off in final in the first instance	(i) Typing might be delayed by interruptions (ii) The wrong format may be used for the proposal (iii) No spelling checks might be operated (iv) Typing may be inaccurate (v) For important documents it might be acceptable to run off a draft at this stage. Routine documents should be run off in final
6. The salesman sends the proposal to the customer	6. *The salesman supplies the proposal to the customer* (a) The customer requires the proposal on his desk within 48 hours of the meeting	(i) Beware the internal mail system for urgent post!

Figure 2.2 Illustration of supplier/customer relationships

(v)   Procedures or instructions on how the proposal should be set out

(vi)   A dictionary or spell-check facility to eliminate spelling errors

(vii) experience or training to be able to type.

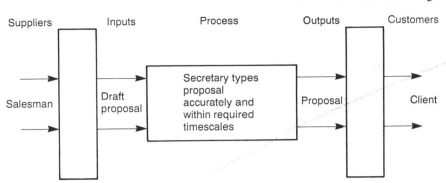

Figure 2.3   Customer-supplier chain

A number of requirements must be satisfied even for a simple process, if the process is to be carried out right first time. Establishing the external customer's requirements is an essential first step. This then establishes the process requirements. For example, if the customer did not require the proposal until a week after the meeting, then the secretary would not need the dictated draft proposal within 24 hours of the meeting.

Understanding processes, how they are linked together in a customer/supplier chain, and the requirements for each process in the chain is essential if processes are to be carried out right first time. This enables an organisation to focus on increasing customer satisfaction and reducing the cost of non-conformance.

Figs. 2.4 to 2.6 illustrate a useful series of questions which need to be answered for each process in order to identify the requirements for that process. It is only by knowing the answers to these questions that a business is able to effect improvements.

PROCESS:

Who are my customers?	What do I deliver to them?	What are their requirements?	What is my current performance?	What actions can I take to improve?

Figure 2.4 Process definition: output to customers

PROCESS:

Who are my suppliers?	What do they deliver to me?	What are my requirements?	What is their current performance?	What improvement can be made?

Figure 2.5 Process definition: input from suppliers

PROCESS:

	What is required?	Does this exist now, reliably?	What improvements can be made?	Who can make this happen?
Skills and knowledge				
Equipment and plant				
Materials				
Procedures, instructions and information				

Figure 2.6 Process definition: process requirements

3 QUALITY COSTS

WHY ARE WE INTERESTED IN QUALITY COSTS?

The objective of a Quality Improvement Programme (QIP) is to develop an approach which ensures goods and services are produced which meet customer requirements for the minimum cost.

This objective may only be achieved by eliminating the costs associated with not getting things right the first time – these are the non-conformance costs of the company. It is only possible to eliminate the costs of non-conformance (CONC) if they can be identified and evaluated. This chapter helps identify the CONC and other Quality related costs.

WHAT ARE QUALITY COSTS AND WHY ARE THEY IMPORTANT?

Quality costs are all the costs incurred by a business to ensure that the total service it provides to customers conforms to the customers' requirements. They include:

(i)   the costs directly associated with providing the end product or service which the customer purchases;
(ii) the costs associated with support activities; and
(iii) the hidden costs such as missed opportunities and poor morale.

A secretary who spends 20 minutes trying to find her boss because he hasn't told her where he is going incurs a cost. She has wasted time which she could have spent more productively. This may also mean that she does not have time today to send out all the letters inviting potential customers to a company product seminar.

An incoming telephone call which is not re-routed to a receptionist when a salesman is out of the office may persuade a customer to place his order elsewhere. Each of these failures may give rise to CONC.

THE IMPORTANCE OF IDENTIFYING THE CONC

Recognising the amount of money wasted on finding and correcting non-conformance at the beginning of a QIP frequently underlines the strategic necessity of introducing the Programme. Findings from a number of businesses suggest that the CONC can amount to as much as 25 per cent of turnover in both manufacturing and service industries. This is certainly a figure which grabs management attention.

Monitoring the CONC can provide a measure of the success of the QIP. However, it should be recognised that when a QIP is introduced, the CONC frequently appears to rise initially. This is because people become more aware of non-conformance and its associated costs as they become able to identify them. Consequently, costs become included which would not initially have been thought of as non-conformance costs.

Knowing the CONC associated with individual activities can be used to help prioritise corrective actions, focusing attention on the highest priority areas.

Being aware of the costs associated with errors will also help every department and individual in their commitment to perform every task right first time.

THE IMPORTANCE OF QUALITY COSTS

Quality costs are important for a number of reasons:

(i)   They are often large. A NEDO survey in 1985 recorded that quality costs in the UK may amount to 10–20 per cent of turnover.
(ii) The size of these costs and where they occur are unknown for most businesses. Fewer than 40 per cent of companies collect information on quality costs.
(iii) The great majority of costs (more than 80 per cent for many companies) are associated with failure and appraisal activities.
(iv) Savings in Quality costs would have a significant, positive impact on the bottom line results.
(v)   The large burden of failure and appraisal activities indicates that

businesses tolerate a large number of defects, which they then have to find and correct. Because appraisal methods inevitably miss a proportion of failures, some non-conforming output will be received by customers. This results in dissatisfied, disloyal customers. Investment in prevention will therefore result in more satisfied customers as well as reducing both failure and appraisal costs.

What does this mean in practice?

Consider the following summary of a company's profit and loss account:

Revenue: £10.0 million
Total costs: £ 9.2 million
Profit   £ 0.8 million

The company incurs a cost of quality amounting to some 25 per cent of turnover (£2.5 million). Of this amount, 80 per cent is incurred on failure and appraisal activities. Therefore the CONC is £2 million.

Consider the options available to this company to increase its profit to £1.6 million.

One very satisfying way would be to increase the volume of sales, so increasing its revenue. To achieve a profit of £1.6 million, however, it may need to double sales revenue. This is unlikely to be possible, especially in a competitive market or a recession.

One other way would be to cut costs. But to increase profit by £0.8 million, they would need to save almost 10 per cent on all activities, or make even larger cuts on selected activities.

A third way is to look at the costs of non-conformance and try to make savings here. To save £0.8 million they would need to reduce the CONC by 40 per cent. Although not an easy task, it seems more achievable than doubling turnover. The advantage of implementing a quality improvement programme which reduces the CONC is that it also reduces the failures seen by the customer, and improves the service which they receive. So it should also lead to an increase in sales revenue.

What have companies found in practice?

The following examples are taken from the DTI booklet 'The case for costing quality' produced as part of their *Managing into the 90's* initiative, and from the bimonthly publication *Quality Update* produced by Philip Crosby Associates as part of its service for clients:

Dairy Crest:	A series of sample surveys in 1988 initially estimated their quality costs at a very conservative £32 million. Although only 3.5 per cent of sales turnover, the figure was certainly high enough to gain management's attention. It was also suspected to be the tip of a much bigger iceberg (*Quality Update*, March/April 1991).
Leyland Daf:	One article in the company magazine, *News Link*, traces the cost of receiving a £1 defective part into the company. At the machining stage it contributes £4 to the CONC; at sub-assembly stage, £36; at assembly stage, £96; and at service or warranty stage, a staggering £870 (*Quality Update*, May/June 1990).
Otis Elevator:	Companies in the European Transcontinental Operations (ETO) of Otis Elevator measured their CONC, based on bad debts, scrap, late deliveries, inventory, breakdowns, cancellation of maintenance contracts and so on. The initial CONC was found to represent 29 per cent of sales. Following implementation of an improvement programme, measurements were made monthly. These showed that for ETO, the CONC reduced by three points between 1987 and 1989. Each one per cent reduction saves $20 million on current ETO sales of $2 billion (*Quality Update*, Sept/Oct 1990).
British Aerospace: (Dynamics) Ltd.	In 1987, after 18 months, BAe estimated its quality costs at 11 per cent of the costs of production. Of these 22 per cent were prevention, 30 per cent appraisal, and 48 per cent failure (DTI, page 8).
Courtaulds:	The Jersey operation reduced its cost of quality from 12.1 per cent to 7.6 per cent of sales, from implementation in 1986. Standfast dyes and printers reduced its quality costs from 20 per cent of sales in 1985, to 7 per cent (DTI, page 13).
Crown Industrial: products	Estimated quality costs in 1986 at 13 per cent of raw material usage costs; by the end of 1988 they were 8 per cent (DTI, page 17).

National   In 1988 Nat West estimated its quality costs at 25
Westminster Bank: per cent of operating costs (DTI, page 30).

WHY MEASURE QUALITY COSTS?

The reason Quality costs need to be measured is because they are large, unknown, and can have a significant impact on profitability and customer satisfaction. Measurements of these costs can also be used for the following purposes:

(i)   The size of Quality costs can be used to attract management attention and shock them into making a commitment to implement a QIP.

(ii)   The reporting of Quality related activities in financial terms generally raises the importance of Quality within the management team and ensures it is given the same attention as any other activity with such a large potential impact on the company's performance.

(iii) Highlighting areas which incur a high cost and which therefore provide ready targets for improvement; once targeted, the results of improvement activities can be monitored.

(iv)   Knowledge of Quality costs and where they occur enables decisions on Quality to be made on a sound basis. The benefits, or otherwise, of any decision can be evaluated according to its effect on quality costs.

CLASSIFYING QUALITY RELATED COSTS

One of the most useful ways of classifying Quality related costs is to distinguish between the costs of conformance and the costs of non-conformance.

Costs of conformance

It is only possible to reduce the CONC by investing in prevention activities. Investing in the prevention of errors enables failure and associated appraisal costs to be minimised.

THIS IS A FUNDAMENTAL DRIVING FORCE BEHIND QUALITY IMPROVEMENT.

However, prevention activities inevitably result in some costs. These are PREVENTION costs, or the costs of conformance. This includes all the costs associated with any activity designed to ensure that the right activities are carried out right first time.

Prevention costs may include those associated with:

(i)   writing procedures defining how tasks are to be performed.
(ii)   process controls, such as Statistical Process Control (SPC).
(iii)   calibrating test equipment to ensure product is produced within specification.
(iv)   training and educating employees so they understand how tasks should be performed.
(v)   maintaining equipment.
(vi)   planning processes to assure quality. Much of the work of the Quality Improvement Team falls under this heading.
(vii)   working with suppliers to improve the quality of goods supplied.
(viii) Audit activities to ensure the continued effectiveness of the pre-vention system (any audit activities associated with the checking or correcting of errors are CONC costs).

The key feature of a QIP environment is that failures are not accepted as a normal occurrence. The root causes of any failures are identified and eliminated by the introduction of prevention activities. Failure is an exceptional occurrence. In this environment we don't need a vast appraisal activity. All that is necessary is a small audit activity to ensure the prevention system is working correctly.

So, after focusing on reducing failure costs we can then look at reducing appraisal costs.

Costs of non-conformance

Costs of non-conformance are all the costs incurred because failures occur. If there were no failures there would be no requirement for appraisal and correcting activities.

These are the costs incurred as a result of either: (i) not doing the right job: for example, the costs incurred by an individual producing a regular report which no-one reads is a CONC, since it does not contribute to the success of the business; or (ii) not completing an activity right first time: obvious costs associated with not doing things right first time include scrap, warranty, repair and similar activities.

Non-conformance costs include the costs of FAILURE and also many APPRAISAL costs which are necessary only because of the high level of failures. Further details of non-conformance costs are included below.

NON CONFORMANCE COSTS

(1) The costs associated with not doing things right first time
The most obvious Quality related costs are those associated with failure to achieve conformance to requirements. These are termed Failure costs.

These costs may arise either before delivery or after the product or service has reached the customer. Examples of Failure costs which are frequently quoted because they are easy to identify include:

- in warranty repairs   – correcting defects after the product has been delivered.

- after sales support   – solving problems the customer has when using a product or service.

- product recall   – repairing, handling and investigating recalled products.

- scrap   – lost material, machine time and labour.

- downgraded product – product sold as seconds at reduced prices.

- rework   – labour, equipment and materials used in repairing or reproducing defective work.

- lost efficiency   – reduction in the effective capacity of the department because of effort diverted to allow corrective action. For example, part of the production line may be tied up with rework when it could be producing a new batch of product.

- customer complaints – smoothing over problems in the field. This may include any incentives offered to pacify a customer, for example, extended warranty, or the reduction of fees.

- liability insurance   – premium paid for product liability and claims insurance, and the cost of settling any claims.

- administration   – all the administration, meetings, paperwork, telephone calls associated with analysing and resolving failures.

Other less visible failure costs which need to be considered include:

- excess inventory
  – costs associated with holding excess inventory because of errors in forecasting (perhaps a marketing or purchasing error); or perhaps as a result of poor material control procedures

- excessive debtor days
  – costs associated with invoices not being paid on time. This might result from inadequate customer vetting; sending inaccurate invoices; or faulty or inappropriate goods.

- obsolete stock
  – costs associated with stock no longer required. This includes storage, overhead and scrap costs. This might result from a marketing, engineering, sales or purchasing error.

- engineering changes
  – costs associated with processing changes in specification. Associated rework costs need to be added to this total.

- overtime
  – the excessive hours worked because of poor planning or controlling of activities.

- excess capacity
  – the extra capacity required to rework or replace failures.

There are also hidden costs associated with failure. These are generally more difficult costs to estimate, but include:

- lost opportunities
  – income lost as a result of customers not placing orders. This may be due to a number of factors, for example:
    – product late to market.
    – previous non-conforming deliveries.
    – poor routing of telephone calls when an office is empty, or a line is busy; or receptionists not passing messages to salesmen.
    – salesmen do not call because they are sorting out problems elsewhere.

- poor employee morale
  – costs associated with excessive staff turnover and reduced efficiency.

Failure costs occur in all areas of the company. However, they are often accepted as part of the normal course of events and so are easily overlooked. It is important to adopt a rigorous approach to identifying failure costs. An example of the typical quality costs associated with key departments is illustrated in Fig. 3.1.

(2) Appraisal costs

The fact that errors occur is widely recognised in industry. In order to minimise the number of errors which reach their customers, many companies operate systems to find these errors. There are inevitably costs associated with finding these errors. These are the APPRAISAL costs. Examples of appraisal activities include the following:

- checking a document for accuracy before approval.
- inspecting goods received.
- testing and inspecting a product between manufacturing operations, and final checking.

Today we commonly expect errors to happen and so we need appraisal activities to find them. If failures were eliminated, the vast majority of appraisal activities would also no longer be necessary.

(3) The costs associated with doing the wrong things

The above illustrate the costs which are associated with the failure to complete activities more efficiently, i.e. right first time. But what about activities that do not really further the objectives of the business. In many cases, these activities can be discontinued. This is an important area which few businesses address adequately. A useful technique for understanding which activities perform a useful purpose is 'functional analysis'. This is described in chapter 4.

In many organisations, meetings are legion. Are they necessary? Are they all held for a pre-defined purpose? Are they managed properly? Is an agenda prepared to ensure everyone is aware of the preparation required, and the proposed output of the meeting? Do the meetings start and finish on time?

How many print-outs do you receive? How many of these do you use? How much more valuable could the print-outs be if you could specify the information you would like, and how you would like to see it presented?

These are examples of activities which currently may not be contributing to the success of the business. If they are not contributing to the success of the business, then the associated costs constitute non-

Quality costs include:
(i) personnel costs;
(ii) overhead costs (light, heat and space);
(iii) consumable materials;
(iv) capital equipment depreciation.

Department	Prevention costs	Appraisal costs	Failure costs	
			Internal	**External**
Design	1. Design procedures 2. Training 3. Functional analysis 4. Setting specifications for materials/products/services 5. Quality function deployment Understanding customer requirements before starting on designs 6. Reliability analysis 7. Design proving 8. Design reviews	1. Design specification for inspection equipment/ procedures 2. Pre-production/prototype trials 3. Checking of drawings and specifications	1. Excess/obsolete inventory (unpopular designs) 2. Design changes 3. Project overspend	1. Product liability (for design failures) 2. Returned goods (for design flaws) 3. Rework/rectification (for design flaws) 4. Customer complaints (regarding design flaws) 5. Downgrading products (for design flaws) 6. Analysis of returned goods (for design flaws) 7. Orders lost because products were not launched on time
Distribution	1. Distribution procedures 2. Training 3. Functional analysis	1. Inspection of finished products/services prior to despatch	1. Rejects/rework due to incorrect packaging	1. Goods delivered to incorrect address

Figure 3.1 Examples of quality costs by department

Department	Prevention costs	Appraisal costs	Failure costs — Internal	Failure costs — External
Finance	1. Finance department procedures 2. Training 3. Functional analysis	1. Internal audit 2. Checking invoices before sending	1. Issuing credit notes to correct invoices 2. Management reports not provided on time	1. Bad debts 2. Overdue accounts (beyond normal credit period)
Maintenance	1. Maintenance procedures 2. Training 3. Functional analysis 4. Scheduled maintenance	1. Inspection of plant	1. Production line stoppages 2. Investigation and repair following complaints, return of goods, warranty claims	1. Non-conforming product 2. Late delivery due to plant down-time
Marketing	1. Marketing procedures 2. Training 3. Functional analysis 4. Setting product or service specification 5. Market research, customer survey	1. Checking letters/questionnaires before sending out	1. Excess/obsolete stock because of poor forecasting 2. Lost customers 3. Fall in market share 4. Poor response time to queries 5. Lost sales because of poor forecasting	1. Product does not meet market requirements
Personnel	1. Personnel procedures 2. Training 3. Functional analysis 4. Staff appraisal 5. Staff surveys 6. Consultative committees	1. Checking appraisal returns 2. Checking candidate reports	1. Recruitment of unsuccessful recruits 2. Failure to fill post on time 3. Staff turnover 4. Employment disputes, strikes 5. Chasing up authorisation to make offers of employment	1. Poor customer relations, due to inadequate training 2. Product not delivered due to plant stoppages

Figure 3.1 Examples of quality costs by department, continued

Department	Prevention costs	Appraisal costs	Failure costs	
			Internal	**External**
Production and materials control	1. Production procedures 2. Training 3. Functional analysis 4. Controls to ensure processes remain 'in control' 5. Specialist handling equipment and procedures 6. Pre-production and prototype trials 7. Evaluation of product/service specification (for production compatibility) 8. Production planning 9. Calibration of test equipment	1. Production/process inspection (on line and finished goods) 2. Inspection/measurement equipment	1. Scrap, waste, rework, rectification of faulty products 2. Replacement of defective product or repeating service 3. Downgrading of product or service 4. Excess/obsolete stock (because of poor production) 5. Reinspection 6. Analysis of failures 7. Excess capacity	1. Receiving, checking, repair and/or replacement of returned goods/services 2. Handling customer complaints 3. Warranty claims 4. Product liability (for production failures) 5. Excess stocks of new materials, work in progress and finished goods 6. Excessive delivery times
Purchasing	1. Purchasing procedures 2. Training 3. Functional analysis 4. Supplier improvement programme	1. Vendor auditing 2. Vendor approval/rating	1. Goods inwards checking 2. Excess stock of bought-in components (from poor buying decisions) 3. Cost of returns to supplier	1. Scrap material (not meeting specification/in excess of requirements) 2. Damages arising from product failure (as a result of inadequate materials)
Quality	1. Quality procedures 2. Training 3. Functional analysis 4. Quality management system 5. Design of process controls 6. Auditing 7. Customer survey	1. Inspection of finished products/services at any stage	1. Quality system failure, resulting in non-conforming product	1. Trouble shooting 2. Handling customer complaints (arising from quality failures) 3. Warranty claims (arising from quality failures) 4. Product liability (arising from quality failures) 5. Non conformances raised by external auditing body 6. Audit deficiencies outstanding

Figure 3.1 Examples of quality costs by department, continued

Department	Prevention costs	Appraisal costs	Failure costs	
			Internal	**External**
Sales	1. Sales procedures 2. Training 3. Functional analysis	1. Checking quotes before sending out	1. Lost customers from inadequate service 2. Lost orders 3. Excess/obsolete stock (from poor sales forecasting) 4. Production overtime (from poor sales forecasting)	1. Handling goods returned as unsuitable 2. Dealing with customer complaints arising from goods returned as unsuitable
Service	1. Service procedures 2. Training 3. Functional analysis 4. Evaluation of product/ service specification (for service compatibility 5. Pre-production and prototype trials 6. Calibration of test equipment	1. Inspection of repairs	1. Lost customers from inadequate service 2. Lost orders 3. Excess/obsolete stock (from poor service forecasting) 4. Warranty after repair	1. Excessive turnaround time

All costs associated with the Quality Department are Quality costs. The objective of the Department is to reduce overall quality costs borne by the business by ensuring:

(i) procedures are in place which ensure that the right actions are taken; all actions are effected right first time; and all output is produced in accordance with pre-agreed requirements.

(ii) the procedures operate effectively in practice.

It is sometimes thought that the full cost of the service department represents a cost of quality. If products were made properly in the first place, there would be no need to service them. However the service departments in a number of industries achieve a healthy income from maintaining equipment in good condition for customers. This chargeable activity is not a true cost of quality. The cost of quality covers non chargeable activities, such as warranty work. The increasing drive towards long term reliability of equipment, and the increasing complexity of equipment are having a conflicting impact on the activities of many service operations.

Figure 3.1 Examples of quality costs by department, continued

conformance costs. They are the costs of failing to control the activities undertaken by the business.

What costs should be included as quality costs?

All costs associated with an activity should be included as part of the cost of quality calculation. The key costs are as follows:

(i) direct labour – standard and overtime rates for employees directly involved in the activity;

(ii) indirect labour – costs associated with the management and supervision of direct labour;

(iii) direct materials – cost of materials used in the activity (raw materials and consumables);

(iv) occupancy costs – cost of space, light, heat and power associated with the activities;

(v) administrative support services – costs associated with payroll, stores, and other support services associated with the activity in question;

(vi) equipment – depreciation on equipment used in the activity.

It is important to capture the full cost of Quality for each activity. Only then will it be possible to understand its full impact on the business. The necessary information generally should be available from the internal management accounts of the business.

HOW TO GATHER QUALITY COSTS

The British Standards Institute (BSI) and the American Society for Quality Assurance have both produced guidance on Quality costs. These are contained in:

(i) BS6143 'The Determination and Use of Quality Related Costs';

(ii) BSI issued a further standard on quality costs in early 1992, to complement the existing standard BS6143. The new standard is BS6143 part 1. This standard adopts a process approach to the analysis of quality costs and focuses on two categories of cost:

    (a) costs of conformance; and

    (b) costs of non-conformance.

      This is a change to the traditional analysis into prevention, appraisal, internal failure and external failure costs in the original BS6143 (which has been re-designated BS6143 part 2); and

(iii) The American Society for Quality Control document 'Quality Costs – What and How'.

Both of these documents provide useful guidelines on collecting and analysing quality costs, but they should not be used prescriptively. Companies should develop a system which works for them.

Each company must decide, for itself, the most appropriate method for collecting and categorising quality costs. It is important to apply the chosen method consistently, and use the information to improve their performance.

The following are useful guidelines when beginning to gather quality costs:

(i)   The starting point is to decide why you want to gather Quality costs. Do you want to know the total for Quality costs across the whole company as a target for overall improvements? Or do you want to identify the activities which are most important to the business, and then carry out a quality cost analysis only in these areas? The reason you want the costs will influence how you should go about collecting them.

(ii) Use existing cost management systems where possible. It may be necessary to adapt the output from the existing system, but don't invent a separate new system. Fig. 3.2 illustrates the range of potential sources for quality cost data.

(iii) To ensure management attention, Quality costs must be included in the regular management accounts. It is therefore important to enlist the help and support of the finance department early on.

(iv) Decide on the appropriate basis for analysing quality costs to suit the business. Use the available guides but don't be restricted by them. Having established the ground rules, apply them consistently, or it will not be possible to monitor progress.

(v)   The first estimate of overall costs does not need to be too detailed. Don't delay the QIP looking for pennies! Once the training and education programme begins, then people will be more enthusiastic and better qualified to identify quality costs. The information can then become more accurate.

(vi) Be prepared for Quality costs to rise initially as people become better at identifying them.

(vii) Attribute costs according to where they occur: for example, by department, supplier or product. This will help guide subsequent investigation and cost reduction.

(viii) Target failure costs at the start.

(ix) Monitor overall Quality costs periodically (perhaps annually). They do not need to be monitored too often as they usually only change relatively slowly.

(x) Quality costs should be gathered more accurately and monitored more frequently (perhaps weekly or monthly), for those areas targeted for improvement.

Quality costs – potential sources of data
(a) Salaries and wages analysis (include direct and indirect staff)
(b) Department cost reports
(c) Departmental budgets
(d) Analysis of overheads (light, heat, power etc)
(e) Product costing data
(f) Space utilisation reports
(g) Scrap reports
(h) Analysis of reworked product/services
(i) Analysis of returned goods
(j) Records of downgraded, scrapped product/services
(k) Staff time reports
(l) Staff travel/expense reports
(m) Labour/equipment utilisation reports
(n) Material usage reports
(o) Register of fixed assets used in departments
(p) Inspection/test reports
(q) Sales reports
(r) Customer complaints log
(s) Records/authorisations for repairs, replacements, refunds
(t) Aged debtors' report
(u) Analysis of credit notes
(v) Cost of capital employed

Figure 3.2 Quality costs – potential sources of data

The role of the Quality Improvement Team

The role of the QIT is to devise a method for identifying the total Quality related costs across the company. It is important that all Quality related costs are included at this stage and not just the obvious costs associated with manufacturing. This analysis can then be used as a basis for measuring progress as the QIP is implemented. It can also be used to reinforce the need for implementing the Improvement Programme when communicating with management and employees. The measurement of Quality costs provides valuable management information and will require the active participation of every manager and supervisor if it is to be a meaningful measure of current business performance.

Quality cost reduction

Quality costs can be used as a basis to target areas for improvement. The first activities to target are those which:

(i)   incur high failure costs; and
(ii) which have the greatest impact on customer satisfaction.

It is then appropriate to target other activities, such as the appraisal activities designed to identify failures.

Significant reductions in the CONC can, and regularly are, being made by companies. This reduction in wasted effort should be publicised and celebrated by organisations. It helps businesses to satisfy the requirements of their customers, and usually makes the work of their employees more interesting. By publicising successes, an organisation helps develop the momentum for the Improvement Programme.

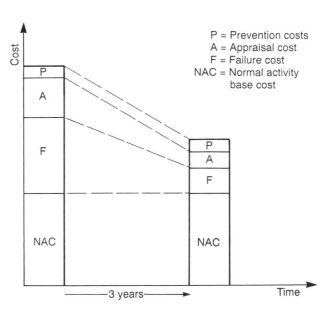

Figure 3.3 Typical quality cost reduction

In the early stages of a QIP, it is useful to focus on reducing the CONC associated with individual activities because a reduction in overall Quality costs can take a long time to flow through to the bottom line. A reduction in overall quality costs to one third of their initial value may typically be made in three years. Fig. 3.3 illustrates the impact of a typical QIP on Quality costs over a three year period. Here, significant reductions have been made in failure and appraisal costs as a result of a small investment in prevention costs.

This illustrates the objective of the QIP, which is to eliminate the CONC by investing in prevention.

4 FUNCTIONAL ANALYSIS

THE PURPOSE OF FUNCTIONAL ANALYSIS

Quality is driven by the needs of customers. Customer-oriented businesses are likely to be the only ones that will continue to exist through the 1990s and into the 21st century. Technologically advanced companies and monopolies may continue in business for a while, but they too have to provide customers with the products which they require.

Functional analysis is the cornerstone of a successful programme of continuous Quality improvement. Businesses rely on their customers: functional analysis drives businesses to focus on satisfying the needs of those customers. Put frankly, any activity that is not directed towards this end may be superfluous, and the resources tied up should be considered for redeployment.

Functional analysis achieves its purpose by identifying:

(i) the purpose of the business as a whole in terms of satisfying EXTERNAL CUSTOMER needs;
(ii) the purpose of each department in the business in terms of satisfying both INTERNAL and EXTERNAL CUSTOMER needs;
(iii) whether or not departments achieve their objectives in a cost-effective fashion;
(iv) the costs associated with any failure to work efficiently; and
(v) areas for implementing corrective actions.

This radical approach requires each department to critically examine its role in achieving the overall objectives of the business. This includes deciding why it exists and what it contributes to further the aims of the business.

FUNCTIONAL ANALYSIS – THE METHOD

The flowchart at Fig. 4.1 illustrates the steps within a typical functional analysis programme, from establishing the requirements of the external customer, to setting detailed targets for improvement within each department. The key activities in each step are described below:

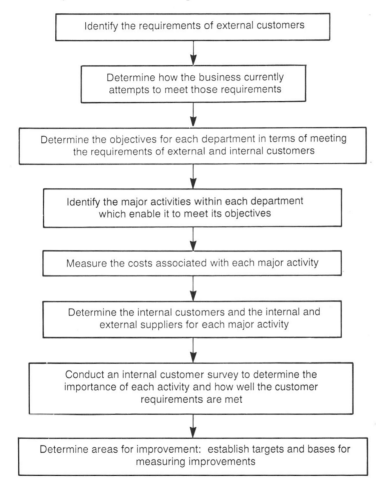

Figure 4.1 Flowchart illustrating the functional analysis method

Identify the requirements of external customers
In view of the importance of this step, it has been considered in detail in chapter 2.

Determine how the business currently attempts to meet those requirements

As a first step, it is essential for senior management to determine why its business exists and what are its aims. Most businesses are set up to increase the wealth of their shareholders. In order to achieve this end they must provide a product or service that satisfies the needs of their customers. It is these commercial, customer-driven aims that interest us here.

A business might manufacture petrol driven engines. If so, is that the purpose of the company? It is quite possible that management consider that this is the purpose of the company – and that they achieve their objective very effectively. But customers might very well look at the business differently. They might be looking for a power source to drive their vehicles. At the moment, petrol engines may be the best form of power supply available; but customers would not hesitate to use a different source in future if circumstances change. If the company does not recognise that it is in the market to supply the customer need for power sources they might well be left behind as technology, or consumer tastes, march on. It is one of the functions of the marketing department to ensure this does not happen!

The whole management team should meet to determine why the business exists and its aims for the future. This vital step guides each function when determining its role within the business. It is useful to record the aims of the business in a mission statement which can be published for the benefit of all employees.

Each manager must demonstrate their commitment to the mission of the business every day and in every action they take. Employees quickly see through management 'initiatives' which are all talk and no action.

The mission statement

This is a definitive statement, made by the senior management team, of why the organisation is in business. It should be short, clear, and focus on the current and future customer requirements which the company must meet to survive.

Determine the objectives for each department in terms of meeting the requirements of both internal and external customers

Having determined the aims of the business, it is necessary to determine why each department exists and what it actually contributes to meeting the overall business aims. Senior management should step back and review periodically (perhaps annually) the purpose of each department and how departments should interact. It is important that the whole management team is involved in determining the role of each department and not just individual department heads in isolation. Each function is both a customer and supplier to other departments and needs to meet the requirements of those departments. Each function also has its own requirements which need to be met by the other departments. It is therefore vital that all the customers and their requirements are identified before the role and purpose of each function is decided. This can only happen if all the potential customers, i.e. all the other department heads, are present and contribute to this discussion.

To understand the purpose of each function it is useful to take each function in turn and brainstorm the questions:

(i)   Why is this function required?
(ii) What does it contribute to achieving the business aims?
(iii) Who are its customers? and
(iv) What are their requirements?

From the answers to these questions, the mission statement for each department can be established in preparation for the next step of the analysis.

At the end of this phase the overall business aims and purpose will have been defined. The role of each function will also have been established in terms of what they do for whom, who their customers are (in many cases these will be internal customers) and how the satisfactory performance of these tasks can be measured. Once these key parameters have been established, each department can examine the activities it carries out. It can also devise means to measure how well it carries out its activities and the Quality costs it incurs.

Identify the major activities within each department which enable it to meet its objectives
Modern businesses have become complex organisations. A typical business might include the following principal functions:

(i)   *The Production department* is the cutting edge of the business – producing the product or service actually required by customers. In a service business this might be the professional staff. In a manufacturing business this would be the production lines.

(ii)   *The Marketing department* is responsible for interpreting the future needs of customers in the light of the capabilities and aims of the business. It should ensure the business produces the right product or service at the right time and the right price.

(iii)   *The Finance department* ensures customers are creditworthy; are invoiced promptly for all supplies at the correct price; purchases are properly authorised and paid for; all transactions are properly recorded; management and financial accounts contain appropriate information and are produced promptly; VAT, PAYE, audit and other compliance issues are handled effectively.

(iv)   *The Personnel department* ensures an adequate supply of appropriate recruits; training needs are considered and effectively carried out; staff are properly treated, appraised of their performance, counselled about their future; and reasons for poor staff retention are investigated.

(v)   *The Design (research and development) department* collaborates with the marketing and production departments to develop designs for new products that will satisfy anticipated customer requirements.

(vi)   *The Service department* continues to meet customer needs once the product has left the factory. This may include installation, customer training, maintenance and resolving customer problems and complaints.

(vii)   *The Quality Assurance department* ensures that the practices and methods adopted throughout the company result in products and services which meet customer requirements first time, every time.

(viii) *The Sales department* obtains orders from customers, establishing requirements for product specification, price and delivery schedules. They are then responsible for the accurate and prompt transmission of this information to production (to make the product) and finance (to invoice the customer for the sale).

(ix)   *The Purchasing department* procures the necessary materials and services according to specification at minimum installed cost.

(x)   *Warehouse and distribution operations* check goods received and despatched; and ensure goods are sent to the right customers on time.

Every department has a range of specific responsibilities assigned to them. Each department will also be responsible for liaising with other departments on specific issues. Thus, for example, the personnel department will need to liaise with each department in relation to their employees. Every department is therefore a customer of the personnel department and it is up to each department to take part in specifying the objectives of the personnel department. The same is true in all cases where departments interact.

Once the overall role of each function has been determined, the department head should work with his staff to identify the major activities performed to meet their overall objectives. The major activities are either those on which most time is spent, or those which the group feels are key to meeting departmental objectives. The investigation of major activities can be time-consuming, so care should be taken to avoid spreading resources too thinly.

At this stage, major activities may well be identified which are not part of the department's role as defined by the management team. It may then be necessary to amend the department's role to incorporate this activity; or it may be decided to transfer the activity to another department; or the activity may not really be required by the business. The decision on what to do should be taken by the whole management team since it affects the primary role of a department.

Once the department has agreed its major activities, these should be recorded so that each member of the department can see how they relate to the overall objectives of the department (see Fig. 4.2).

Fig. 4.3 illustrates the functional analysis approach as it is applied to a number of practical examples.

Measure the costs associated with each major activity

When implementing a programme of continuous quality improvement one frequent difficulty is the collection of quality costs and the use of these as a basis for introducing measurements of performance and improvement. It is relatively easy to determine the obvious quality costs associated with the product, such as rework, scrap and customer returns but significant costs are also incurred in less obvious administrative tasks.

The total Quality related cost should be determined for each activity. Quality costs may fall into the following principal categories:

(i)   Employment costs associated with time spent on quality related activities;

(ii) The cost of plant and equipment; materials and components used in processes;

(iii) The cost of the associated accommodation, power, communications and other services; and

Department	Manager	No. in Dept.

The mission of this department is:

Major activities to fulfil this mission

No.	Activity	Percentage of time spent on this activity	Importance of this activity 1=important 5=not important
1			
2			
3			
4			
5			
6			

Figure 4.2 Functional analysis: major activities

(iv) the overhead costs associated with support functions.

Each major activity can be broken down into smaller sub-activities and the Quality related costs incurred can be analysed as either prevention, inspection or waste. Each department should define these for their own activities using the following guidelines.

Prevention costs relate to ensuring errors are not made when carrying

Activity	Considerations	A possible way forward
1. Raw materials and component stocks held by a manufacturing company	1. Stock costs money. Working capital is tied up; accommodation and staff are required to manage it; and it may deteriorate	1. Consider just-in-time arrangements 2. Benchmark best practice *Consider this example:* Japanese car manufacturers maintained stock amounting to 0.2 days' requirements according to a survey in 1989. European car manufacturers maintained stock amounting to 2 days' production. This provides an obvious opportunity for savings
2. Repair areas at production sites	1. If all products were made correctly first time, there would be no need for any repair area or associated personnel	1. Develop a strategy to reduce the number of repairs. It will then be possible to reduce the size of the repair area 2. Benchmark best practice *Consider this example:* Japanese car manufacturers employed an area equivalent to 4.1% of the assembly space for repairs in 1989 European car manufacturers employed an area equivalent to 14.4% of the assembly space for repairs Repairing products is: (i) more expensive than making them correctly the first time around; (ii) ties up working capital in stock as the goods cannot be sold; (iii) may mean the goods can only be sold at a reduced price, as seconds; (iv) is unlikely to capture all errors. This means that customers will be exposed to buying faulty product; and (v) increases the likelihood that product will be scrapped as defective There are obvious opportunities for savings here

Figure 4.3 Illustration of the functional analysis approach (data from Table 7.1)

Activity	Considerations	A possible way forward
3. Employee training	1. Training employees is costly in terms of: (i) the cost of the training course; and (ii) the opportunity cost of time spent training 2. However, training may be cost effective if: (i) effective productivity increases. This may be a result of reduced scrap or increased throughput; (ii) the value of output increases; or (iii) more sales can be made profitably	1. Benchmark best practice *Consider the following example:* A comparison of Japanese and European car plants in 1989 showed the following: |	*Japanese plant*	*European plant* | Productivity (hours per vehicle) 16.8 36.2 Assembly defects (per 100 vehicles) 60 97 Absenteeism (%) 5 12 Training of new workers (hours) 380 173 It is possible that there is a correlation between these statistics. Perhaps training does increase productivity, reduce absenteeism, and mean fewer errors are made in the production process
4. Service activities	1. In warranty service activity costs money and the business does not receive any additional income as a result 2. The need for in-warranty service gives products a bad name. Customers will tend to avoid buying goods from manufacturers who have a reputation for producing non-conforming product. 3. Out of warranty service activities are frequently a profitable line of business. Measures to enhance and develop this activity should be undertaken if this is so	1. Identify the factors giving rise to in-warranty service work. These may include: (i) poor production methods; (ii) inadequate operator training; (iii) poor user manual; or (iv) incorrect usage 2. The factors giving rise to in-warranty service activities should then be eliminated by introducing preventive measures

Figure 4.3   Illustration of the functional analysis approach, continued (data from Table 7.1)

out a task. This might include verifying that requirements haven't changed, checking that the materials and facilities required for a process are available; preparing and reading the procedure or instruction handbooks; indeed anything designed to ensure tasks run smoothly.

Inspection costs relate to checking for errors either in the inputs received from suppliers, your own work, or anyone else's work output before releasing the work from the department.

Waste costs relate to repeating an activity because of an error or simply not working at all, perhaps because a meeting was cancelled at the last minute or was late starting.

In many cases, the largest single cost for these activities is the payroll cost. A reasonable estimate may frequently be obtained by analysing the time spent on each of these activities. Employees should therefore be asked to record a daily time log for each activity for a period (perhaps a month) chosen because it is representative of the year as a whole. At the end of this period the time costs associated with these activities can be calculated by the department manager (see Figs. 4.4 and 4.5).

Using time records, the department manager can extrapolate to determine the approximate annual quality costs for their department. This is done by multiplying the times for the period under review by the hourly rate (including overheads) and grossing up to represent a year. Fig. 4.6 shows this calculation from the information recorded in Fig 4.5.

The other Quality costs, such as the cost of materials, plant, equipment, power and accommodation should then be added to arrive at the total annual quality related costs. This figure provides the group with an idea of the target for improvement.

Before they begin to implement this exercise, management must determine the purpose of collecting these costs. Any potential saving in time by employees might be seen as a threat to the workforce. If management plan to retain the existing workforce and redeploy personnel to more productive roles, then they must explain this message clearly in order to avoid misunderstandings.

Determine the customers/suppliers for each major activity

A process model (see Fig. 2.1) should be drawn for each major activity to identify the process, its customers and suppliers.

For each major activity the group should identify who needs what they produce (their customers), why and how they need it. They should also decide what they need to enable them to carry out the activity (their inputs) and who supplies these inputs (their suppliers).

Department	Major activity	Date

Time → / Sub-tasks ↓	Time spent on each sub-task Each block = 30 mins											Quality related time (hours)			
	08	09	10	11	12	13	14	15	16	17	Sum	Prevention	Inspection	Waste	Sum
TOTALS															

Figure 4.4 Daily time log

DEPARTMENT		PERIOD COVERED	

Time (hours)	Week 1						Week 2						Week 3						Week 4						Period total					
	NAT	'Quality time'					NAT	'Quality time'					NAT	'Quality time'					NAT	'Quality time'					NAT	'Quality time'				
Major activity	Sum	Prev	Insp	Waste	Sum		Sum	Prev	Insp	Waste	Sum		Sum	Prev	Insp	Waste	Sum		Sum	Prev	Insp	Waste	Sum		Sum	Prev	Insp	Waste	Sum	
No. 1																														
No. 2																														
No. 3																														
No. 4																														
No. 5																														
No. 6																														
TOTALS																														

NAT = Normal activity time

Figure 4.5 Monthly sum of time spent on major activities

Department	
Department Head	
No. in Department	
Major tasks: 1. 2. 3. 4. 5. 6.	

For the period   to   , the following time was spent on these major activities and their associated 'Quality Related Activities':

Total time recorded against all major activities for the period (from Fig. 4.5)		hours
Total hours worked by the department. (No. in department × hours in the period)		hours
Time spent on Quality related activities during the period (from Fig. 4.5)		
a) Prevention		hours
b) Inspection		hours
c) Waste		hours
d) Total		hours
Estimated annual Quality costs $\frac{hours\ worked}{time\ recorded}$ × $\frac{total\ Quality}{time}$ × $\frac{hourly}{rate}$ × $\frac{no.\ periods}{per\ year}$	£	
Add on any other Quality costs such as waste material ⇒estimated Quality costs for this department	£	

Figure 4.6 Annual quality costs

Conduct an internal customer survey

Once the outputs and customers have been identified for each major activity the group should then talk to each of their customers to determine how important the activity is to them and how well the output from the process satisfies their needs. Each customer and his requirements can be identified using the table at Fig. 4.7 as a model. Fig. 4.8 forms a useful basis for recording the results of a customer survey. At this stage the answer to the question 'how well are we satisfying your needs' is often a

Department	Activity Ref. No.	Activity

No.	Customer	Customer requirements	What measurements are applied, or could be applied, objectively to measure quality of output
1			
2			
3			

Figure 4.7 Customer survey (1)

Activity no.	Customer 1 Importance 1=Strong 5=Weak	Customer 1 How well met 1=Well 5=Badly	Customer 1 Sub-total	Customer 2 Importance 1=Strong 5=Weak	Customer 2 How well met 1=Well 5=Badly	Customer 2 Sub-total	Customer 3 Importance 1=Strong 5=Weak	Customer 3 How well met 1=Well 5=Badly	Customer 3 Sub-total	Customer 4 Importance 1=Strong 5=Weak	Customer 4 How well met 1=Well 5=Badly	Customer 4 Sub-total	Dissatisfaction index — sum of subtotals / No. of customers
1 Example	$5/_1$	× 2	= 10	$5/_5$	× 4	= 4	$5/_2$	× 2	= 5	$5/_4$	× 4	= 5	$\dfrac{24}{4} = 6$
2	5/	×	=	5/	×	=	5/	×	=	5/	×	=	
3	5/	×	=	5/	×	=	5/	×	=	5/	×	=	
4	5/	×	=	5/	×	=	5/	×	=	5/	×	=	
5	5/	×	=	5/	×	=	5/	×	=	5/	×	=	
6	5/	×	=	5/	×	=	5/	×	=	5/	×	=	

The higher this index the greater the need for improvement

Figure 4.8 Customer survey (2)

subjective judgement by the customer. To help in the assessment of performance it is useful to try and identify with customers an objective means of measuring how well the group meets their needs. This measure can then be targeted as a basis for future improvement.

For each major activity a customer satisfaction index can be calculated based on the number of customers, how important the activity is to each customer and how well each customer's requirements are being met. This information can later be used as part of the decision making process to target areas for improvement.

Later, once the group fully understands their customers and how to meet their requirements, they can talk to their suppliers about what they require from them.

Determine areas for improvement: establish targets and bases for measuring improvements

Having completed the customer survey and gathered data on the time spent on each activity, each department can target the areas which require improvement. This may be a complex decision based on a number of factors, such as the costs associated with an activity; how important the activity is to its customers; how well the activity is currently being performed; and the scope for improvement. The group may then nominate areas for improvement. Each group will then decide who will form and lead improvement groups. These groups will develop a proposed course of action to eliminate unnecessary activities, and improve performance in important activities. The group will also recommend how improvements should be measured.

THE BENEFITS OF FUNCTIONAL ANALYSIS

In summary, functional analysis achieves the following major benefits for all businesses:

- It identifies the requirements of external customers, and focuses all activities towards meeting those requirements.
- The overall aims and purpose of the business are established.
- The role for each department in meeting those aims is established.
- The major activities each department carries out to fulfil its role are determined.
- The internal and external customers, and their requirements, are identified for each major activity.

- The performance of each activity is measured.
- The Quality costs for the major activities within each department are collected. These may be aggregated with the product related Quality costs to determine the Quality costs for the business as a whole.
- Areas requiring improvement can be targeted and improvements measured.
- The whole process starts with top management and gradually involves everyone. This demonstrates management involvement and commitment to quality improvement, and at the same time ensures everyone is involved.
- Individuals better understand the business and its aims, and how their daily activities help to advance those aims.
- Individuals understand how their output is used by their customers. This leads to a greater understanding of the customer/supplier chains within a company and the inter-dependency of functions.

THE APPLICATION OF FUNCTIONAL ANALYSIS TO KEY DEPARTMENTS

Functional analysis describes a method for analysing the role of each department within an organisation to ensure it is focused on meeting the requirements of external customers.

This section records the results of functional analysis as it might be applied to a number of key departments in a business. Each organisation is unique and will have its own way of working. The purpose of this section is to provide an illustration of the functional analysis approach in order to stimulate ideas about what can be achieved in practice.

Each example follows the same basic format:

(i)   The mission of each department is described.
(ii) The principal roles of each department are defined.
(iii) The customers for each major activity are identified.
(iv) Key customer requirements are described.
(v)   Key measurements are identified which may be used as a basis for comparing performance against customer requirements.
(vi) Useful tools are identified which could help improve the ability of the department to meet the requirements of their customers, first time, every time.

The mission of the sales department is to:

(i) maximise the value of profitable sales made by the company;
(ii) accurately forecast order rates for production scheduling and financial forecasting purposes; and
(iii) ensure orders are placed within an appropriate timescale.

Role	Customer	Customer requirements	Objective measurements	Useful tools
1. Maximise the value of profitable sales made by the company	1. Sales manager 2. Shareholders	1. Maximise the value of profitable sales taking account of production and distribution constraints 2. For the purpose of monitoring performance it is usually appropriate to consider the value of sales orders secured; the value converted into sales; and the amount of cash received. A sale is of no value until the cash is received	1. Value of sales orders 2. Amount of cash received from sales made 3. Accuracy of quotes, measured as: (i) profit achieved compared to budget; (ii) cost overruns	1. Sales order procedures. These should cover the making of sales, and describe the liaison necessary between the sales team and, for example, the credit control department prior to effecting a sale
2. Ensure orders received are transmitted for production quickly and accurately	1. Production 2. External customer	1. The accurate and timely transmission of orders to the factory	1. Time taken to transmit orders to factory 2. Number of (or some measure of the cost of correcting) errors in orders received by the factory	1. Standard order procedures 2. Electronic transmission of orders 3. Accurate product database

Figure 4.9 (a) The sales department

Role	Customer	Customer requirements	Objective measurements	Useful tools
3. Effective management of customer accounts	1. External customer	1. The professional management of the customer interface: (i) Salesman is contactable whenever necessary (ii) Salesman ensures the customer is supplied with product that meets his real requirements (iii) The company should ensure delivery of product conforming to the agreed requirements at the right time, at the right place, for the agreed price	1. Time taken to acknowledge orders from customers 2. Number of errors in quotations received by customers 3. Time taken to send quote to customer from the date of receiving the invitation 4. Percentage of quotes sent to customers within the agreed deadline	1. Secretary should know whereabouts at all times 2. Standard quotation procedure, incorporating standard terms of trade 3. Accurate product database
4. Minimise the cost of securing each order	1. Sales manager	1. Minimise the cost of securing each order	1. Number of successful (or unsuccessful) quotes 2. Value of successful (or unsuccessful) quotes 3. Percentage of successful (or unsuccessful) quotes 4. Cost of each quote; or the cost of getting each order	1. Sales procedures
5. Forecasting sales order volume for each product	1. Production 2. Finance	1. Accurate and timely forecast of anticipated orders for the next period	1. Accuracy of order forecasts used for production scheduling or financial budgeting purposes (orders received as a percentage of orders forecast) 2. Timeliness of order forecasts, measured as percentage received on time, number or percentage received late	1. Sales procedures

The mission of the finance department is to ensure that:

(i) all customers are creditworthy;
(ii) all sales are invoiced promptly and accurately;
(iii) all transactions are accurately recorded in the accounting records;
(iv) all purchases are properly authorised, paid and accounted for;
(v) VAT, PAYE, audit and other compliance issues are handled correctly, efficiently and promptly;
(vi) Appropriate management information is produced accurately and in a timely manner.

Role	Customer	Customer requirements	Objective measurements	Useful tools
1. All customers are creditworthy	1. Management team 2. Shareholders	1. Customers are good credit risks 2. Customers settle outstanding accounts promptly	1. Excessive debtor days 2. Value of debts outstanding over 1 (2 or 3) months 3. Cost of bad debts 4. Debt collection costs 5. The cost of the credit control department 6. Number (value) of customer accounts in solicitor's hands	1. Credit assessment procedures 2. Debt collection procedures
2. All documents (confirmation of order, delivery notes, invoices, statements of account, and credit notes) are accurate	1. External customer	1. All documents are issued promptly and accurately	1. Number of errors on invoices etc received by customer 2. Number/value of credit notes or other documents issued to correct invoicing etc errors 3. Number of errors on invoices corrected prior to sending	1. Standard invoice format 2. Documented invoicing procedures

Figure 4.9 (b) The finance department

Role	Customer	Customer requirements	Objective measurements	Useful tools
3. Minimise the time between sending goods/service to customers and the receipt of the full amount of cash outstanding	1. Accounts receivable	1. Invoices are issued promptly and accurately so customers have no excuse for late payment 2. Minimum delay between shipping goods and the receipt of cash	1. Number of days between the delivery of goods/service and the despatch of the invoice 2. The cost of capital tied up in overdue accounts 3. The number of days between completion of order and despatch of goods 4. Number of days between the delivery of goods/services and the receipt of cash 5. The cost of chasing overdue debts 6. Value of outstanding invoices (broken down into 'less than one month', 'one month', 'two months', and so on)	1. Standard invoice format 2. Documented invoicing procedures 3. Routine, enforced billing schedule
4. All purchases are properly authorised	1. Purchasing	1. No unauthorised purchases are made	1. Number of unauthorised purchases	1. Documented, enforced procedures relating to purchases of goods and services, governing: (i) authorisation of purchases; (ii) expenditure limits; (iii) documentation (eg purchase orders)
5. All transactions are accurately recorded in the accounting records	1. Shareholders	1. All transactions are properly recorded in the accounting records	1. Number of errors in the accounting records	1. Internal audit procedures 2. External audit

Figure 4.9 (b) The finance department, continued

Role	Customer	Customer requirements	Objective measurements	Useful tools
6. Appropriate management information is produced accurately and in a timely manner	1. Senior management team	1. Timely delivery of accurate reports containing agreed management information	1. Late delivery of reports (number of days) 2. The number (value) of errors in reports 3. Time wasted producing/reviewing unnecessary/inappropriate reports 4. Time wasted looking for important information	1. Agreed timetable for preparation and delivery of reports to management 2. Agreed list of key information for each report
7. VAT, PAYE, audit and other compliance issues are handled correctly, efficiently and promptly	1. All employees 2. Regulatory bodies	1. Accurate and timely handling of PAYE, VAT etc procedures	1. Delays in receiving salary 2. Errors in salary/PAYE/VAT returns 3. Time taken to correct errors 4. Time taken corresponding to the Inland Revenue/HM Customs 5. Value of professional fees on these issues	1. Documented procedures

Figure 4.9 (b) The finance department, continued

The mission of the personnel department is to ensure:
(i) an adequate supply of appropriately qualified recruits;
(ii) training needs are identified and effectively implemented;
(iii) staff are properly treated; appraised of their performance and counselled about their future;
(iv) the terms of engagement (salary, hours, job description and conditions of employment) for all staff are agreed with all staff members.

Role	Customer	Customer requirements	Objective measurements	Useful tools
1. Recruitment of suitably qualified staff at the time required	1. All departments	1. Replacements are identified promptly after requirements have been specified	1. Number of days in each department at less than full headcount 2. Excessive overtime costs resulting from staff shortages 3. Number of days/cost of training for new staff members in excess of standard requirements 4. Time spent interviewing inadequately qualified candidates by: (i) personnel department; and (ii) each operating department 5. Time taken to recruit each vacancy 6. Performance rating of recruits after 6 months' employment	1. Formal record of agreed target headcount for each department 2. Budgeted overtime levels 3. Training budget for new staff grades 4. Recruitment procedures: * pre-selection * interviewing
2. Ensure training needs are identified and effectively implemented	1. All departments	1. Staff receive adequate, relevant training	1. Number of days training per department 2. Expenditure on training for each department 3. Number (or value) of operator errors resulting from inadequate training 4. Time taken to effect agreed training requirements 5. Rating by participants of training received	1. Training budget for each department 2. Training schedule for each member of staff 3. Training policy and documented procedures 4. Consideration of training requirements at staff counselling

Figure 4.9 (c) The personnel department

Role	Customer	Customer requirements	Objective measurements	Useful tools
3. Staff are properly treated; appraised of their performance and counselled about their future	1. All employees 2. All departments	1. Staff are properly treated, appraised of their performance and counselled about their future 2. Reasons for poor staff retention are investigated and overcome 3. Staff are informed of, and involved in company decisions	1. Number of staff complaints (by department) 2. Number of staff who are not appraised (by department) 3. Time devoted to appraisal and counselling of staff 4. Staff turnover (numbers and as a percentage of headcount) (by department) 5. Recruitment costs 6. Number of instances in which post resignation counselling is not performed 7. Number/length/cost of strikes or other disputes 8. Percentage negative comments from employee surveys	1. Staff handbook explaining procedures and standard terms of employment 2. Job specifications for all staff 3. Formal appraisal and counselling procedures (covering existing employees and resignations) 4. Records kept of agreed follow up action from counselling session 5. Staff consultative meetings 6. Employee surveys of (dis)satisfaction with the company's procedures

Figure 4.9 (c) The personnel department, continued

The mission of the warehouse/stores is to ensure raw materials, components and products are:

(i) subject to appropriate procedures on receipt from internal and external suppliers (completion of delivery advice note, inspected, recorded, and stored);

(ii) stored safely and securely under appropriate conditions until required;

(iii) goods required by customers (whether internal or external) are accurately identified and made ready for collection when required.

Role	Customer	Customer requirements	Objective measurements	Useful tools
1. Receipt of goods from internal and external suppliers	1. Production	1. Goods should be received in good condition	1. Number/value of damaged goods received into stock	1. Goods inwards checking procedures 2. Ship to stock status for approved suppliers
2. Storage of goods	1. External customer 2. Production	1. Goods should be properly identified 2. Goods should be stored in the correct location 3. Goods should be stored securely 4. Goods should be protected from damage and deterioration	1. Number/value of items stolen, damaged or subject to deterioration in storage 2. Time taken to pick stock items	1. Packaging and handling procedures 2. Stock management procedures
3. Checking and despatch of goods (i) raw materials and components (ii) finished goods (iii) replacement goods	1. External customer	1. The correct items are received undamaged and at the right time	1. Time to despatch goods after receipt of request 2. Number of errors in goods despatched	1. Packaging and handling procedures 2. Despatch procedures
4. Receiving, checking and sorting returned goods for replacement or repair	1. External customer 2. Production 3. Service 4. Design/engineering	1. All goods returned to be identified; replacements sent out and the investigating department informed	1. Time taken to send out replacement goods 2. Time taken to inform investigating department	1. Documentation procedures governing the receipt of returned goods

Figure 4.9 (d)   The warehouse/stores department

The mission of the quality department is to help ensure that all departments in the business manage and exercise their responsibilities for quality effectively. Each department is responsible for the quality of its output, and the quality of its internal workings. The quality department is responsible for advising and supporting other departments to achieve their quality objectives. It is also responsible for auditing their quality management systems to confirm compliance with procedures.

Role	Customer	Customer requirements	Objective measurements	Useful tools

1. Management of the quality management system	1. All departments
	2. External assessment body
	3. External customers
		1. Quality procedures established and followed for all departments	1. Number of audits carried out to schedule
			2. Average time to implement corrective actions
			3. Number of instances of non-compliance with procedures
				1. Quality manual setting out:
				  (i) the quality policy of the business
				  (ii) the responsibilities of each department
				  (iii) quality procedures to cover all operations
				2. Approved quality management system
				3. Quality audit timetable
				4. Quality audit checklist
				5. Documented quality audit procedures
				6. Audit training

2. Training personnel	1. All departments	1. Adequate, interesting, relevant training carried out to ensure all employees understand their quality role	1. Participant rating of education programme 2. Number of personnel trained (in each period/cumulatively)	1. Set formal objectives for each training course. These should be agreed with the head of the departments from which participants will be drawn 2. Attendance rating for courses

Figure 4.9 (e)   The quality department

Role	Customer	Customer requirements	Objective measurements	Useful tools
3. Establish appropriate means of communication to keep all staff informed of the progress made by the quality programme	1. All employees	1. Interesting and accurate information about the quality programme to enable them to: (i) understand how they fit into the wider picture (ii) see the benefits accruing to the business, and hence to them as employees from their efforts (iii) motivate them to continue to strive to improve performance	1. Employee awareness of quality 2. Rate of turnover of information on notices	1. Quality noticeboard 2. Quality publication (newspaper/magazine/newsletter) 3. Quality section at key meetings
4. Facilitating the reduction in the cost of quality in each department	1. All departments	1. Accurate information on how the cost of quality is broken down by constituent activities 2. Accurate and timely calculation of the cost of quality in each department and for the business as a whole	1. Reduction in the cost of quality each period (by department and by the business as a whole) 2. Cumulative reduction in the cost of quality (by department and by the business as a whole)	1. Quality cost analysis

Figure 4.9 (e) The quality department, continued

Role	Customer	Customer requirements	Objective measurements	Useful tools
5. Advise each department on quality issues	1. Each department	1. Prompt, commercial advice on quality issues as they affect: (i) the external customer; and (ii) internal operations	1. Number of occasions advice is sought from the quality department 2. Positive comments from customer departments on the promptness and value of the advice from the quality department 3. Average time to respond	1. Log of advice sought maintained by the quality department 2. Periodic (say 6 monthly) evaluation of the value and promptness of advice from the quality department by all other departments
6. Analysing and interpreting customer feedback on the whole service provided by the business	1. All departments	1. Prompt, accurate feedback on customer perception of quality	1. Number of customer reports obtained 2. Customer rating of overall service	1. Source data for analysis: (i) customer questionnaire (ii) customer complaints log (iii) warranty claims (iv) product liability cases

Figure 4.9 (e) The quality department, continued

5 QUALITY MANAGEMENT SYSTEM STANDARDS

An effective Quality Management System (QMS) is a key building block for Total Quality. It is, however, only one element in a Total Quality Management organisation. It describes a controlled, documented system of procedures, designed to ensure that only conforming products or services are released to customers.

This can be achieved either by preventing errors occurring in the first place or by checking the product or service to ensure that non-conforming product is not released to the customer. A typical traditional QMS often relies heavily on a series of checking activities to identify instances of non-conformance. The errors are then corrected.

A traditional QMS does not generally cover other service and administration activities, such as finance or personnel. In order to picture the key differences between a typical QMS and a Total Quality environment, it is helpful to compare their key features as illustrated in Table 5.1.

A number of quality system standards have been developed to describe the requirements for an effective QMS. This chapter describes how the UK quality system standards originated; how they developed; and how they are applied today.

THE ORIGIN OF THE UK QUALITY SYSTEM STANDARDS

During the late 1950s and early 1960s, the UK armed forces suffered an unacceptably high level of equipment failure in the field. This compromised their ability to perform their designated military role and, more importantly, led to considerable potential danger to the life and welfare of both service and civilian personnel. The high cost of military equipment meant that the direct costs of equipment failure were very high; and the costs in terms of human life were unacceptable.

	A traditional Quality Management System	*A Total Quality Management Culture*
Areas covered	Typically only product-related activities.	All activities within a company, including service and administration activities.
Focus on errors	Typically checking to ensure errors do not reach customers.	Preventing errors occurring in the first place.
Responsibility and involvement	Typically the responsibility of a quality department to audit the system and recommend necessary changes.	Everyone is responsible for quality and striving for continuous improvement in all activities.
Benefits	Establishes basic controls over performance of activities. Reduces errors to customers and begins to reduce internal waste.	Builds on QMS. Focuses on eliminating errors and waste in every activity.
Customer focus	Focus directed at reducing errors in products or services received by the external customer.	Strives to ensure conforming outputs for all processes, whether for internal or external customers.

Table 5.1 Comparison of the key features of a traditional Quality Management System and a Total Quality Management culture.

In order to ensure their suppliers produced equipment to specification, the Ministry of Defence (MoD) introduced a series of design and manufacturing control requirements. These specified a range of quality procedures which had to be documented and controlled. The most comprehensive range of controls was applied to suppliers which were completely responsible for the design and manufacture of an item. A less comprehensive set of controls was applied to equipment stockists. These control requirements were set out in the Defence Standard 05–21 series. This series of standards has since been replaced by equivalent AQAP standards which are recognised throughout NATO for all defence related suppliers.

The use of formal Quality System standards to control the quality of products rapidly spread to the nuclear and process plant industries. Here, too, the consequential losses arising from equipment failure could be very high. Failure at a nuclear plant could result in a huge loss of life or terrible injuries. The cost of delaying the commissioning of a power station could be enormous. As a result, failure in these industries could not be tolerated. This led to the development of quality standards, such as

BS5882, covering the particular issues associated with nuclear plant design, manufacture, installation and commissioning.

These early standards were developed for industries where the potential costs associated with product failure could be enormous. The requirement that formal Quality Systems be adopted by suppliers to these industries was the most effective way to minimise the risk of equipment failure.

As the benefits of Quality Systems became apparent, both to customers (by assuring the delivery of conforming goods) and to suppliers (by improving customer satisfaction) the need for a Quality System Standard which could be used by industry in general was recognised. This led to the development of BS5750 in 1979. This standard was largely based on the NATO AQAP series of standards. Initially, a relatively small number of (mainly manufacturing) companies were approved to the standard. The growing importance of Quality as a basis for competitive advantage has led to a rapid increase in the number of companies applying for BS5750 approval. There has also been an increasing awareness of its application to service industries.

In 1987, a number of countries ratified an agreement recognising an International Quality System Standard, the ISO9000 series. This is directly equivalent to the BS5750 (1987) series and is recognised throughout the world. This rationalisation of national Quality System standards is a key step in the removal of barriers to free trade. Still very much based on the NATO series, ISO9000 includes a number of standards each of which is appropriate to a different business activity. These range from ISO9001 for companies who design and manufacture products, to ISO9003 for stockists.

Because these standards have to be applied across a wide range of industry and commerce, their requirements are framed in general terms. In order to expand and interpret specific clauses in the standards a number of Quality Assessment Schedules (QAS) have been developed for particular industries by BSI and industry representatives. The QAS provides the details necessary to apply the standard to a particular business sector. These schedules are, however, guidelines and are not part of the standard.

THE POSITION TODAY

Today the MoD continues to assess and approve its suppliers against the AQAP standard. For many companies, this is the only Quality System approval which they hold. However, in the light of the costs to the MoD, and also possibly as a result of Government pressure for greater recognition of the ISO9000 series, the MoD has stated its intention to phase out its approval to AQAP standards. Although large defence suppliers, such as British Aerospace and GEC, may continue to be directly assessed and approved by the MoD, all other suppliers are being encouraged to apply for ISO/BS approval. This approval is certified by independent, approved bodies and paid for by the assessed companies.

This move away from AQAP assessments will leave ISO9000/BS5750 as the principal approval standard in the UK.

ISO9000/BS5750 – THE APPROVAL BODIES

ISO9000 and BS5750 are directly equivalent standards. The British Standards Institute (BSI) is responsible for the issue and control of the standard in the UK. A number of independent assessment organisations, including BSI, Lloyds Register and Yarsley have been assessed and approved by The National Accreditation Council for Certification Bodies (NACCB) to assess companies against these standards and to award approvals, in specific industry and business sectors. The purpose of the NACCB is to ensure, on behalf of the Secretary of State for Trade and Industry, that the approval bodies themselves have a quality system and the technical ability to carry out competent assessments.

ISO9000/BS5750 – THE APPROVAL PROCESS

Conformance to one of the Quality System standards may be specified between two parties as a contractual requirement. In this case conformance to the standard may be assessed by the customer placing the contract (second party assessment). Alternatively, and more commonly, an independent assessment of a company's QMS can be carried out by an approved body (third party assessment).

Any company may apply to an accredited body for approval. The company should ensure that the scope of the accredited body's approval covers the business activity concerned. It should then supply a copy of the documentation for their QMS to the approval body for review. The approval body will notify the company of any deficiencies in the documentation and seek agreement on measures to rectify them. The approval body will then undertake an intensive audit of the operations of the company and either award a certificate or notify the company of the deficiencies found and seek agreement on measures to rectify them. Following approval, the company is subject to periodic compliance audits by the approval body. The costs of the initial approval and subsequent compliance audits are met by the applying company.

THE BENEFITS OF AN APPROVED QUALITY MANAGEMENT SYSTEM

An approved QMS provides assurance to customers that the company is committed to quality and is able to supply products and services in accordance with their requirements. The standards only define what must be controlled, and not how individual processes must be controlled. Accordingly, a company which understands why they are introducing a QMS can implement a flexible system which suits themselves and realise the benefits an effective QMS can bring.

An effective QMS should ensure that the activities of the business are controlled and documented. This enables everyone to know what they are doing and how to do it. As a result, inefficiencies and waste may be targeted and eliminated. The benefits of an effective QMS are many but they can only be realised by a company which recognises them; is committed to the QMS; and takes the time and trouble to implement a well-thought out system which suits the company and advances its business objectives.

The following are typical of the benefits of a well-thought-out effective QMS:

(i)   Satisfied and loyal customers because goods and services are always produced according to their requirements.
(ii) Reduced operating costs as waste is eliminated and efficiency increased as a result of eliminating non-conformance.
(iii) Improved competitiveness and profitability as operating costs are reduced.
(iv) Improved employee morale as they are working efficiently.

An ineffective QMS is usually seen by everyone concerned as time-wasting and inefficient with no real benefit to the company except keeping the customer happy. This position may arise if management decide to implement a QMS without paying adequate attention to the requirements of the attention to the requirements of the business. This might happen if, for example, the company implements a QMS because of pressure from their customers to seek ISO/BS approval. This provides the customer with assurance that only conforming products or services will be delivered by the supplier. However, unless the QMS is adequately planned, it may well be implemented without realising the many benefits which an effective Quality Management System (QMS) would bring. In the worst case, a company might finish up with a system that is difficult to manage and does not advance its commercial objectives.

Unfortunately, this type of QMS will not advance the aims of the business and will not even keep the customer happy for long because people will always try to find a way round it and so non-conforming goods or services may well be released at some time.

An effective QMS can be implemented without being approved to a quality system standard. However, in addition to providing information and guidance on how an effective QMS should operate, approval to a recognised standard has significant commercial benefits:

(i) It provides evidence to customers that the QMS has been independently assessed as effective. This is increasingly important as a marketing edge over competitors.

(ii) It avoids duplication of customer assessments. Most customers accept and recognise the BS5750/ISO9000 approval. Independent approval saves time and money for both the customer and supplier. The companies can then concentrate on specific requirements for particular contracts or orders.

(iii) It provides evidence of a responsible attitude to quality and product liability requirements.

THE REQUIREMENTS OF THE BS5750/ISO9000 STANDARDS

There are three levels of approval within the ISO series:

(i) ISO9001/BS5750 pt1 – Quality systems specification for design/ development, production, installation and servicing

(ii) ISO9002/BS5750 pt2 – Quality systems specification for production and installation

(iii) ISO9003/BS5750 pt3 – Quality systems specification for final inspection and test

The appropriate approval standard depends on the activities of the company. Guidance is given in the introduction to each standard and in the guidance document, ISO9000, to help select the correct standard.

Each standard defines the activities for which a company must define appropriate controls. These range from ensuring the Quality policy of the company is stated and there are sufficient, qualified personnel to carry out this policy; to ensuring that whenever defects occur they are reported and actions introduced to prevent their recurrence. Most well-run companies will already carry out a number of the required procedures in order to control their business.

Once a company has determined the appropriate standard, it is necessary to ensure that its QMS conforms to it. One of the major activities when seeking approval for a QMS in a well organised company is preparing documentation to describe all the quality related procedures, and then controlling and amending the documents as the business evolves. It is important, as far as possible, to make the QMS reflect existing procedures, rather than change what is done to conform to a pre-determined system. For this reason it is important to involve the whole company in documenting and implementing the QMS. A consultant can play an important role in training and interpreting the standards for the company. But beware the 'off-the-shelf' QMS, whether produced internally or by a consultant! These may act as a strait-jacket and will generally fail in the longer term.

The key requirements for an effective QMS are: commitment from the top; a manager responsible for quality with sufficient resources to support him; documented procedures and records; and periodic, rigorous review of the system.

These issues should be clearly addressed in the Quality Manual.

DETAILED REQUIREMENTS OF BS5750 pt1/ISO9001

ISO9001 is the most comprehensive of the ISO9000 series. It contains the requirements for an organisation involved in the original design, development, production, installation and servicing of products. A brief description of the principal features of ISO9001 is set out below. The other two standards contain appropriate elements from ISO9001. The requirements of each standard are detailed in Fig. 5.1.

Number of clause / Title of clause	ISO 9001/ BS5750 PT1 Design and manufacture	ISO 9002/ BS5750 PT2 Manufacture	ISO 9003/ BS5750 PT3 Final inspection and test
Management responsibility	4.1	4.1	4.1
Quality system	4.2	4.2	4.2
Contract review	4.3	4.3	–
Design control	4.4	–	–
Document control	4.5	4.4	4.3
Purchasing	4.6	4.5	–
Purchaser supplied product	4.7	4.6	–
Product identification and traceability	4.8	4.7	4.4
Process control	4.9	4.8	–
Inspection and testing	4.10	4.9	4.5
Inspection, measuring and test equipment	4.11	4.10	4.6
Inspection and test status	4.12	4.11	4.7
Control of non-conforming product	4.13	4.12	4.8
Corrective action	4.14	4.13	–
Handling, storage, packaging and delivery	4.15	4.14	4.9
Quality records	4.16	4.15	4.10
Internal quality audits	4.17	4.16	–
Training	4.18	4.17	4.11
Servicing	4.19	–	–
Statistical techniques	4.20	4.18	4.12

Figure 5.1 Requirements of the ISO9000/BS5750 series of standards

MANAGEMENT RESPONSIBILITY

Quality Policy
To ensure that Quality is taken seriously by all members of an organisation, senior management should define and publish the company's Quality Policy. This defines the quality objectives for all employees and helps demonstrate the commitment of senior management to Quality. Senior managers are then responsible for ensuring this policy is understood and implemented throughout the company.

Organisation

To ensure an effective QMS is implemented, it is essential that the role and responsibilities of all functions which affect quality are defined. This is usually achieved by means of an organisation chart and job specifications. When considering the organisation required to assure Quality, the company should identify the test, inspection and other monitoring activities required (including audit and design review) and ensure sufficient, trained personnel are available to carry them out.

It is also important to nominate one manager with the necessary authority, resources and responsibility to ensure the QMS is implemented and maintained. The manager should have sufficient freedom to carry out this task without conflicting with his other responsibilities.

To ensure the QMS is properly implemented, and continues to meet the requirements of ISO9001, a system of quality audit and management review procedures should be implemented.

QUALITY SYSTEM

Having nominated a manager and decided on the organisational structure to assure Quality, the company should consider the Quality Management System it will introduce. This system should be fully documented. The activities which the system should control are detailed in the remainder of the standard.

QMS documentation

To ensure a system of standard procedures is applied to control the quality of product or service, a comprehensive set of documentation is required to describe appropriate procedures. The different types of documentation may effectively be illustrated as a pyramid as shown in Fig. 5.2.

The Quality manual describes how a company ensures conformance to ISO9001. It usually starts with a statement of the Quality policy and a definition of how this is put into practice by addressing each of the requirements of ISO9001. Detailed control procedures and other documents are referred to as appropriate. The manual is a formal declaration by the company of how it assures quality and forms a documented set of managerial instructions on Quality matters.

Control procedures define in detail the methods and controls adopted

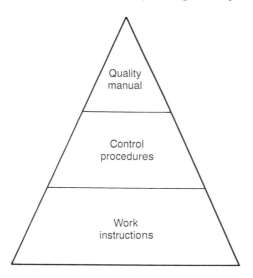

Figure 5.2 Pyramid of documentation

throughout the organisation to assure Quality, and might include Quality procedures, design procedures and standards, manufacturing procedures, sales procedures and data processing procedures. These procedures generally affect a number of people or departments, and frequently cover interfaces between functions. Individual work instructions are referred to where appropriate.

Work instructions define procedures for specific tasks or processes. They generally apply only to one task or to a small group of people. Examples include specific inspection instructions, test specifications, drawings, planning instructions and calibration methods.

For example, consider the procedures required to define how 'in-process testing' is controlled. The Quality manual may discuss the overall policy on testing and may refer to a routing procedure to describe in detail how the process is controlled. The routing procedure may define who takes a decision on what testing is required for a given item and how the system ensures that the item follows this routing. The routing procedure may state that all testing is carried out in accordance with the appropriate test specification. The test specification then describes what tests a particular item is subject to at a given stage during its manufacture.

Quality documentation is one of the keys to running an effective QMS. As a result, it is important to define how each level of documentation is controlled. It is also important to understand the relationship between documents to ensure any changes take account of all the knock-on effects which might occur.

CONTRACT REVIEW

Once documented and implemented, the QMS defines how an organisation assures the quality of the product or service it expects to provide. When accepting an order or contract to supply a product or service it is important to ensure the company is capable of meeting the specific requirements. Accordingly, all orders or contracts should, therefore, be reviewed before acceptance to ensure the requirements are capable of being met. Orders or contracts should not be accepted unless the company is capable of meeting the requirements. The following issues need to be addressed at this stage:

(i)   Are the processes and equipment used capable of meeting the requirement?

(ii)   Does the company have sufficient, skilled personnel?

(iii) Are the methods currently used for testing, inspecting and monitoring output adequate to meet the requirements?

(iv)   Are the equipment and methods currently used for taking measurements and testing capable of the required accuracy?

(v)   Does the company fully understand the acceptance criteria? All those items which determine whether or not the item meets the customer's requirements should be written down and fully understood. This includes a proper definition of any subjective judgements such as 'smooth finish', 'scratch-free', or 'blue'.

(vi)   Are all the necessary processes (including design, production, inspection and test) compatible and capable of producing the product/service in accordance with requirements?

(vii) Do procedures exist to produce appropriate records?

A documented system should exist to ensure this review is undertaken before an order is accepted. The system should ensure the following points are checked:

(i)   The requirements are clearly stated in writing;

(ii)   Any differences between the order and the original quotation/tender are resolved; and

(iii) The company is capable of meeting the requirements.

It is usually possible to implement a fairly simple procedure to check points (i) and (ii) when standard or repeat orders are received. It may then be possible to restrict checks to identifying unusual features and ensuring the version required is fully documented before accepting the order. A more rigorous procedure should be implemented whenever new orders, non-standard orders, or special contracts are received. This will require a more detailed check against the above criteria. A documentary record should be kept to demonstrate that this review has taken place. For companies which do not usually produce standard items but work to specific contracts, the above points are often documented as part of a Quality plan prepared specifically for individual contracts.

DESIGN CONTROL

The standard contains detailed requirements on how the design process should be controlled, and specifies that procedures to cover the following activities should be fully documented:

Planning
It is essential that everyone understands their role and responsibilities in the design process and how they interface with other groups. The standard specifies that:

(i) The organisation for each design activity should be documented so responsibility for each activity and interfaces between activities are defined; and
(ii) The person responsible for each activity should have the necessary qualifications and sufficient resources to carry out the activity.

The standard requires procedures to specify how and when information is transmitted between groups. The timely flow of controlled and accurate information is essential to ensure the design process is carried out effectively and without errors in cases where a number of groups work on specific elements of complex designs.

Design input
Design requirements may be received directly from external customers or from internal sources such as the marketing department. Before

accepting a design requirement, the design department should review it to ensure it is sufficiently detailed to enable them to know what is expected from the design process.

Design output

Output from the design process may consist of drawings and specifications supported by calculations, analyses, tests and reviews to demonstrate that the design conforms to the input requirements. Design procedures should ensure that the design output:

(i)   Meets the input requirements. It is only possible to do this if the input requirements are adequately specified;

(ii) Contains instructions to define how conformance of the product or service can be verified during production;

(iii) Meets all the necessary regulatory requirements. The design process should ensure that all regulatory requirements are considered, not only those specified as part of the input requirements; and

(iv) Meets necessary safety standards. The design department should identify all parts of the design which are safety critical so they can be carefully monitored during the production process.

Design verification

Procedures should exist to ensure the design output conforms in all regards to the input requirements. Design verification should be planned, performed and the results fully documented as part of the design process. A number of methods may be acceptable depending on the circumstances. Typical methods include:

(i)   Holding design reviews;

(ii) Undertaking tests;

(iii) Carrying out checking calculations; and

(iv) Comparing the new design with similar, proven designs.

Typically, a combination of these methods might be adopted. The company should consider carefully which methods are most appropriate for any given design project. Unless a design is proven before it is released for production, it is likely that significant rectification costs and wasted time will arise during the production process.

Design changes

Whenever a change is made to a released design, for example a new material is introduced, the change should be proven, approved and communicated to everyone concerned in a controlled way. The procedures necessary to control design changes usually form part of the system for document control.

DOCUMENT CONTROL

An effective QMS ensures that all activities are carried out in a controlled way, so that everyone knows what they are supposed to do. This requires documentation of how tasks should be performed. Because many processes are related and interdependent, it is important to ensure any change is implemented by everyone at the same time. This requires a system to ensure documents are controlled so that: (i) Everyone who needs to use a document has easy access to it; and (ii) Only the current version of a document is available at any time. This avoids confusion and mistakes.

Procedures should cover the origination and amendment of documents, detailing who holds the document; who may authorise changes; how documents are reissued; how obsolete documents are withdrawn; and a system for verifying the current version (perhaps using a master list). Key documents which need to be controlled include: (i) the quality manual and procedures; (ii) department manuals and procedures; (iii) work instructions, including test, inspection and planning documents; and (iv) drawings and specifications.

PURCHASING

To ensure the Quality of the end product or service it is important to ensure the quality of bought-in services and materials. This applies equally to component suppliers and sub-contractors. The buying company is responsible for ensuring that the Quality system of his supplier is effective, and should ensure that:

(i)   The supplier is capable of meeting the customer's requirements. This may be established by supplier assessment, verification of third party approvals, and review of past performance;
(ii)   The supplier is provided with sufficient written data to enable a complete understanding of the requirements;
(iii) Products and services can only be purchased from approved suppliers; and

(iv) A supplier's performance is regularly monitored and corrective actions introduced where appropriate.

PRODUCT SUPPLIED BY CUSTOMER

Items may sometimes be supplied by a customer to be built into the end product. The company should introduce a procedure to ensure these items are checked, identified, securely stored and used as specified in the contract.

PRODUCT IDENTIFICATION AND TRACEABILITY

All companies should implement procedures to enable them to identify each product, sub-product, component and raw material at each stage in the manufacturing process, from goods inwards to final despatch. This helps avoid the possibility of products or components being mixed up and perhaps fitted in the wrong place. Unique part numbers and revision numbers are a common means of achieving this objective.

In some industries it may be necessary to apply more rigorous procedures. For example, in the defence and aerospace industries it may be necessary to be able to trace every component back to its original manufacturing batch to enable component failures to be investigated or to trace all other critical users so replacements can be fitted before further failures arise. A system to ensure full traceability can be very costly and time consuming to implement. As a result, it is not a mandatory part of the standard. Traceability should generally be specified in individual contracts unless it is required as part of the industry QAS.

PROCESS CONTROL

A system should be implemented prior to commencing production to ensure process controls are adequate to ensure products and services conform to specification. The system should ensure that:

(i) The activities and equipment required to produce the output are identified;
(ii) Instructions are prepared describing how activities are to be performed. These instructions should include details of:

(a) training and skills required;

(b) set-up/start-up procedures;

(c) the order in which activities should be carried out;

(d) material and equipment requirements;

(e) how the process is to be monitored; and

(f) maintenance requirements.

(iii) Instructions describe how the output from a process is assessed to ensure it conforms to requirement. This can include tests, inspection methods and workmanship standards.

Process control may be applied equally to the administrative activities carried out in the organisation. 'Special processes' such as heat treatment, non-destructive testing and welding are employed in some industries. The output from these processes cannot be fully assessed by subsequent inspection or testing. Deficiencies may only show up after the product is in use. These processes may well be critical in the manufacture of products such as, for example, pressure vessels. In order to ensure product quality in these circumstances it is necessary to apply additional special control procedures during manufacturing. Detailed standards exist for a number of processes governing the qualification of operators, appropriate procedures and the records required to demonstrate conformance to procedures. These standards only apply to certain industries.

INSPECTION AND TESTING

Inspection and testing are means of assessing whether or not processes have been carried out correctly and the product conforms to specification. The standard requires that inspection and testing should be considered at all stages in the production process, and be carried out where necessary. Records should be kept as evidence of the tests performed.

The standard focuses on three principal areas in relation to test and inspection:

Receiving inspection

Incoming goods should be checked to ensure they conform to requirements. The type and level of inspection depends on the controls exercised by the supplier, and his previous performance.

In-process inspection and test

In-process test and inspection procedures should identify all non-conforming product. Activities which monitor process parameters and indicate a likelihood of non-conforming product are generally more cost effective than inspection or test activities that only detect non-conforming product after production. In service activities, the term 'non-conforming product' applies to instances where the required service levels have not been met: for example, if 72 hr delivery is promised but not achieved.

Final testing and inspection

The appropriate level of final test and inspection may vary in the light of the overall control environment and should include a check to ensure that all the specified operations have been carried out.

Inspection is generally carried out after an activity has been completed. As a result, it does little other than sort 'good' product from 'bad'. Companies should therefore consider carefully the level, nature and quantity of testing/inspection introduced. Where possible, effort should be directed at preventing errors occurring in the first place. Merely finding errors once they have occurred is expensive (in terms of time and material wasted) and does nothing to prevent errors occurring again in the future.

The standard is concerned to ensure adequate controls exist to ensure products and services conform to specification. It is permitted to modify the control environment to take account of changed circumstances. Individual inspection and testing activities to ensure product conformance may be removed provided it can be demonstrated that prevention activities ensure the errors concerned no longer occur. To operate a cost-effective QMS, procedures should be subject to periodic review to identify appropriate prevention activities which may replace test/inspection procedures.

INSPECTION, MEASURING AND TEST EQUIPMENT

The performance of measuring and test equipment is vital to product integrity for all companies which rely on test and inspection procedures to verify product conformance.

Equipment used to verify that a product conforms to requirements must be reliable and capable. The standard requires that a system is introduced to ensure the right equipment (regularly calibrated to ensure readings are reliable and accurate) is used in the right way. The system should address the following issues:

(i)   Appropriate equipment should be selected for the measurement required;

(ii) Equipment used to assure product quality should be regularly calibrated, and the calibration status should be obvious to the user;

(iii) The calibration methods should be documented to ensure traceability of the calibration to national standards. Re-calibration should be performed sufficiently frequently that it occurs before equipment goes out of calibration;

(iv) A system should be in place to assess the validity of any measurement taken using an instrument which is subsequently found to be out of calibration; and

(v) Calibration records should be kept for each item of measuring equipment.

INSPECTION AND TEST STATUS

It is important that product is labelled clearly and unambiguously to ensure anyone who may need to use it knows the inspection/test status of the item. This ensures that only proven, conforming product passes to the next stage in the process. Methods such as tags, stamps, labels, route cards, colour-coding and location may be used to indicate the three test states: awaiting inspection/test; passed inspection/test; and failed inspection/test.

CONTROL OF NON-CONFORMING PRODUCTS

Non-conforming product should be clearly identified to ensure it is not used. A procedure should describe who is authorised to decide the means of disposal for non-conforming material (rework, repair, use in another application or scrap); how the decision is communicated; and how subsequent operations are controlled. This information should then be used to drive the corrective action activity. For service activities, 'non-conforming product' applies to areas where service levels have not been met; for example a client report not issued on time or containing errors.

CORRECTIVE ACTION

A key element of any QMS is the continuous improvement of quality. The system should ensure that actions are introduced to prevent problems from recurring, the effectiveness of the prevention activities are verified, and any change in procedures is properly documented and implemented. A procedure should define the responsibility for initiating and implementing corrective actions. Where possible the system should allow anyone who discovers a problem or error to highlight the need for corrective action. Specific areas where procedures are required include:

(i)   investigating the causes of non-conforming product and introducing actions to prevent recurrence. For service activities this applies to recording any instances where service levels have not been met, and implementing corrective action.

(ii) analysing processes, concessions, quality records, service records and customer complaints to detect trends and introduce actions to prevent non-conforming products or services.

HANDLING, STORAGE, PACKAGING AND DELIVERY

A procedure is required to ensure the product is adequately packed, handled and stored to prevent damage or deterioration at all stages from the receipt of goods to safe delivery to the customer. Protection measures might include site security to prevent vandalism or theft; packing or handling procedures to protect the finish on a product; or special handling techniques to prevent, for example, damage to electronic components through electrostatic discharge.

QUALITY RECORDS

Records may represent the only evidence that designated Quality procedures have been applied to any given product or service. As a result, it is important to decide the nature of the records required to demonstrate this compliance, and the procedures to ensure they are properly maintained and stored. These procedures should describe:

(i)   The records required to demonstrate compliance with the requirements of the standard.

(ii)   Record storage and retrieval procedures.

(iii) The period for which records should be retained.

INTERNAL QUALITY AUDITS

To ensure the QMS is properly implemented and continues to meet the requirements of ISO9001, procedures should be defined covering two key activities:

(i)   Management review to ensure the QMS continues to meet the requirements of the standard. It is pointless ensuring that everyone is working to the QMS if the QMS itself is not adequate to fulfil the requirements laid down by the standard. Senior management should undetake a regular review of the current system and implement corrective actions. This may include a review of audits, quality costs, outgoing/in-process quality measurements and customer complaints. A record should be kept of the review, together with resulting actions.

(ii) Quality audits to ensure everyone is working in accordance with the QMS. The quality audit procedure should define the following points:

(a) audit methods;

(b) responsibility for scheduling and carrying out audits;

(c) how the audit schedule will be determined;

(d) how audit results will be recorded; and

(e) corrective action and follow up procedures.

Auditing is a key requirement of the standard because it is only through auditing that a company can determine whether or not the QMS is being properly implemented. It is a skilled process which should be carried out by trained personnel if it is to yield positive, beneficial results.

TRAINING

Individuals should have access to the correct procedures, tools and skills in order to carry out tasks in accordance with requirements. The appropriate skills may be acquired through a combination of qualification, training and experience. A system should be designed to identify the training needs for any activity affecting product or service quality. Detailed records should be maintained of an individual's capability to carry out specific assignments.

SERVICING

Where servicing is an important part of customer requirements (for example the regular servicing of heating equipment, or the installation of computer networks), the above procedures should be applied to the service activity to ensure it conforms to requirements.

STATISTICAL TECHNIQUES

Statistical techniques may sometimes be applied to verify the acceptability of a product or process. Where these techniques are used they should be thoroughly understood and documented. Statistical techniques may include:

(i)   Inspection sampling plans (governed by BS6001) where the acceptability of a batch of product is determined by the inspection of a sample.
(ii) Statistical Process Control where the control of a process is achieved by monitoring the control parameters.

6 A STORY OF CONTINUOUS QUALITY IMPROVEMENT

INTRODUCTION

For many companies, the costs of not getting things right first time, the non-conformance costs, can amount to 25 per cent of turnover. Eliminating this unnecessary burden enables a company to improve profitability in the short term and enhance competitiveness in the longer term.

Non-conformance costs may arise in any department. All departments spend some time doing things over again or rectifying other people's errors. Consequently all departments are involved in Quality Improvement; no-one is exempt. Each and every individual is involved in ensuring that the right things are done right first time.

The objective of Quality Improvement is to continuously improve Quality by eliminating non-conformance in every activity throughout the company. The benefits which can accrue from the implementation of a successful Quality Improvement Programme are enormous: improved customer satisfaction; elimination of error and waste; reduction in operating costs; increased motivation and commitment of employees; increased profitability and competitiveness: indeed the very survival of the company may be at stake.

Implementation of a Quality Improvement Programme is, however, not a step to be undertaken lightly. It demands absolute commitment from everyone, starting with senior management, if it is to succeed. It frequently requires a change in company culture and a radical rethink of every activity being performed in the company. The commitment of senior management is the most important factor in ensuring the success of the programme, and is also the most difficult to achieve. There is no easy method for achieving this commitment. It requires constant attention, persuasion and powerful evidence of the benefits which can accrue from Quality Improvement.

The effort required to implement a successful Quality Improvement

Programme is considerable; but the cost of not implementing one can be catastrophic. Inadequate attention to consistently meeting the requirements of customers frequently results in business failure. Total Quality is only for survivors!

ALPHA SYSTEMS

This story follows the steps taken by Alpha Systems to implement a Quality Improvement Programme. Although the company is fictitious the story reflects the experiences of a number of real companies. The basic approach adopted by Alpha, and the problems it encounters, are common to many businesses, whether manufacturing or service, large or small, high technology or traditional.

However, the story only represents one possible way of implementing Quality Improvement. Every company is unique. Consequently, every Improvement Programme will be unique. The aim of this chapter is to provide an insight into what is possible. Whatever methodology is used there are a number of key steps which any Programme must include:

(i) *Planning for Quality Improvement*: this phase is key to the success of any Quality Improvement Programme. The objectives of this phase are to:

   (a) secure the active commitment of senior management to the continuous improvement of quality.
   (b) determine the most appropriate means of implementing Quality Improvement within the organisation.
   (c) develop a detailed plan to guide the implementation of the Quality Improvement Programme.

(ii) *Understanding customers*: companies only exist because they serve the needs of their customers. Quality improvement is about improving the ability of a business to meet customer requirements. In order to improve quality, it is essential to:

   (a) understand the external customers, their requirements and how well they are being met.
   (b) identify how internal processes work to meet the needs of the external customers. It is only by improving the performance of these processes that a business can better meet the needs of its external customers, at minimum cost.

(iii) *Understanding quality costs*: non-conformance costs arise because things go wrong. Activities which generate high quality costs are either not satisfying customer needs, or not working efficiently. It is therefore essential that the Improvement Programme identifies the magnitude of quality costs and where they occur. This information can be used as a focus to drive the Programme.

(iv) *Quality awareness*: a Quality Improvement Programme relies on the complete commitment of all employees. Every individual must be educated to ensure they understand their role, and how they can contribute to Quality Improvement. Employees also need to be kept informed of progress

(v) *Measurement of performance*: it is only possible to focus on improving performance if the current performance of processes is measured. Improvement goals can then be targeted and improvements monitored.

(vi) *Prevention*: businesses have traditionally relied upon checking output for errors and then correcting them; this is a very inefficient way to run a business. The cornerstone of Quality Improvement is the recognition that errors are not inevitable, they can be prevented. Action is necessary to ensure any problems which prevent quality improvement are identified and corrective actions implemented to eliminate them. A system is required to achieve this on an on-going basis.

The following story illustrates how a business might implement a Quality Improvement Programme incorporating these key requirements.

SETTING THE SCENE

Alpha Systems designs, manufactures and services electronic instruments. It has been reasonably successful over the years. The case study begins a couple of weeks after the annual strategic planning programme has been completed.

The personnel involved:

Michael Wright	General Manager
Richard Harrison	Manufacturing Manager
Jane Reed	Purchasing Manager
David Morgan	Engineering Manager
Ian Gray	Service Manager

Tom Webster   Sales Manager
Julie Ford   Quality Manager
Alan Peters   Human Resources Manager
Adrian Cole   Financial Controller
John Fergus   Programme Administrator

RECOGNISING THE NEED FOR IMPROVEMENT

Michael Wright has been the General Manager of Alpha Systems for three years. He had been promoted from sales manager in another division of the Alpha group. Michael had set himself the objective of revitalising the company and achieving a significant improvement in profitability. He hoped to achieve this within five years.

Since his arrival, Michael had systematically examined every activity in the business. He had restructured, modernised, introduced new systems and methods and carried out training at all levels in the company. The products seemed to be what the market required and everyone was working hard, but still there was no significant improvement in the profit being generated.

Michael wondered what he could do next. He was running out of ideas and began to wonder if he really had what it takes to turn the business around. Whenever things seemed to be going well a new problem emerged. Things just never seemed to run smoothly.

The previous year they had lost a major US order because the tender didn't arrive on time. They had been asked to bid late. The sales and marketing people had done a great job putting together a detailed presentation at short notice and the customer seemed very impressed with the product. As long as the price was right it looked like the order was in the bag. The salesman put the order in for typing and marked it urgent – he also spoke to the sales office in advance so they could rush it through when it arrived. Unfortunately, he only included the customer's name on the order and not their address. The sales office looked up the address on the database and sent the quote off. The quote went to a division of the company with whom Alpha had previously done business, not the division which had requested the quotation. By the time the mistake had been discovered the tender closing date had passed and the order lost.

Then, six months ago, the manufacturing line came to a complete halt. The display panels used on all the instruments had cloudy windows instead of clear ones. This made the display very difficult to read. The Quality Manager reacted swiftly. She withdrew the whole stock of windows and had them individually checked. This yielded enough clear panels to start the line again. She took the remaining panels to do battle with the supplier. But the supplier had never been told how clear the panels had to be and had no means of checking them for clarity. Alpha relied on checking them when fitting them to the instrument. This problem batch of panels had particularly thick windows which made them appear cloudy. As soon as he knew of the problem, the supplier's inspector visited Alpha and determined visually how clear the window needed to be to ensure a clear display. He then assured the Quality Manager that no more cloudy windows would get past him. The problem was resolved and the line has now been running for six months with no further problems. However, the line had lost two days' production.

Michael called a management meeting to discuss the continuing lacklustre results. He did not see why the rest of the team should not share the responsibility. The team agreed they had done all the right things in restructuring and modernising Alpha. They had just run into bad luck recently with a series of 'one-off' problems. Now these had been resolved (the Quality Manager gave details of the actions taken), an improvement in profit should soon be seen. Michael was somewhat reassured and closed the meeting in a more positive mood.

On returning to his office he found Adrian Cole, his Financial Controller and longest serving team member, waiting for him. Adrian was worried. He had been with the company for ten years and had seen these 'one-off' problems throughout that time. He did not see why they were miraculously going to disappear this time. Sure, there was a lot of activity, and a lot of problems had been resolved. But as soon as one lot of problems was resolved another crop would appear. They were all becoming experts at resolving problems. He often wondered how come they never saw the problems coming so they could prevent them arising in the first place?

Michael felt his spirits drop again. After Adrian left he went on a tour around the company to talk to some of the old timers and see how they felt. If Adrian was right, then something radical had to be done. They could not spend every day staggering from one crisis to the next, never moving forward. Alpha was in business to produce electronic instruments, not to become expert trouble shooters. Perhaps that was where his profit was going. He was running a 'ghost factory' whose mission was to solve problems. There had to be a better way.

A few days later Michael called the Quality Manager into his office.

'Julie', he began, 'since the management meeting I've been thinking a lot about quality and the problems we've been having. I think we may be talking ourselves into believing that things are getting better. I was talking to Fred, the buyer, last night about the great work your team has done to resolve the 'panel display' problem. He said a similar problem arose about five years ago and he would expect it to happen again another five years from now! It really made me think about the value of all the effort we're spending solving problems. We seem to spend a great deal of our effort finding and fixing problems rather than preventing them occurring in the first place. If all we do is keep fixing problems there will always be new problems to take their place. What ideas do you have about what we could do?'

Julie thought for a while before replying ' I've been meaning to talk to you for a while, Michael, about the possibility of implementing a Quality Improvement Programme. I think we spend all our time fixing problems because that's the way we've always worked. We haven't got any systematic means of preventing errors occurring. So we wait for them to occur and then go round fixing them. A Quality Improvement Programme would completely change our way of working so that we invest effort in getting things right up front. That way we prevent errors occurring, rather than fixing them afterwards.'

'Have any other companies that you know implemented this type of Programme? And what have they achieved?'

'A couple of recent seminars have given me some useful details about companies which have implemented this type of Programme. They seem to have gained significant benefits. Would you like to read the information and see what it's all about?'

'Yes, that would be interesting. If we did decide to go down this route, how long would it take you to get it all underway? We could certainly do with some quick results on this.'

Julie drew in a breath, 'It's not quite as simple as that, Michael. We only get one chance at this. So we need to make sure we understand what we're doing before we rush into it. The one thing that comes through loud and clear from my reading is that this is not a quick fix motivation campaign. It's about changing the culture of the Company and everyone in it. We need to make everyone believe that preventing defects is possible and is what we, the management, want them to do. It will need the full commitment of everyone in the company, starting with you, if we are going to succeed. It certainly isn't something that I can implement alone. There's no formula or management technique to make it happen. We need to make those changes one step at a time, taking everyone in the Company with us at each stage. A number of different approaches have been developed for implementing Quality Improvement. I think you should read the material I have pulled together and then we can decide how to proceed.'

'OK, Julie. You've convinced me that I need to slow down and take things one step at a time. I'll read that material over the weekend. Perhaps we could meet first thing on Monday to discuss where we go from here. There's just one thing before you leave; why doesn't our Quality Management System achieve it all for us? It's approved to BS5750; I thought that was all about preventing defects and ensuring conformance?'

Julie thought before replying, 'Quality Standards like BS5750 are designed to prevent customers from receiving non-conforming products or services. They do not really focus so much on achieving those requirements without errors or rework on the way. Also they do not cover all the other activities where we generate errors and waste; such as accounts, personnel and administration. Although we involved the workforce when we implemented the Quality System we never really sold them the idea that they are personally involved in improving their own activities. To some extent they feel that the Quality System will do it all for them. Provided they work within the system, conforming products and services will result. I think the Quality System is essential because it establishes a baseline and framework; but now we want to involve the workforce in making improvements in the way we all work. This builds on the Quality System and takes it to the next level.'

'Oh, I see. Or at least I think I do. The Quality System has resulted in a controlled way of working in those areas associated with the products and services we sell to our customers. What we want to do now is to release the creativity in our people to improve the way we work in every activity we carry out. Then we can continue to meet our customers' requirements; but do so without all the errors and waste on the way. I've certainly got a lot to think about. I'll see you on Monday morning.'

PLANNING FOR QUALITY IMPROVEMENT

Purpose of this section

Before a Quality Improvement Programme (QIP) can be successfully implemented, senior management must recognise the need for Quality

Improvement and must understand the total commitment required from them if it is to succeed.

Having committed themselves to implement Quality Improvement, they then need to put together a detailed plan to guide the implementation of the Programme.

Management commitment and involvement

Having recognised the need for Quality Improvement, the first objective it to secure management commitment to the new company culture, focusing on preventing errors, rather than merely fixing them once they have arisen. The commitment required from management to a QIP is absolute if the Programme is to succeed.

It is then necessary to gain the support and commitment of the entire workforce. The attitudes and actions of employees are generally determined by what they believe management wants of them. It is therefore essential that management defines clearly and unambiguously its requirements in relation to Quality. This is recorded formally in the Quality Policy of the Company.

The Quality Policy is an important statement of management's intention as regards Quality. But it is the demonstration by every manager in their day-to-day work that they are *never* prepared to compromise their commitment to the Quality Policy that will make a Quality Improvement Programme succeed.

Gaining the support and commitment of senior management is not easy and is one of the major reasons for the failure of a Quality Improvement Programme. The go-ahead to implement a Programme may be relatively easy to attain. It is the personal commitment and involvement from every manager that is difficult. Gaining this commitment requires persuasion, practical examples, reports on the benefits of a QIP, and continuous effort! Any and every means possible should be used. These may include:

- estimate of the cost of non-conformance. This demonstrates the cost of not committing to Continuous Improvement.
- obtain customer input on current performance and how well their requirements are being met.
- describe accounts of other companies' experiences and the benefits they have realised.
- consider using videos, articles and press clippings on Quality Improvement to reinforce the message.
- training and seminars.

- a pilot run in a department committed to Quality Improvement to demonstrate the benefits.

Although management commitment may be difficult to attain, it generally gets easier as the Programme develops and the benefits of success begin to be realised. The publication and celebration of early successes is an essential part of increasing the momentum of a Quality Improvement Programme.

Quality Improvement Structure

In most companies, significant changes are required when implementing a Quality Improvement Programme (QIP). In order to plan and pilot the implementation of the Programme most companies form a Quality Improvement Team (QIT). The team should be composed of a chairman, an administrator, and a representative of each department.

Selection of the chairman and administrator is important since they will become deeply involved in the Programme and will direct the running of the QIT. The role of the QIT is described in more detail in Chapter 7.

CASE STUDY
PART 1: in Michael's office

Julie turned up at Michael's office on Monday morning and was pleased to find Michael obviously expecting her. Too often in the past she turned up for appointments with Michael to discuss Quality matters only to find something more important had come up and Michael was not available. Perhaps this was a sign that things were really changing!

'Morning Julie,' said Michael, 'I spent quite some time over the weekend reading about Improvement Programmes. They certainly seem to have produced impressive results elsewhere. I have decided that we will launch a Programme here and it seems that the first thing we need to do is to determine our Quality Policy and then get the rest of the management team to understand and sign up to it. Once that is achieved we can form the Team and really get underway. I have had a go at writing a policy. In fact I all but copied it from one of the examples which was included in the information you provided, and I would like your opinion.'

Michael passed over the following statement for Julie's comment:

> The Alpha Quality Policy is to understand our customers' requirements and ensure we meet those requirements first time, every time.

Julie read the policy several times and then smiled. 'It seems absolutely fine to me, Michael. We could include a lot more on customer satisfaction, reducing costs and the like, but I think that will just confuse the issue. This way it is short and to the point and no one can misunderstand what we want them to do. It looks good, although we will need to make sure everyone understands that they may have internal and external customers.'

'Excellent,' replied Michael. 'I suggest we arrange a meeting of the management team next Tuesday to convince them of the need for an Improvement Programme and get them to sign up to the Quality Policy. I would also like to agree who will be the chairman and administrator of the QIT since they seem to be important roles. I suggest we spend some time discussing that now. I know from our discussions on Friday that you can't implement the Programme alone but shouldn't you at least be the chairman of the Team?'

'I would certainly like to be, but I don't think it would be appropriate, Michael. If we really want to get the message across that Quality is the responsibility of everyone and not just the Quality department then we should elect someone else as chairman. I do agree that it should be a senior member of management. Perhaps you should do it?'

'That might be a good idea. Certainly, I have to make sure it succeeds. If it doesn't then I may not have a business to run in a few years. But, if I do it, people might agree just because I suggest things rather than being really committed and involved. I think, if possible, we should think of someone else.'

Julie thought before replying, 'What about Tom Webster, the sales manager? He's obviously very close to our customers and could provide valuable feedback on how they view us as a company. He often has to pick up the pieces when things go wrong, and pacify the customers. Somehow, I don't think he'd agree to do it, though.'

'Tom would do an excellent job,' Michael replied. 'The only problem with having Tom is that it might make people believe the Programme is solely about the external customer, in effect a Customer Care Programme. We also need to get the message across that to eliminate errors and waste we need to satisfy internal customers at every stage; the person next in line who receives the output from our activity. I think Tom would bring valuable expertise to the Team but I don't think he should be chairman.'

'Just a minute. I've had an idea,' Michael exclaimed. 'What about Adrian? He was the one who put the idea into my head in the first place by suggesting that we ought to be able to see problems coming and so prevent them. He's a long standing and well respected member of the management team. He has high personal standards and would be invaluable in putting a cost to the current levels of waste and errors we are suffering. He is genuinely concerned that we're becoming a company of trouble shooters and I think he would welcome the opportunity to do something about it.'

'If we can convince him that the Quality Improvement Programme will be implemented everywhere, including his finance department, then I think he would be an excellent choice. If we get him on board it will convince a lot of the others that the Programme has a good chance of success. Adrian has a reputation for only backing those projects which are dead certs. What about one of my Quality engineers as the administrator? John Fergus would be an excellent choice. He's bright, good with people and a born organiser. I think he'd relish this sort of opportunity.'

'OK,' replied Michael. 'I'll get Val to organise a meeting. If you bring John along we can introduce him to the management team. I suggest we save asking Adrian to be the chairman until the end of the meeting.'

PART 2 : The initial management meeting

Julie introduced John to each of the management team as they arrived but at this stage did not explain what he was doing at the meeting. Michael welcomed everyone and opened the meeting.

MICHAEL I'm pleased you could all make it this afternoon. I would like to discuss the proposal that we implement a Quality Improvement Programme within Alpha. Let me briefly outline our position. For the past three years our sales have been around £40M despite the expanding market for our products. So we are losing market share to our competitors. Our profit for the year is forecast at £610K, only 1.5 per cent of sales. When I took over, I firmly believed that within five years we would return at least 5 per cent of sales. If we don't improve our profits then not only will I be out of a job but the Alpha group will probably be looking for somewhere more attractive to invest their money. We need to improve our ability to satisfy our customers and also improve our profitability by reducing internal costs and increasing sales. The recent problems we have had with Quality have really made me think about where we are going and seem to tie up with our poor profitability. Unless we deliver to our customers what they ordered when they require it then we will never be able to increase our sales. We also seem to spend a great deal of our time and effort solving problems and virtually no time at all preventing problems occurring in the first place. Julie and I have found some very positive information on companies who have recognised similar problems and have implemented a Quality Improvement Programme with some impressive results. I would like us to implement such a Programme here and this is what I would like to discuss today.

TOM I agree, Michael. We need to greatly improve the products that manufacturing deliver. I will certainly support a Quality Improvement Programme in manufacturing.

MICHAEL Thank you, Tom. But you know it's not just the manufacturing area that is involved in generating errors and rework. Although we do have problems with some of our products, we also have problems in the non-manufacturing areas. Product Quality isn't enough. Every task performed and decision taken has to be of a high Quality. To survive today, we need to get the whole act right, not just the product. Do you remember last year when we lost that big order in the States because the tender did not arrive on time? I know your people did a great job on the proposal and presentation. But we just failed to send the proposal to the correct address. That had nothing to do with the product at all. I'm sure we all know of other examples where silly errors have caused us real problems. In fact, Julie has estimated that, in common with many other companies, as much as 25 per cent of our effort in all departments may be involved in doing jobs over again. We need to be able to harness all that effort productively.

DAVID I agree with you that every department generates errors and rework, but I really can't believe that a quarter of my people's effort is being spent on unproductive tasks.

RICHARD Well, you're always moaning about your people spending time in production sorting out problems. Perhaps if the product was right in the first place they wouldn't need to waste that time. Also my chaps wouldn't have to sit around waiting for your people to turn up!

TOM I suppose if we even look at this meeting, there's been a lot of wasted time. Two people turned up ten minutes late so the rest of us had to sit around and wait. Just think what that must have cost. I do agree, though, that 25 per cent seems a bit far-fetched.

MICHAEL Maybe 25 per cent is too high, but perhaps we shouldn't get too bogged down with the exact percentage just yet. As part of the Programme we will find out what it really is and I expect we'll all be quite surprised. I don't suppose we're that much better than other companies, so I do expect our Quality costs will be approaching 25 per cent. Let's accept 25 per cent for the moment. Then, given our current salary bill of £12M, we are spending £3M doing things over again. That doesn't include scrap material, or costs associated with excess inventory and the like. £3M certainly seems a target worth working for. Even if we only eliminate a proportion of it, it'll do a lot to improve our profitability.

ADRIAN I agree we won't be able to save the whole £3M. We have to invest some money in running the Programme and training people. But if we really can eliminate errors and rework, then we should also see additional benefits. People get really fed up doing rework and solving the same old problems over again. I think the Programme would have a beneficial effect on people's morale and their loyalty to the company. I've read a bit about Quality Improvement Programmes, and a lot of attention seems to be given to getting people to work together in teams and giving them the power to make changes.

MICHAEL I think at this point I'll ask Julie to tell us a bit about the Programme.

JULIE Before we start on the Programme, I'd like to spend a bit of time discussing what Quality means. In normal conversation, we all seem to use the term Quality in a vague way to denote some measure of goodness or worth. We also confuse Quality with elegance, luxury and all sorts of subjective things. Everyone uses Quality in a different way and none of us really understands what the other means. When I started looking at the Quality Improvement Programme, I realised that defining Quality in subjective terms doesn't really mean anything. Before we can have a Quality Improvement Programme we must define clearly what Quality means in objective terms. Quality to us must mean conformance to requirements. Then everyone can understand what it means. If we want something to be more elegant or more powerful then we must change the requirement; but Quality must always mean conformance to requirements. Using this definition also makes it easier to understand that Quality applies to everything, not just the product.

DAVID It certainly makes sense to me to have a clear definition of Quality. I know in the past I've always had difficulty describing what Quality is. I usually finish up being rather vague and waving my hands around a lot.

TOM It would certainly make for fewer complaints from our customers if we always made everything conform to their requirements. But isn't it going to cost a lot of money?

JULIE If we don't do it then it's going to cost more than money, it's going to cost us our business. If we don't supply to our customers' requirements then someone else will; and eventually we won't have any customers left. But the second fundamental of the Improvement Programme is that it is always cheaper to do things right the first time rather than correct them later. So we are going to have to change the way we work. We will need to invest effort up front getting things right. We will then save the money we currently spend fixing things.

MICHAEL Julie and I have spent some time drawing up a Quality Policy. I'd like you all to read it and decide if you can commit to it. If we can't all commit to it then the Programme cannot go any further.

Michael handed round the Policy and they all spent some time silently reading it.

DAVID It seems to summarise what you have just told us about the Programme. If we are to keep our customers and reduce costs then it seems to me that we have no time to lose. You can certainly count me in.

TOM If we do decide to go ahead, how long will it take to get this thing up and running?

JULIE This is not something we can do overnight. It will take a lot of careful planning. The first thing to do is to set up a project team to plan how we will implement the Programme. I think that if we started now we could have the team formed within two weeks and could begin training them straight away after that. The whole Programme may well take a year to really get going. This is just the start of a never-ending commitment to Quality Improvement. But before we can start we need to select a chairman for the QIT.

MICHAEL I think this is where I come in. Julie and I have discussed it and we would like you, Adrian, to head up the Improvement Team.

ADRIAN But I don't know anything about Quality Improvement.

MICHAEL Neither does anyone else here, so we'll all be learning together. I think you've already shown that you believe we need to improve and that the aims of the Programme are achievable. That's the main qualification you need. Also, John here will act as administrator, so you'll get a lot of help from him.

ADRIAN OK, I'll do it. But, I've got a lot of questions. What do I do? Can I pick my own team? How much time will it take? And what's all this about training?

JULIE You'll be the chairman of the Improvement Team, whose job is to plan and pilot the Programme. I expect it will take about 20 per cent of your time. But we thought that probably wouldn't be too much of a problem as you've got your MBA student on secondment for the rest of the year. Yes, you can pick your own team in conjunction with the department heads. Every department should be represented on the team and the person chosen should have the authority to make commitments on behalf of the department. Once chosen, you and the rest of the team will spend four days learning what the Programme is all about.

ADRIAN Well. That's a bit clearer. As far as the team goes, shouldn't it be the people here?

JULIE You don't have to have the people here on the team. We could involve other members of each department instead.

ADRIAN I don't mind that. There are a few people I can think of that I am sure would do well on the team. But I do need to know that they have the full support of each of the managers here. It can't just be used as a way of the manager opting out of the Programme.

MICHAEL OK Adrian, we'll leave it to you to talk to each of the departments and come up with a team, and then Julie will arrange the training. I suggest, though, that you keep Julie on the team, I think we could do with her help. And Tom could provide some very useful input on our customers' perceptions of us.

ALAN What about the union? If they don't co-operate then we'll be in real difficulties.

MICHAEL I agree. It's vital that we involve them as soon as possible. Let's give Adrian a few days to think through the Programme and then Adrian, Alan and I will talk to the union. I don't really anticipate any problems provided we explain what we're doing and why. They're generally a pretty sensible bunch.

DAVID Just a minute. I think we're getting a bit ahead of ourselves here. I for one feel that I'm being steam-rollered into something I don't really understand. We really need to think about this and discuss it a bit more before we go ahead.

MICHAEL Do other people feel the same way as David?

There were a couple of nods and a few people looked away at this point.

MICHAEL OK, I suggest we get someone to come in and talk to us in further detail about Quality Improvement, the benefits and what's involved. I've just been reading about what other companies have achieved, so I'm all fired up and can't wait to get on with it. Julie, would you please arrange for someone to come in and talk to us early next week. Also I suggest you let everyone have a copy of those articles you lent to me so they can be prepared.

UNDERSTANDING CUSTOMERS

Purpose of this section
This section focuses on customers, how their requirements are identified and how these requirements are communicated throughout the business.

The importance of customers
Organisations only continue to exist because of their ability to meet their external customer requirements. The needs of external customers must drive all the internal processes within the organisation. It is no good continuously improving the effectiveness of the internal processes if, at the end of the day, they are not producing the outputs which the customer requires. It is essential that organisations understand:

(i) Who are their external customers and what are their requirements.
(ii) What are the internal processes which produce the service or product required by the external customer.

(iii) Their customers' perceptions of current performance.

(vi) How performance can be improved.

When implementing a Quality Improvement Programme, it is easy to fall into the trap of becoming focused internally; concentrating resource on improving internal processes and reducing costs at the expense of the needs of external customers. Understanding customer requirements is an essential part of any QIP.

Understanding the customer

It is essential that a comprehensive picture of customer requirements is determined. This is not restricted to the product or service delivered to the customer, but covers the total service required from the organisation as a supplier. There may be a number of different customers to consider, even within the same organisation. The person who places the order has requirements; the receiving department where goods are delivered has requirements; the user has requirements; the person who pays the invoice has requirements. A company which wishes to succeed must be aware of all these requirements and constantly improve its ability to meet them.

There are a number of sources of information on customer requirements. Examples include:

- Customer surveys and trials
- Trade surveys and trials
- Working with selected customers
- Competitor analysis
- Focus groups
- Benchmarking
- Customer complaints
- Legal and guideline standards (for example, British Standards)
- Informal customer, or potential customer comments received from sources such as: the sales force after customer visits; feedback from other employees; and comments heard at conferences, training courses and trade exhibitions.

Every contact with an existing, or potential, customer at any level in the organisation is an opportunity to learn more about their requirements. It is important that this information is tapped and used to improve the ability of the business to meet customer requirements.

Internal processes

An external customer requirement can only be met if internal processes within an organisation are set up effectively to deliver the requirement. A breakdown in the internal supply chain often results in failure to meet external customer requirements. An important part of Quality Improvement is the analysis of the whole organisation to ensure it is set up effectively to meet the requirements of its customers. The following steps are a useful guide to achieving this:

(i)   Identify the basic purpose and objectives of the business. What customer requirements does it exist to fulfil?
(ii) Identify existing and potential future customers of the business. Tap as many sources as possible to ensure their requirements are understood. This includes understanding why potential customers are not actual customers!
(iii) Identify the overall role each department plays in meeting customer requirements and business objectives. This may reveal that changes are required in the roles of departments within the organisation.
(iv) Identify the internal processes which link together to meet the external customer requirements. Ensure the external customer requirements flow back through the supply chain to determine the customer requirements for each internal process. Only by doing this at each stage in the supply chain can the external customer requirements be met.
(v)   Measure performance overall, and for each process.
(vi) Introduce improvements to each process to improve performance.

CASE STUDY
PART 3: The management meeting

> MICHAEL Adrian, you have asked to discuss the concept of functional analysis at the meeting. Perhaps you could tell us all a bit about it – I certainly haven't used it before.
>
> ADRIAN Functional analysis seems to be an important element in the Quality Improvement Programme. It helps ensure we understand our customers' requirements and are set up to meet them. Basically, it requires that we identify the purpose of our business – the customer needs we exist to fulfil; and how we go about fulfilling them. Then we develop this to decide the objectives of each department within the business – their reasons for existing. We can then identify the specific tasks each department carries out to meet its objectives and decide whether or not these tasks are carried out

in the most effective way. We can then target areas for improvement and introduce measurements to monitor the improvement.

TOM I don't quite understand what you are driving at, Adrian. Surely the purpose of Alpha is to produce products which the customers want to buy. The marketing people should identify what people want to buy. The engineers should design the product; production should make it; and the sales team should sell it.

ADRIAN You are probably right, Tom. That is broadly what we do today as a business and within each department. However, functional analysis requires us to put aside what we have always done and take a radical look at our business. What customer needs do we fulfil? We do not exist to supply electronic instruments; we exist to fulfil a customer need to make accurate fluid flow measurements. In a few years from now that need may not be fulfilled by electronic instruments at all, some other technique may have replaced it. If we take our eye off the ball of customer needs we may continue to make bigger and better electronic instruments which no-one wants any more.

We need to apply this way of thinking to each of our functions and decide what customer needs, whether internal or external, they exist to fulfil. We should forget what each of us have always done and start again from basics with our focus on customer needs and requirements.

MICHAEL You certainly sound very enthusiastic about this concept, Adrian. It requires each of us to look again at why Alpha exists and how we organise our business. It sounds very exciting to me and seems to achieve a great deal – if we can carry it out successfully. I suggest we have a go now at deciding why we exist as a business – perhaps a brainstorming session would be a good way to start. We may not come up with our definitive mission today but at least we will be underway.

RICHARD I agree that our business must always be focused on meeting customer needs but I don't think that, at the moment, we know enough about our customers to do that. Our marketing people are involved with customers when drawing up the product specification; but there must be more to it than that.

JULIE You're right, Richard. The customers have many more requirements than just those associated with the product. Last week I logged a complaint from a customer finance department. He was annoyed that many of the invoices he receives have an error on them. The product we are supplying may be excellent, but the impression we are giving to the finance guy is pretty poor. All these people have an influence on whether the customer continues to do business with us. Although the product may be good we are costing them (and us) a lot of money to sort out problems on our invoices! We need a method to ensure we understand all the customer requirements.

TOM I've got an idea which might help get this off the ground. Why don't we organise a meeting, or a series of meetings, with our customers and find out what they really need from our business. It won't give us all the answers but it should at least point us at areas where we need to dig a little deeper.

MICHAEL That sounds like a good idea, Tom. It will also help start getting us closer to our customers. I suggest that we consider having a series of breakfast meetings, and invite, perhaps, a dozen people to each. We'll need to look at a cross-section of companies, and a cross-section of functions. Perhaps we could look at each of the functions in turn at a separate meeting? Julie, will you and Tom get together and come up with a suggested list. Perhaps you could start by having a look at your complaints log and invite some of those companies.

IDENTIFYING QUALITY COSTS

Purpose of this section
The objective of the Quality Improvement Programme is to develop an approach which ensures goods and services are produced which meet customer requirements for the minimum cost.

The objective is to eliminate the costs associated with not getting things right the first time, the costs of non-conformance (CONC).

The importance of identifying the CONC
Recognising the amount of money devoted to the CONC at the beginning of a QIP frequently underlines the strategic necessity of introducing the Programme. Findings from a number of businesses suggest that the CONC can amount to as much as 25 per cent of turnover in both manufacturing and in service industries. This is certainly a figure which grabs management attention.

Monitoring the CONC can provide a measure of the success of the

QIP. However, it should be recognised that when a QIP is introduced the CONC frequently appears to rise initially. This is because people become more aware of non-conformance and its associated costs as they become able to identify them. Consequently costs become included which would not initially have been thought of as non-conformance costs.

Knowing the CONC associated with individual activities can be used to help prioritise corrective actions, focusing attention on the highest priority areas.

Being aware of the costs associated with error helps every department and individual in their commitment to perform every task right first time.

Calculating the Quality related costs

One of the most useful ways of classifying Quality related costs is to distinguish between the costs of conformance and the costs of non-conformance. Costs of non-conformance are all the costs incurred because failures occur; if there were no failures there would be no requirement for the activity. Costs of conformance are all the costs associated with preventing non-conformances arising.

Cost of non-conformance (CONC)

The most obvious element of CONC are the costs associated with failure to achieve conformance to requirements – the *failure costs*.

Failure costs occur in all areas of the company. They are often accepted as part of the normal course of events and so are easily overlooked.

The fact that failure costs exist is generally well recognised in industry. In order to minimise failure costs many companies operate systems to find failures. There are inevitably costs associated with finding these errors. These are the *appraisal costs*.

Today many of us expect failures to happen and so we need appraisal activities to find them. If failures were eliminated the vast majority of appraisal activities would also no longer be necessary.

Cost of conformance

To reduce the CONC we need to invest in prevention activities. Prevention activities inevitably result in some costs. These are *prevention costs*. Investing in the prevention of failure enables failure and associated appraisal costs to be minimised. This is the fundamental principle underlying Quality Improvement.

The key feature of a QIP environment is that failures are not accepted as a normal occurrence. The root causes of any failures are identified and eliminated by the introduction of prevention activities. Failure is an exceptional occurrence rather than the norm. In this environment we do not need a vast appraisal activity, we only need a small audit activity to ensure our prevention system is working correctly. So after focusing on reducing failure costs we can then look at reducing appraisal costs.

The role of the Quality Improvement Team

The role of the QIT is to devise a method for identifying the total Quality related costs across the company. It is important that all Quality related costs are included at this stage and not just the obvious costs associated with manufacturing. This analysis can then be used as a basis for measuring progress as the QIP is implemented. It can also be used to reinforce the need for implementing the Improvement Programme when communicating with management and employees. The measurement of quality costs provides valuable management information and will require the active participation of every manager and supervisor if it is to be a meaningful measure of current business performance.

The objective of the QIP is to eliminate the CONC by investing in prevention.

CASE STUDY
PART 4: A QIT meeting

> A QIT meeting, following their introductory training course. Adrian calls the meeting to order.
>
> ADRIAN Well, after our training course, I for one was staggered at the number of activities which we have all accepted as being part of our normal business, but which actually are only necessary because we keep getting things wrong.
>
> DAVID I agree, it's quite depressing to think that we've been managing the business so badly all these years.
>
> JANE At least we've now recognised it and are doing something about it. I'm sure there are a lot of people out there who haven't even got to that stage yet.
>
> ADRIAN Since the last meeting, I've been doing some work on our Quality related costs and reckon that, just looking at the obvious costs, they are about 10 per cent of sales, or £5M. Of course, some of these costs will be prevention costs; but I think that's only a very small part of the total. I'm sure the amount we spend on inspection

and rework far outweigh what we spend on prevention. Anyway here's a copy of the figures. They are far from the true total but at least they provide a basis for discussion.

	£000
Field service	850
QA dept	340
Inspection	600
Scrap	1200
Warranty	1500
Rework	300
	£4790 K

JULIE They are very interesting figures, Adrian, but I agree that they are too low. They are probably only about half of the true total since they involve mainly the production-related areas; and many errors occur in the other departments.

DAVID I can see quite easily how we can arrive at the CONC in manufacturing, but I don't see how it can apply to a creative area like design where you exist by developing original ideas.

JANE What about designs which are not implemented? And what about all the changes you carry out once the design has reached production? Those cost a fortune and always seem to delay the launch of our new products.

DAVID Those changes are almost always because manufacturing cannot make the product. They're nothing to do with engineering. We only do the changes to make life easier for them.

JULIE What about introducing a prevention activity? By ensuring manufacturing are included at the earliest stages of your designs, we will know we can manufacture a product before you release the design from engineering and won't need all the changes. The costs of all the changes are certainly a non-conformance cost resulting from a failure to prevent errors at the design stage.

RICHARD I agree with that, Julie, and am sure there are similar examples in every department. Would you, Adrian, spend some time between now and the next meeting discussing non-conformance costs with each department head? That way we will have a more realistic figure to discuss at the next meeting.

IAN One thing that worries me is that the whole of my service department has been included as a CONC. Does that mean that they will all be out of a job as the QIP progresses?

JULIE All my department is included as a CONC as well. We need to make sure we understand what will happen in these areas as the QIP progresses and CONC is eliminated.

ALAN Yes, we are certainly not going to get much support for the Programme if people feel their jobs are threatened – especially the union people.

JOHN The position is obviously quite complicated. But in principle if we improve the Quality of our products and services we will increase our sales and profitability because we will give customers what they require all of the time. The money we save from the reduction of CONC can be invested in growth. The QIP will highlight activities and specific job functions which are no longer required; but as we grow we should be able to redeploy those people in more productive jobs. For example as we improve our outgoing quality we will no longer need so many field service engineers. But we may be able to use them advising customers and salesmen of new applications for our products. Their role could change from customer repair to customer support. This is an area where we are very weak now. It should also help us to win more orders.

ALAN Thanks, John, that's helped set my mind at rest. I hadn't really thought of it that way before.

JULIE I agree that the QIP is not a head count reduction programme. We want to keep all our people and develop them in roles which are more productive for the whole company. But whatever happens we need to succeed with the QIP. If we don't we will all be out of a job as another business folds. And no one wants that to happen.

ADRIAN Thank you everyone. If no one has anything further I suggest we close. The next meeting is in three weeks time. That will give me plenty of time to put together details of the Quality related costs in conjunction with each of you. I for one can't wait to see them. I think they will be very interesting.

QUALITY AWARENESS

Purpose of this section
This section explains the importance of involving everyone in the Quality

Improvement Programme and describes effective means for achieving this objective.

The individual commitment to Quality

To be successful, a Quality Improvement Programme often requires a complete change in the way an organisation is run:

(i) All employees require a greater understanding of customer requirements and the internal processes required to meet these requirements;

(ii) It will no longer be acceptable to rely on finding and fixing errors. The organisation will have to become committed to investing resources in preventing errors arising; and

(iii) Individuals should be empowered to take actions to improve the Quality of output from their own work areas.

To achieve these changes requires the commitment of every employee within the company. The required level of personal commitment is only likely to be achieved if every individual understands the aims and benefits of the Programme, the role they can play, and how they can implement improvements in a successful QIP. A number of activities can help achieve this personal commitment to Quality Improvement:

(i) Education. Individuals need to understand the reasons for the change, what it will mean to them and how they are equipped to contribute. The training must be relevant, interesting and enable people to understand and participate in Quality Improvement.

(ii) Communication. A constant flow of information is necessary, describing progress made by the QIP, how and when individuals will be involved, and the successes achieved.

(iii) Recognition. A system to recognise and publicly reward those who make an outstanding contribution to Quality Improvement can play an important part in encouraging employee commitment.

Education

After the management team agrees on the need for Quality Improvement, and accepts the Programme in principle, the QIT should attend an intensive training course. This course should explain their responsibilities for implementing the Quality Improvement Programme, and ensure they thoroughly understand how it can be implemented. This course may be run internally or by an external trainer depending on the level of existing expertise within the company.

Having been trained, the QIT should plan the education programme for the rest of the workforce. It is important that the whole workforce is included in the training programme. Everyone has their part to play in a company. A receptionist may help to gain or lose a customer as easily as a manager. If a message is not passed on quickly, the customer may choose to look elsewhere for his needs. Production line staff are likely to know more about the things that are wrong where they work than their managers and supervisors. They have probably been living with the problems and fixing things for a number of years.

Experience has shown that the most effective approach to training within a company is to cascade the learning process from the manager to the supervisors and then to individual employees. The duration and content of the education programme depends on the individuals being trained. But they should all understand why the Programme is required and their personal involvement in the drive for Improvement. At each stage the supervisor should be actively involved in the training. This ensures that the supervisor fully understands the Programme and how it affects his area of the business. It also provides an important opportunity to demonstrate his commitment to the Programme to his team. This approach has the added advantage of helping to develop a team approach in all areas of a company. This can result in a dramatic improvement in performance as people become personally committed to their team.

Once teams form and begin looking at areas requiring improvement they will need training in how to analyse and resolve problems. It is no good asking people to make improvements if they have not been given the tools to enable them to do so. The training programme should be designed to enable them to use the essential problem solving tools. The techniques taught will depend on the business, but may include functional analysis, data gathering, Pareto analysis, brainstorming, fishbone diagrams and process control.

In view of the time and experience required to produce training material, many organisations use externally generated training material. If external material is used it must be adapted to ensure it is relevant to the organisation and to the individuals being trained.

CASE STUDY
PART 5: Following the QIT training course

Adrian is talking to Julie and John following the QIT training course.

ADRIAN Now we have been trained I think I understand what's involved in the Programme but I'm a bit unsure of where we go from here on education. I know we are supposed to train our next line of management. But is the QIT really supposed to do that? If we are, then what are we going to do about material. I certainly haven't got time to generate all that along with everything else.

JOHN I understand why it's important to educate everyone but why don't we just get the people who did our training to come and do the training for us – that would certainly save us an awful lot of time and effort.

JULIE We could do that and, as you say, it would save a lot of effort but I don't think it's the right thing to do. The cornerstone of the Programme is the commitment of every manager. Because we want to change attitudes and minds it isn't something we can use outsiders for. What's really needed is to convince our people that we, the managers and supervisors, have really changed. We must demonstrate that we are working in a different way and want them to do the same. Sure, a consultant could come and tell them that we've changed but I don't think they would believe it.

JOHN I suppose that if managers don't train their people themselves, then they could opt out of the Programme altogether. If they are responsible for training their people, they will really have to understand the principles and believe in it.

ADRIAN OK, I agree. Each manager should do his own training. But what about material. We can't expect each manager to generate their own and I haven't got time – what about you Julie?

JULIE I suggest we ask the consultants to generate the training material, under our supervision of course. Then each manager can add local examples to suit the group he's training.

JOHN That sounds good to me. Everyone gets the same basic message but with local examples. The managers don't have too much preparation to do and we don't delay the Programme for weeks whilst we generate our own material. Would you like me to talk to the consultants about it?

JULIE Thanks, John, that would be useful.

A few weeks later Richard arrived in Julie's room – he was looking pretty perplexed.

RICHARD Julie, I've just had a conversation with John, and he has told me we will be spending time this year training everyone in the department. I can understand that the supervisors need to know about the Programme but surely it's a bit over the top training my girls on the line. I don't see that they'll be interested. I thought I'd just issue a memo to them all to let them know what's going on and leave it at that.

JULIE I know it's a big investment, Richard, but I think it's worth it. This Improvement Programme is all about changing the culture of the company and we can only do that if we can change the attitude of everyone in the company. Your girls are just as important in this as you and me. When it comes to Improvement I bet your girls know far more about the things that are wrong in their work area than you or your supervisors. They are the ones who've been living with the problems and fixing them for years. If we want them to make improvements we have to help them to believe they have the ability to do so. Education about the need for improvement and some techniques they can use to analyse and solve problems will give them confidence they can do it. I think that once they have been trained and we show them we want their support, you'll be surprised at just how much they contribute! And to make things easier we can schedule the training for less busy times in the month.

The essential role of communication

The objective of the communication step is to explain the need for improvement to all employees and prepare them for the commitment required to the Improvement Programme.

At some point everyone will receive training on their involvement in the implementation of the Programme. But it is important to keep everyone involved right from the start. The most effective means of developing commitment is to ensure people know what is going on. If people are not kept informed from an early stage they may feel left out of the Programme. This could result in the belief that the Programme is not for them. This could undermine the Programme and may lead to resentment by some employees. The early involvement of everyone helps to generate the enthusiasm and commitment necessary to ensure the success of the Programme.

In the early stages it is particularly important to communicate any successes achieved as a result of the Programme. This encourages all employees to become involved, and helps encourage those who are currently struggling to introduce improvements.

An important part of the Improvement Programme is to develop a team approach between employees and their supervisors. Ensuring key messages are communicated to employees by their immediate supervisor helps this team building process. It also demonstrates his involvement and commitment to the Programme.

Effective methods for communicating

The communication activity has two essential ingredients, both of which need to be planned by the QIT:

(i) General information about the Quality Improvement Programme can be communicated through posters, competitions, a company magazine, or special events. It is important that this material is interesting, varied, and kept up to date. A steady stream of information should be supplied to employees to keep them informed of progress and developments. If this stream dries up it is likely to be seen as yet another management fad implemented without commitment. This will undermine its continued success.

(ii) Regular meetings between employees and their supervisor should be used to reinforce the general information produced by the company on the Improvement Programme, focusing on the particular department in question. These meetings should also be used to discuss specific non-conformance problems affecting the department and the necessary corrective actions. As well as producing results this also primes employees for the education and operational steps of the process.

CASE STUDY
PART 6: At a QIT meeting

Adrian is standing in front of the team at a regular Quality Improvement Team meeting.

ADRIAN The most important thing about communication seems to be that everyone must receive sincere and easily understood messages. The most effective way to achieve this is through their supervisors and peers since these are the people they work with every day and have most influence over their opinions. If we get this step right, it will make our job much easier because people will become enthusiastic about the Programme and want to be actively involved.

DAVID What about organising a meeting where Michael talks to everyone about what we're doing? The supervisors could all be there to signal their support for the Programme and everyone will hear the same message at the same time.

JOHN I think individual meetings with the supervisor would be better although it will require more effort than just having one big meeting. We need such a change in the way we work that it is essential we explain the situation carefully to everyone and that each person hears it from his supervisor. Any other way and people might not feel involved or they might feel their supervisor is not involved. If they do not feel involved then they cannot become committed.

JANE I think John's right. At a big meeting people can just sit back and listen without really becoming involved. At a meeting with their supervisor, who they know well, they are much more likely to challenge him and ask questions which should result in their being more involved and committed at the end of the day.

JULIE We also want to ensure the communication meetings are a regular event so people understand that this is an ongoing process and not just a nine day wonder. That wouldn't happen if we just had a big meeting with Michael. I think John's right; we should do it through the supervisor. If we encourage regular meetings between the supervisor and his people, then we've started to build a means to enable groups to look at their activities and identify areas for improvement. If we can all agree that the supervisor is the best person to give the message, we can then discuss the message we want him to get across.

DAVID OK, you've convinced me. The supervisor is the key to getting our message over so that the workforce will really believe we're serious about this whole thing. I think the message needs to be simple and clear. We, the management team, have recognised that we have never clearly told the workforce that we require every job to be done right the first time. That is what we are now asking them to do and we will help them by fixing the problems they identify and investing time and effort in preventing failures. If we all work on it together we can eliminate errors. The Programme is just a means to ensure we achieve that goal.

RICHARD That sounds a clear basis for our message, David. I think the supervisors will believe in it and the workforce will understand what it's all about and will respond positively.

ADRIAN Having been briefed earlier by John on the advantages of the supervisor holding regular communication meetings with his people, I've already spoken to Michael on how we might handle this and we have come up with the following suggestion. Michael and the QIT will meet all the managers and supervisors next Thursday to explain the Programme and its importance to the future of our company; the steps we need to take to improve our operations; and the fundamental role played by managers and supervisors in ensuring the success of the Programme.

We will then ask each of them to organise regular meetings with their teams to discuss the Improvement Programme and begin identifying and introducing improvements. We will provide information on the Programme, the measurements which have been introduced so far and the costs of non-conformance which we have identified to date.

IAN That sounds like an excellent first step. But how do we know that the supervisors will actually hold regular meetings?

JULIE They will only continue to hold the meetings if they believe we, their managers, are interested. We, therefore, must also hold regular meetings with our immediate subordinates to discuss the Programme, the measurements they are making, the problems they are finding and the corrective actions introduced. I suggest we then report back to the QIT. That way we will get a much better feedback on how the Programme is being received and the progress being made.

TOM I think we all agree on involving the supervisors in regular communication meetings. If we take up Julie's suggestion and all hold regular meetings with our people, that should ensure supervisors know we are committed. That should encourage them to continue to hold their meetings. What about organising some general information on the Programme which we could display around the building. That way we'd keep the message in front of everyone all the time.

IAN That sounds like a good idea, Tom. I think we need someone to be responsible for co-ordinating the information, making sure the material is always fresh and up to date. Perhaps Alan could do that if we all provide ideas and information.

ALAN   That's fine by me, provided everyone comes up with information and keeps it up to date. Nothing signals to people more clearly that a Programme is running out of steam than a pile of out of date information.

JOHN   I've already ordered some posters. I also had an idea last night that perhaps we could organise a competition to design some more. It would help generate enthusiasm and would certainly be a lot cheaper than getting them done outside.

ALAN   Good idea, John. I'll see about arranging a competition. We could discuss it at the next meeting. Where do you suggest we display the posters you've ordered once they arrive?

TOM   Not on the existing noticeboards, that's for sure. I think we should invest in some new noticeboards just for QIP information. That way we won't get lost among the darts results!

JULIE   I think the budget could stretch to a few noticeboards; I'll get them organised. But I think we need a bit more than a few posters. We've now established measurements in all departments. I suggest that in addition to reviewing them at QIT meetings we could also put up the charts showing progress on the noticeboards.

JOHN   I'm not sure that just putting up all the measurements will be very meaningful. What about featuring one department each month? Each department could describe the measurements they have introduced, what they have achieved and their experience of the QIP.

IAN   That sounds like a good idea. It should certainly generate interest. But perhaps rather than making a decision now we should use the time before the noticeboards arrive to think about what we are going to put on them. Meantime what about getting Michael to do an article for the company magazine on the Programme?

ALAN   I could ask Michael to do that for us. I could also arrange to set aside a regular slot each month for a feature on a different aspect of the Improvement Programme.

ADRIAN   Excellent. I think we've made great progress today. Perhaps we should decide on the next few topics for the magazine, and who will write them, at our next meeting. And now, if no one's got anything else to discuss, I suggest we go and tell our managers and supervisors about Thursday's meeting.

A couple of weeks later the assembly and production control supervisors are talking:

CARL How did your production control people react to your communication meeting, Harold?

HAROLD Well, to begin with they all had their 'quality is nothing to do with me' look on their face, so I knew I had some work to do. I told them all about the Programme, what's happened so far, what's planned from now on and how it will involve them. Then I told them about your problem with missing components in the printed circuit board assembly area. We talked for a while about how this could be caused and eventually worked round to the point where they recognised that some of the problems could be caused by us. We are responsible for planning the flow of every item through that area and touch every component and piece part several times on its journey through to test. So we could be responsible for the wrong components being in the bins. Once we got to this point they became more interested and I even had some suggestions on how we could improve things to avoid the problem in future. I think we will make progress but it's going to take time. They need to know we are serious about it before they put any effort into it themselves.

CARL The supply of information seems to be the key to success. I told my assembly people about the problems the test guys find with our boards and they were staggered. They've never had that sort of information before because things have always been put right by repair. Jack suggested that from now on they do their own rework so they know about the problems and can prevent them happening again. It sounded like a good idea so I'm going to speak to Richard about it tomorrow. I must say I've been quite surprised by the response. I thought they'd be pretty cynical about the whole thing but so far they've been very positive. There aren't too many ideas at the moment and I seem to do most of the talking but I think that will change once we've been meeting for a few weeks and they're more confident.

HAROLD My people were all keen to know when their training will take place. Do you know anything about that?

CARL No. We're meeting Richard tomorrow, why don't you raise it then. I expect everyone will be interested in knowing.

HAROLD OK, I will. It should be an interesting meeting. I'm going to raise the training issue; you're going to talk about having rework done by assembly people themselves instead of going to repair; and I know Arthur from test is going to query those costs of non-conformance figures we were given at that meeting with Michael last week. I'm looking forward to it!

Recognition

The need for recognition
Most people want to get more out of a job than just their wages or salary. Job satisfaction, and whether they feel their efforts are appreciated, can be just as important.

A QIP increases the involvement of all employees in their work; and gives them a say in how their job can be done more effectively. Many organisations also adopt some form of recognition for significant contributions to Quality Improvement.

The monetary value of any award is not generally particularly important. The key feature of any award process is that it allows management to signal to all employees that they treat the award seriously. An individual needs to know that management appreciates his contribution and his contemporaries know that he has made an exceptional contribution.

Fundamentals of recognition
When implementing a recognition system the following features are important:

(i)   How much an individual values the award depends not on its monetary value but on how seriously management takes the award. Try to make the award something the employee can remember or keep. Something the employee can wear or use at work is a good idea. This will be noticed by his contemporaries and mark him out as an award winner.

(ii) Make a big thing of presenting the award and ensure everyone knows about it. In addition to making the individual concerned feel good this also generates further enthusiasm for the Programme and keeps the momentum going.

(iii) Ensure everyone knows how the award can be won; who makes the decision, the selection criteria and how an individual or group is nominated.

(iv) Ensure the selection system is fair and is capable of recognising all significant contributions whether these are by a group or an individual.

CASE STUDY
PART 7: The QIT meeting

ADRIAN The purpose of today's meeting is to discuss how we should reward those people who make an outstanding contribution to Quality Improvement. Hopefully it should be fairly straight-forward. Any suggestions?

JANE I think that if people are going to value the award it needs to be something worth having, cash or a holiday. Also we need to make a big deal of it and let everyone know who's won.

JULIE I agree that we should make a big thing of it, but I don't think we should spend a lot of money on the award itself. I think what people really value is honest appreciation for their efforts and for everyone to know that their contribution has been recognised. The way to do that is to be involved and interested in what they've done, not just to throw money at them.

RICHARD I think Julie's right on this one, Jane. It's a bit like presents at Christmas. The one that you really appreciate and value isn't necessarily one that costs a lot of money, it's the one that some-one's really thought about that counts. I think it will be the same here. We need to show appreciation for their efforts, not try to buy their involvement in the Programme!

ALAN Yes. It's like the long service awards which the departmental managers give out. If they just leave it on someone's desk or even send it through the post, the guy wonders why he bothered staying all that time. If the manager organises a presentation and perhaps lunch for a few friends, the person feels important, remembers the day and wears the award with pride. That's what we want to achieve with the Quality awards.

ADRIAN I also think we should concentrate on the dignity of the presentation rather than on the value of the award. John, you've been looking at this. What have you found?

JOHN I think you are right, Adrian. What really counts is how the award is treated by senior managers and how the presentation is carried out. We certainly don't want them sent in the post! The most important factor is that the individual feels management takes the award seriously and that everyone in the company knows about the award and the winners. The award doesn't have to be expensive, but it should be something the recipient can be proud of. I suggest we hold a lunch for the award winners where the presentation will be made. We should also make a big feature of these awards in the magazine. We have already introduced an award for the best Error Cause Removal idea adopted each month which has gone down well. The winner and his suggestion are featured in the company magazine and Michael presents him with a bottle of champagne at a presentation in the department. Actually the department seems to appreciate the chance to meet and chat to Michael as much as the winner appreciates the champagne! I suggest for the other awards we have a Quality cup on which the winners' names will be engraved. This can be permanently displayed in reception with a feature on the current winners. We could also give a small award to each individual for them to keep, perhaps a pen or a pin which they could wear. I propose we set up a formal recognition system to award exceptional performance in the following areas: groups which meet their improvement goals; individuals who make an outstanding contribution; and selection from the ECRs submitted. That way we have group and individual recognition. We encourage individuals to contribute, we keep progress groups going and we stimulate the ECR activity. We could make the awards each quarter.

JANE   You certainly have done a lot of work on this, John and have come up with some good ideas. One suggestion I'd like to make is if we are not going to give awards of greater value why don't we ask one of the directors to present the awards. We rarely see them here and I think it would make the recipients feel pretty special to meet them.

ADRIAN   I agree, Jane. I'll ask Michael to talk to the corporate people and see if one of them could come to the awards lunch to make the presentations and talk to the winners. Also, John, I think it's important that the selection of award winners is seen to be fair. I would like you to choose an awards committee whose members are drawn from across the company. This committee will then select the award winners. I'd like to review the committee's proposals on how they will select the award winners and whether they agree with your proposals on the awards to be given, at our next meeting. Perhaps they will have some different ideas. It's important that we can publish the selection criteria so everyone can see they are fair. They will all then have an equal chance of winning and know how to nominate someone for an award.

MEASUREMENTS AND TARGETS FOR IMPROVEMENT

Purpose of this section
This section explains the importance of introducing objective measurements in all departments throughout the organisation, and then setting targets for the improvement of performance.

Objectives of performance measurements
Accurate measurement of the quality of all processes is the cornerstone to improvement – until we know where we are today, we cannot improve.

Objective measurements enable management and employees to focus attention on areas of weakness and to monitor progress.

Since all departments are involved in meeting customer requirements and in generating and fixing errors, all departments should be involved in the Quality Improvement Programme, and all departments need to introduce appropriate measures to enable performance to be monitored.

Measurements can be used to highlight opportunities for improvement and also to monitor the success of the Programme. It is important that all measurements which are introduced fulfil two primary objectives:

(i)   They should be meaningful to the business. Improvements in these areas should lead to improved business performance.
(ii) The measurements should be owned by individuals or work groups.

It is often difficult to define measurements which meet both these objectives. As a result, the introduction of measurements is often best approached from two angles:

(i)   From the top down. These are the initial measurements introduced and owned by managers and their departments. They are key functional measures where improvements will result in direct, tangible benefits to the business. These measurements effectively define the 'big picture' into which the other measurements will fit.
(ii) From the bottom up. These are measurements introduced directly by individuals and work groups as the Programme progresses and individuals become involved in the Programme. They are often measurements of smaller, more personal activities which are often more meaningful to the individuals than the 'big picture' measurements.

With any Improvement Programme it is important to have both types of measurement; one without the other reduces the benefits of the Improvement Programme. Bottom up measures on their own can trivialise the Programme as the benefits to the business may be relatively small. Top down measurements on their own can limit the extent to which individuals become involved in Quality Improvement. This can prevent individuals from realising they have an important role to play.

Fundamentals of top down measurements

Before introducing new measurements at the beginning of the QIP, it is essential to focus attention on those areas which have a real impact on the business. This helps set the scene for a forward looking Programme, which individuals can recognise is driven by business needs. Once the Programme has been running for a while, individuals and groups will begin to introduce measurements of their own.

The following sequence has been found, in practice, to provide an effective way to identify appropriate measures:

(i)   Identify the basic purpose of the business and its objectives. The whole management team will need to be involved at this point. The results of this analysis should then be interpreted for each department. Functional analysis is a key technique to use at this stage.

(ii) Identify the key measures of performance for each department. For example, one of the key measures for the personnel department might be to ensure that each of the other departments has its full quota of staff. The appropriate measure in this case might be variances from target head count.

(iii) Each department then establishes a number of functional measures. Functional measures reflect the major activities of each department to meet the key objectives for the department. For the personnel department one of the functional measures might be the time taken to agree the job specification once the vacancy has been identified. Improvement in these functional measures can then be monitored. Progress in the functional measures supports the department's overall business objectives.

(iv) As the Programme cascades through the organisation these measurements will be developed and added to until everyone has established performance indicators within his own work area.

(v)   These measurements should be reviewed as part of the annual business planning cycle to ensure they continue to reflect the overall business objectives.

Each measurement should be agreed and owned by the department being measured. Only then is the department likely to take the measurement seriously.

Measurement is only effective if it produces information which people can easily understand and use. Data must, therefore, be accurate and the operating and reporting methods must be straightforward.

Once accepted by the departments concerned, all measurements should be prominently displayed for everyone to see. This ensures commitment to the measurements by the department being measured, and allows an opportunity for everyone interested to participate in the improvement programme. Measurements are not just for managers, they are for everyone involved in the process.

Measurements should be made regularly. The frequency depends on the specific measurement being made.

The measurement of Quality in practice

Most companies operate systems to measure performance within manufacturing divisions but have difficulty in deciding on measures to use within other areas. The following are examples of measures which may be appropriate within other areas:

Engineering:	Number of engineering changes.
	Software bugs reported in released software.
	Number of weeks projects slip.
Sales:	Time to respond to requests for quotations.
	Percentage of orders incorrectly entered.
	Comparison of actual orders against forecast.
Service:	Turn-around time for repairs.
	Warranty claims after service.
	Excessive service spares inventory.
Accounts:	Incorrect invoices raised.
	Debtor days outstanding.
Personnel:	Time to fill vacancies.
	Staff turnover rates.
Administration:	Number of items returned due to typing errors.
	Number of hours late producing the typed copy.
	Time taken to pass messages to the recipient.

One of the most useful ways to display measurements is by the use of trend charts. These charts should be posted on a regular basis (daily, weekly, monthly) to record progress over time.

The charts however only record status and progress. It is the action taken as a result of the information on the charts which results in improvement.

CASE STUDY
PART 8: At the QIT meeting

ADRIAN OK everyone, the purpose of today's meeting is to discuss how we will implement the measurement step. I've asked John to summarise the purpose of the measurement step and then we can discuss it.

JOHN The measurement step is one of the most important in the Programme since it is through measurement that we can target and monitor improvement. Improvements in performance in each department are the visible evidence to everyone of how we are progressing with Quality Improvement. The first step is to ensure each department proposes a number of measurements of their performance which they will commit to improving. Once the measurements have been agreed, we can then make sure they are prominently displayed for everyone to see.

JANE I can't see the point in doing that. It's just asking for trouble. Surely measurements are for us, the managers, to use.

RICHARD Maybe that's how it used to be. But from what I understand we are now asking everyone to improve things. It will be difficult to get them interested in improving things if we don't give them any information on how they're doing. Besides, no-one will want their measurement to be getting worse, will they? I think that if they are displayed, people will be more committed to improving them.

JANE Within the purchasing area all we can measure is how well our suppliers are doing. I can't see any supplier being happy at having his reject rate displayed for all to see – especially his competitors!

ALAN Surely there are some measurements of how well your department does it's job? What about measuring how long it takes to process a purchase requisition or the number of times a part is ordered from a non-approved supplier? As far as suppliers are concerned, I suggest we tell them what we're doing and agree with them how the measurements will be made and then help them with improvements. After that if they don't like it, or don't improve, I suggest we start looking for another supplier.

ADRIAN So what we're asking for is a proposal from each department of the measurements it will make and display for all to see?

JULIE That's right, Adrian. Measurements that the departments themselves agree with and own.

DAVID What concerns me, Julie, is that departments may choose things that are fairly easy to improve so they will look good; but which are so trivial that people think the whole Programme is a bit of a joke. We could be sunk before we've even begun.

RICHARD Does it really matter how trivial they are as long as they improve?

ADRIAN I think that once the Programme is more established you may be right Richard. But at the moment all people can see is how much we are going to spend on training this year. They will want to see us getting our money back by making improvements in significant areas. David's right. We need to make sure the measurements are significant. What do you suggest, Julie?

JULIE I've got a couple of suggestions. One is that we need to involve Michael and the rest of the management team who are not part of the QIT on this issue. We need the management team to define the overall business objectives and the role each department plays in ensuring those objectives are met. Then we can devise the significant measures in each department that actually advance those objectives. My other suggestion is that we get Tom's people to devise and carry out a customer survey asking them what they think of our total performance as a supplier. This will need to include questions that are not related to the product itself – things like what they think of the time it takes us to return calls. We could use this information to determine areas where we need to intro-duce measurements and improve performance.

ADRIAN That sounds an excellent idea. What do you think, Tom?

TOM It's something we've never done before and will need careful planning to ensure we get the information we need. If it works it could provide vital information on the areas where we need to take action to improve our customers' perception of us. I'll get my people to have a look at it and report back at the next meeting. I think they'll be quite excited at the prospect, but I think we'll need some help when it comes to actually carrying out the survey.

ADRIAN Good. If you can let me have the relevant information, Julie, I'll tackle Michael about organising a management meeting to discuss it. I suggest we all read the material carefully so that when it comes to the meeting we're prepared with some ideas!

The fundamentals of bottom up measurement

Once the QIP is underway, the training has begun and measurements introduced, individuals will begin to see evidence of the value of the Programme in their work. This will help generate enthusiasm for the Programme. It is important to turn this enthusiasm into action. Only then will the Improvement Programme be able to develop fully throughout the company.

At the outset of the Programme, the department heads will each have identified a number of top-down measures to be used as a basis for improvement. Their staff will have been set the objective of improving their performance against these measures. However it is possible that the initial measures may seem remote to the workforce, and so not fully owned by them.

To maintain the enthusiasm of employees it is important that they are fully involved in the Programme as soon as possible. Perhaps the best way to achieve this is to let them identify a set of objectives that they take ownership for. Each group will then be responsible for introducing corrective actions and measuring improvement.

The supervisor in each group should sit down with their team and agree on improvement goals. Wherever possible these goals should come from the group itself although it may be necessary for the supervisor to set the ball rolling by suggesting possible goals. The goals may be for the group as a whole or for individuals within the group. The goals should be specific and measurable.

Once selected, goals should be posted in a conspicuous place and progress monitored. It is important that managers monitor and encourage improvements and that they should be widely publicised.

CASE STUDY
PART 9: A sales department meeting

The sales department was holding its regular Quality meeting. They spent some time discussing improvements against existing departmental measures before Sally, the sales team leader, continued.

SALLY So far, we've all been trained and have been meeting for a few months to discuss how we might improve our performance against the measurements suggested by Tom. Now we have the opportunity to introduce our own measurements and set our own targets for improvement. This is the time that we try to identify for ourselves any other areas in which we can make improvements. It will then be up to us to decide what activities we want to improve and introduce measurements to monitor progress.

JACK It's all very well for us to decide on new areas to improve, but what about the measurements we've been taking to date. Do we just drop those?

SHIRLEY Oh no, I don't think we should drop those. They seem to be pretty important and we're already starting to make improvements. For example, we've seen a great improvement in the accuracy of our sales forecasting. We are now at the stage where we can give manufacturing a firm idea of the number of items we expect to ship in the next month. In the past I know they have been pulling their hair out because they could not plan their production schedules on the figures we were giving them. I used to see differences of ± 30% between confirmed sales orders and our forecasts. Now, although we are down to ± 15%, we cannot rest on our laurels. I think it's essential we keep trying to improve on this. The drive on the shop floor to turn orders round within a month depends on accurate forecasts.

SALLY OK, if everyone else agrees then we will continue to measure and improve our sales forecast accuracy. I agree that it is a vitally important area. But what other measures should we introduce. One idea I had, after a complaint from a customer the other day, was to measure the time it takes us to send out a quotation. If a customer doesn't receive the quote promptly, we might not even be considered for the order.

JEREMY What about keeping a measure of the total number of minutes people turn up late for meetings. We spend ages hanging around for people before we can start, especially at the monthly sales meeting. I expect if we just start measuring it we will see an improvement without taking any other action at all!

SHIRLEY Maybe people turn up late because the meetings are not very productive. Maybe we could devise some means of assessing each meeting for its effectiveness. We could give each meeting a score and monitor that.

JEREMY You mean we could give points for things like; was a meeting necessary? Was an agenda circulated before the meeting? Were people properly prepared? Had the actions from the previous meeting been completed? Did the meeting run to time? It sounds like quite a good idea to me considering how long we all spend at meetings. We would need to make sure the scoring method was sensible and simple.

LIZ One thing that would really improve life for us secretaries is if we didn't have to keep retyping things because the salesman has made changes. It's really annoying to get a piece of work back for changes when you think you've seen the last of it.

MARIAN Yes, I'd agree with that, especially for long proposals. Maybe we should concentrate on those and measure the number of changes that are made once a proposal has been typed.

LIZ Another thing that causes difficulties for us in the office is when we can't get hold of a salesman because we don't know where he is. We usually need to get hold of them because a customer has a query so it's annoying for them as well.

JEREMY As far as the salesman is concerned, we are often criticised by customers for not getting back to them quickly enough. It's usually caused by our not receiving messages from the message desk promptly.

LIZ Maybe we should measure both the delays in messages reaching the salesman and the number of times the salesman is uncontactable – because I expect they could be linked.'

SHIRLEY I'm usually on the receiving end of complaints from the shopfloor because there are errors on sales orders. They are always coming up here to say that a certain part number doesn't exist or we haven't included the version which the customer needs. It would certainly make my life easier, and theirs no doubt, if we could resolve this.

Sally looked round to see if there were any more ideas before she joined in.

SALLY Well, I didn't know there were so many problems! There are bound to be some areas in that lot where improvement could make a real impact on the business. But we don't want to try to do too many things at once or we are almost bound to fail. I think we should select two or three measures in addition to the sales forecast measure and really concentrate on making significant improvements in those areas. I've made a note of all the suggestions. I'll ask Susan to type them up, with no changes of course, and get her to circulate them to you all. I'd like you to think about them and then, at next week's meeting, we can decide on the ones we will implement.

PREVENTION

Purpose of this section
This section focuses attention on the need to adopt prevention as the system for Quality Improvement throughout the organisation. It explains the Zero Defects concept, and the importance of introducing effective corrective action systems to eliminate the causes of non-conformance and prevent their recurrence.

The Zero Defects concept
The implementation of a successful Quality Improvement Programme requires a company to adopt prevention as the system for managing Quality. Prevention requires everyone within the company to believe that errors are not an inevitable part of working life; that correct systems, training, equipment, materials, and, above all, personal attitudes, can prevent errors occurring. This belief is summarised in the Zero Defects concept. There is some question as to who first propounded the Zero Defects concept, but it is most closely associated with Philip Crosby, and has been extensively used by him, and his consultancy organisation, in implementing Quality Improvements in many organisations world-wide.

The fundamental principal underlying the Zero Defects concept is that it is possible to do all operations right the first time. Zero Defects does not mean that everything has to be gold plated or the place has to be crawling with inspectors. It simply means that each and every one of us has to believe it is possible to carry out activities without error. Errors are not inevitable. We should not anticipate errors and then build up massive systems to find and correct them. If we expect errors to occur and build systems to deal with them, they will happen. We are then effectively saying that errors do not matter. We will find and fix them. This is a very costly path to tread.

If errors are not expected to occur, and preventive actions are introduced to eliminate problems, then errors will not happen. The new attitude is that errors are not tolerated. A big fix-it outfit should not be available, just waiting for errors to happen. Everyone will be more careful and will work to eliminate the causes of errors so that eventually they will no longer occur.

In our personal life we do not expect to put on odd shoes in the morning on a given number of days in a year. If we did expect this to happen then we could ask our partner to check our shoes every morning before going out and then rectify any errors found! This would prove very costly in terms of our partner's time and patience. We do not, however, expect this to happen because we implement a preventive action such as putting our shoes in pairs when we take them off.

The Zero Defects philosophy requires us to apply our personal standards to our work and asks everyone else in the company to do the same.

By adopting the Zero Defects concept, employees underline their commitment to the attitude and belief that errors are not inevitable. Errors can be avoided by applying prevention techniques.

The fundamental importance of effective corrective action systems

The fundamental objective of corrective action is to ensure that having identified a problem the action taken ensures it does not recur. The corrective action should be designed to prevent the same type of error from happening again, not just today but for ever. Although at the start of a Quality Improvement Programme it is important to focus attention on major problems, in the long run no error is too small to require corrective action.

We have already discussed the need to introduce measurements of performance in all areas of the company. These provide raw data to enable us to identify and evaluate the impact of problems. The correct use of effective measurements enables us to monitor the progress resulting from corrective actions taken to eliminate problems.

However, it must be stressed that measurements only provide information. It is the actions taken as a result of this information which produce the necessary improvements. We therefore need to make sure that an adequate system is in place to ensure that effective corrective actions are taken when a problem is identified.

The failure of typical existing corrective action systems

Most companies already operate corrective action systems. The resolution of audit deficiencies, and meetings with suppliers to review the reasons for reject components and improve performance are two typical examples. However, existing systems in many companies fail to succeed for three main reasons:

1. The actions taken as a result of problems are often not really preventive actions. They may fix today's problem but generally do not introduce the long-term improvements necessary to prevent the problem recurring in the future.
2. Many companies do not operate a mechanism for collecting details of the day-to-day problems faced by employees. This can be countered by introducing an Error Cause Removal (ECR) system.
3. The typical approach to resolving problems in many companies is to form a team of managers and supervisors. These teams are formed on an ad hoc basis and meet to try and resolve significant problems as they are identified. By only using managers and supervisors in these teams we restrict the number of problems which can be tackled, and frequently do not get the benefit of the practical experience of the people actually doing the job on a day-to-day basis.

Features of an effective corrective action system

To be effective it is important that corrective actions are properly planned and carefully designed to result in the elimination of the problem concerned, once and for all. The following features typically need to be present in order for a corrective action system to be effective:

(i) An effective mechanism must exist to identify the problems to be solved. It is important systematically to analyse the features of a business and examine whether processes could be carried out more effectively. It is also important to establish a mechanism to identify practical problems facing the workforce (the ECR system).

(ii) Once a problem has been identified it is important to involve all the people concerned with the problem in developing corrective actions (corrective action groups).

(iii) Someone within each group, frequently the supervisor, needs to have some knowledge of problem solving methods.

(iv) The outcome from these meetings should be reported to team members regularly.

(v) Corrective actions should be carefully assessed to ensure they are the most effective means to eliminate the problem once and for all. Once introduced, the results of the corrective action must be monitored to ensure they achieve the objectives set for them.

(vi) Management must support the activity and demonstrate their commitment by taking an interest in the progress made.

Corrective action groups

In addition to improving the existing corrective action systems, it is generally necessary to consider introducing formal problem solving groups. The two most important types of group are:

(i) Progress Groups (also known as Quality Circles): A progress group is generally a small group of individuals from within one department who carry out similar work. The group meets regularly to identify, implement and monitor the progress of corrective actions for problems arising within their work area.

(ii) Corrective Action Task Force: Complex problems frequently arise during the course of a Quality Improvement Programme. A Corrective Action Task Force is an inter-departmental group with a member from each department affected by the problem.

The Error Cause Removal System

An important feature of a successful Quality Improvement Programme is the introduction of a simple method which allows any individual to bring out into the open problems which prevent him performing error-free work. These problems can then be targeted by management with the objective of finding a solution. This is the error cause removal (ECR) system. This type of system differs from a suggestion scheme because, in this case, the employee need only identify the problem. In a suggestion scheme an individual is only asked to contribute if he can also propose a solution. In this way a whole host of problems go unidentified and unresolved. Many companies already operate an ECR system. In some cases this has fallen into disrepute because there is no real management commitment to solving the problems identified. As a result, individuals have to wait a long time for what is often an unsatisfactory answer. Eventually the system is no longer used. Like quality circles, an ECR system is only likely to be successful as part of a Quality Improvement Programme. In this case management actively wants to know about problems and is committed to effecting solutions.

Fundamentals of an ECR system

The following features should be present for an ECR system to work effectively:

(i) The ECR system should be introduced early in the Quality Improvement Programme, so it is available for individuals to use as they become involved in the Programme.

(ii)   The forms should be short, simple to complete and readily available.

(iii) ECRs should initially be submitted to the individual's supervisor. An ECR should be acknowledged within two days of receipt.

(iv)   If the problem cannot be resolved by the supervisor, then the form should be sent to the department responsible for the problem. The individual should receive a reply from the department within two weeks. This should give details of the decision or a report on the actions taken so far together with an estimated completion date.

(v)   Whenever it is decided to do nothing about an ECR this should be cleared with at least the next level of management. The individual must be given a clear explanation of why no action is being taken.

(vi)   Every ECR should be taken seriously. No one should be criticised for raising an ECR.

(vii) All corrective actions introduced must resolve the problem permanently through preventive action. They should not just fix the problem in the short term.

(viii) The system should ensure that each ECR is resolved at the lowest possible level of supervision. Of all ECRs raised, experience has shown that 85 per cent can frequently be resolved by the first level of supervision, 13 per cent at the next level and only 2 per cent might need to be referred to the department head or the QIT.

(ix)   The efficiency of the system should be monitored by the QIT. They should look particularly at the response time and the actions taken. If either of these is unsatisfactory, individuals will cease to use the system and the Improvement Programme will lose its credibility.

CASE STUDY
PART 10: The QIT meeting

ADRIAN   I have been asked by the magazine editor what we would like to say in the next issue of the company magazine. Does anyone have any suggestions?

ALAN   What about featuring the progress made by the Task Force we set up three months ago to look at why it takes so long for new product designs to reach the customer? If you remember we had a heated discussion with just about everyone being blamed from manufacturing to engineering, purchasing, marketing and back again. In retrospect it was a pretty tough task to set for our first problem. But they have made excellent progress so far and are proposing some radical changes in the way we approach this whole activity.

DAVID I understand they will have finished their report next week and I suggest we wait to hear what they've got to say before we publish a report. If we wait, we could run a far better story in the next issue. They have apparently had a lot of difficulty estimating the CONC. It was particularly difficult to estimate the cost associated with lost customers through our not having a new product available when we said we would. But I believe they've now come up with a rough figure that they're happy with, although they wouldn't tell me it. They want to save that until they do their formal presentation to us; so I guess it must be quite interesting! Anyway they feel they are now ready to present their proposals to us for our approval to implement. I would like to have a special meeting of the QIT next Tuesday for this, if everyone can make it.

IAN What about the Progress Groups then? Have we got any information on how they're going?

ADRIAN John, have you any information?

JOHN I haven't yet completed a review of the current status in all departments, but I can give you my general impressions. Most areas are continuing to hold regular communication meetings with their supervisor. But in some areas these are becoming a bit stale and no real progress is being made with identifying performance measurements or implementing corrective actions.

JANE From the experience I've had with my people the process gets a real boost once people have been educated about the Programme. Maybe part of the problem is that our education timetable has been slipping?

JOHN I think you're right, Jane. We certainly haven't trained everyone yet.

ADRIAN Right, I've been monitoring progress on the education step and frankly we could do a great deal better. I think this is something we should tackle straight away. I would like each of us here to commit to completing the training of all our people within the next three months. This means we need to draw up a timetable and tell each individual the date their training will take place. That way we're likely to stick to it! Perhaps for the next issue of the magazine we could do an article on education. Jane, you seem to be the furthest ahead in this area, would you draft an article on the experience in your department?

JANE That's fine by me. I should be able to finish it in time for the copy deadline which is next Wednesday. I will let you have a look at it before then.

JULIE I would also like to suggest that once a month at the QIT meeting each member summarises the progress made on each of the Improvement steps within his area.

ADRIAN That sounds an excellent idea to me, Julie. I think it would have been a good idea to do that from the beginning but I didn't think of it. It's another example of how we need plan carefully every step we take and implement preventive actions! Before we go I'd like to ask John to bring us all up to date on the ECR system we have introduced. What's happened so far, John?

JOHN Well as you know we introduced the ECR system a month ago. In the first month we have received 110 ECRs.

RICHARD That seems a lot. How on earth will we be able to keep up, especially if they keep coming in at the same rate?

JOHN Fortunately we set up the ECR system so that most of the problems could be dealt with by the first level of supervision. That has spread the load. The supervisor can either solve the problem directly himself if it is within his control, or he can refer it to his counterpart in the department who is responsible for the problem. Many of the ECRs raised in this first lot have been dealt with by the individual's own Progress Group. Although outside the individual's direct control they are within the control of the Progress Group. Supervisors have picked these up and referred them directly to the Progress Group. In future, hopefully, individuals will refer these sorts of problems directly to the group instead of raising an ECR.

DAVID Are there many that can't be dealt with by the supervisors?

JOHN There have been a few. At the end of the first month there were ten that had been passed up to a manager. What I have done this month is just circulate a brief description of the ECRs raised so you can all see the sorts of problems being highlighted.

ALAN It's amazing that there are so many problems out there making life difficult for people when most of them can be resolved relatively easily once someone knows about them.

ADRIAN Unfortunately, that was a fact of life under our old system of working; we used to just live with the problems. Now, we have committed to ensure that problems preventing error-free work are resolved. Is there any way to monitor the ECR system to ensure problems are resolved speedily? That way we can establish our commitment to the Programme. If ECRs are not acted on promptly then the system will fall into disrepute. Can you have a look at a way of doing that, John?

JOHN   Yes. It'll take me a little while to set up. By the end of next month I'll start reporting the ECR status.

A sample of the initial ECRs received at Alpha was as follows:

- Why is the soldering machine so far away from assembly? By the time the boards reach me half the components are loose. I have to push them all back in place before they can be soldered.
- The orders we receive from sales only have the customer's name not their address. Some of the customers have more than one address so we have to contact the salesman to find out the correct address.
- The person who unloads at Goods Inwards can't recognise components. The paperwork is never with the right goods and we spend a lot of time sorting this out.
- There is always a queue to use the Fax machine. I spend a lot of time waiting there. Why can't we buy another one?
- The front panels come packed in lots of ten. We issue them in lots of five which means unpacking them and then packing them up again. Why can't the supplier send them in batches of five?
- We leave the lights on when we go home because the bank of switches isn't marked to show which switch turns off which lights. Why can't they be marked so we can turn the lights out and save electricity?
- My PC and printer are different from the other secretaries. Why don't we all have the same models so that if one breaks down we could use someone else's?
- The customer database only has the company name and not the buyer's name. Whenever I want to call a customer that I don't know I have to scout around to see if anyone knows the buyer's name before I call him.

7 QUALITY TOOLS

STATISTICAL PROCESS CONTROL

Statistical Process Control (SPC) is a means by which an operator can determine whether a process is producing, and is likely to continue producing, conforming output. It achieves this by measuring key parameters for a small sample of the output produced at intervals whilst the process is operating.

This information can be used as a basis for making adjustments to the inputs or, if necessary, to the process in order to prevent non-conforming output from being produced.

SPC also enables a business to reduce the variations in the output from a process, although relatively few organisations use SPC in this way.

Producing products which are just within the specification may be acceptable today but any variation from the target nominal value may result in rejects and rework further along the chain. Variations from the nominal value can also cause significant problems in view of the inter-dependence of components in complex products. SPC enables businesses constantly to improve the performance of the process in order to reduce the variation in output. This ability to reduce variation from the nominal value may provide a distinct competitive advantage, and may enable premium prices to be charged for products.

Features of an SPC environment

In a traditional quality control environment, the quality of output is assessed at the end of each process by answering the question: Has the output been produced according to the specification?

This question leads to appraisal and correction activities. The business has to check the output from each process to see whether, or not, it conforms to requirements. If it does not conform, then it has to be reworked or replaced. These activities are an admission of the failure to define and control processes to ensure they produce conforming output.

SPC represents a preventive approach to the manufacturing process. In an SPC environment, the quality of output is assured by concentrating on the design and operation of the process itself rather than waiting until the output has been produced and then inspecting and sorting it.

The key questions asked when using SPC methods are:

(i)   Is the process capable of producing conforming output?
(ii) Is the process actually producing conforming output? (checked by examining in-process samples); and
(iii) Can the process be improved to reduce variability?

In order to benefit from SPC, management must invest the necessary time and money in equipment; and in training and educating employees so they understand both the philosophy of prevention and how to operate the SPC equipment. An effective SPC environment is one which constantly strives for the continuous improvement in the operation of processes, and reduction in variation in output.

In order to operate an SPC environment, the following conditions need to be satisfied:

- the requirements of the process must be defined.
- the process should be set up so that it is capable of producing conforming output.
- the operator should be provided with equipment to enable him to monitor critical attributes of the process whilst output is being produced. This information enables him to assess whether the process continues to produce output which meets the requirements.
- the operator should be trained to make the necessary adjustments to the process or its inputs if the process moves away from producing output at the nominal specification.
- the process should be constantly monitored. This enables the operator to fully understand it, so that opportunities for improving its performance (by reducing variation in the output and increasing conformance to the required nominal specification) may be identified and implemented.

Achieving the required level of commitment and cultural change is a long-term activity and it may take a number of years before a complete change is achieved.

What are the benefits of SPC?

The implementation of SPC offers significant advantages for many types of business:

(i)   It reduces the quantity of non-conforming output. Concentrating on the process itself rather than on post-process inspection also reduces the amount of wasted time and materials expended on rework and repeating processes; the inspection effort required; and improves the quality of the working environment. This can have an important positive impact on employee morale if managed correctly. No-one likes reworking or repeating processes which were not adequately controlled in the first place.

(ii) Most inspection processes miss some non-conforming output. Even where all output is inspected, some 15 per cent of the errors which exist are commonly missed. These non-conforming products will then be sold to customers. By preventing non-conforming output arising in the first place, customers are less likely to receive non-conforming products or services.

(iii) The continuous improvement of processes and reduction in the variation in output enables businesses to compete in terms of both performance and price.

What benefits have companies seen in practice?

The DTI booklet on Statistical Process Control, published as part of the *Managing into the 90's* initiative, includes three examples which illustrate the benefits achieved by the Port Talbot works of British Steel as a result of implementing SPC:

'On the pickle line, where the thin film of oxide on the surface of the steel is removed by acid, and the coils are subsequently trimmed, the steel is weighed as it enters and leaves the process. The VDU presents the operator with an instant reading of the percentage weight loss of each coil. This has improved the yield of the process by approximately one third of one per cent – which gives a saving of about one third of a million pounds a year . . . that alone has paid for the system.'

'On one occasion, a sudden increase in the conductivity of the oil and water emulsion which lubricates the steel during cold rolling, and provides a measure of the impurities in it, gave warning of a major leakage in the cooling system. In the old days, this might not have been discovered for several days, and would have led to quality problems. Immediate action retrieved the situation before any damage was done.'

'On the galvanising line . . . the system continuously monitors the coating on the steel. If the coating is thicker than specification, it is wasteful of expensive zinc; if it is not thick enough, then the product is inferior. Either way, early warning saves money.'

What is a process?

SPC requires the careful design and monitoring of processes. In order to understand SPC it is therefore essential to understand the meaning of the term 'process'. (Fig. 2.1 illustrates the principal characteristics of a process.)

Inputs are received from a supplier (the requirements for these inputs need to be defined). The process transforms these inputs into outputs for delivery to a customer (the customer requirements also need to be defined). The outputs may be a product (for example, a set of accounts, a typed letter or an assembled printed circuit board), or a service (such as answering the telephone or delivering a training seminar).

In order to produce conforming output, the process may need to make use of:

(i)   Direct inputs such as a draft letter, a bare printed circuit board, components or financial data;
(ii) Equipment and facilities (such as a manufacturing plant, typewriter, computer, calculator or training room);
(iii) Skills and job knowledge;
(iv) Procedures describing how the process is to be performed; and
(v)   A specification defining the performance standards required of the process.

Once a process has been defined, SPC can be used to ensure the output conforms to requirements. However, SPC methods can only be used once a process is 'in control' and capable of producing conforming product. For a process consistently to produce conforming product it must be:

- capable of producing conforming product; and
- operating under control so only conforming products can be produced.

Non-conforming output is produced because of variation in the inputs or the process itself.

When a process is first set up, it may not be 'in control'. In this case, it will be necessary to investigate the reasons why the process is not capable of producing conforming product so that the causes can be identified and eliminated. Chapter 8 describes a comprehensive practical problem solving methodology which may be useful in these circumstances. The principal methods described in chapter 8 are:

Process flowcharting
Brainstorming
Cause and effect diagrams (Ishikawa diagrams)
Voting and weighting
Histograms
Pareto analysis
Scatter diagrams
Force field analysis

The remainder of this chapter focuses on the use of control charts.

The causes of variation in a process

Variation can arise as a result of two principal factors:

(i) 'assignable' or 'special' causes. This form of variation is assignable to a specific cause such as differences between the performance of different machinery, operators or materials. This type of variation is not random and can lead to excessive process variation. If assignable causes of variation exist in a process then the process is defined as 'out of control'.

Variation due to assignable causes is often excessive and SPC methods cannot be used to predict these variations. Before control charts can be used, therefore, the process must be adjusted so that it becomes 'in control'. All assignable causes of variation must be eliminated.

(ii) 'random' variations arise as a result of the interaction between a multitude of factors, such as temperature, atmospheric pressure and the normal operating tolerance of the machinery. These variations are random, generally small and cannot be assigned to any specific cause. A process is said to be 'stable' or 'in control' if process variability is the result of random variations alone. SPC monitors random variations and, by plotting the trend in this variation, predicts the point at which the process is about to produce nonconforming product. The operator can then make the necessary adjustments to ensure the process continues to produce conforming output.

Attributes and variables

If the output of a process can be measured as a continuous variable, for example, the voltage of a power supply, diameter of a wire, cycle time, then no two measurements will be identical and the variation will generally follow a normal distribution curve. The parameters of this curve are well understood and it is the characteristics of this curve which are used as the basis for control charts for variables.

Where the output of a process cannot be measured as a continuous variable but only as a discrete value (for example the number of typing errors in a report, number of customer complaints, number of wrong components assembled), these are termed attributes. In this case the variation in the parameters follows a binomial distribution. This is used as the basis for control charts for attributes.

Characteristics of the normal distribution curve for variables

A normal distribution will result if variations in the parameter being measured are randomly distributed – i.e. variations are just as likely to be upwards as downwards from the central value. A normal distribution produces a symmetrical bell-shaped curve as illustrated in Fig. 7.1. This curve can be defined by two parameters:

(i)   The mean (μ). This is the central value. It is calculated by dividing the sum of the individual values by the number of observations.

$$\mu = \frac{\overset{n}{\underset{1}{\sum}} x_n}{n}$$

(ii)   The standard deviation (referred to as σ) is a measure of the spread of values around the mean. It is calculated by summing the squares of the differences between each measured value and the mean; dividing this sum by the number of observations and then taking the square root of the result.

$$\sigma = \sqrt{\frac{\overset{n}{\underset{1}{\sum}} (x_n - \mu)^2}{n}}$$

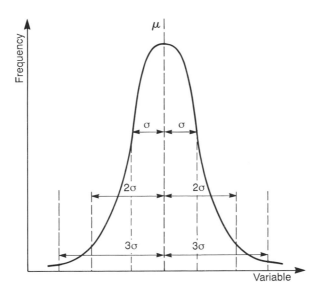

Figure 7.1 Normal distribution curve for a continuous variable

The standard deviation is a key parameter in setting control limits for SPC purposes because a known proportion of the population lie within a range specified by the standard deviation from the mean:

(a) about 68.3 per cent of the items in the population lie within a range defined by 'the mean ± one standard deviation.'
(b) about 95.4 per cent of values are in the range defined by 'the mean ± two standard deviations'.
(c) about 99.7 per cent of values (i.e. virtually all the values) are in the range defined by 'the mean ± three standard deviations'. This range defines the so-called 'natural process capability' of the process. The process produces output within ± three standard deviations of the mean virtually all the time.

These values are used to predict the point at which the process is about to produce non-conforming output so the operator is able to implement preventive actions and keep the process within limits.

Establishing the capability of the process
Before control charts can be constructed, it is essential to ensure that the process is consistently capable of producing conforming product.

The natural capability of a process can be compared to the output specification using a number of measures:

(i)   A simple index. Cp compares the actual range achieved by the process with the acceptable range or tolerance. It is calculated as follows:

(ii) Process capability $Cp = \dfrac{\text{Tolerance range}}{\text{Actual range } (6\,\sigma)}$

If Cp is greater than one it means that at least 99.7 per cent of the outputs from the process are contained in a range which has the same breadth as the acceptable range.

However, this measure does not take into account that the process mean may not conform to the required nominal value. So, the process may produce output which does not conform to requirements. A second index, Cpk, takes into account both the range and the centring of the process. It is defined as follows:

$$Cpk = \frac{\text{upper limit} - \text{nominal}}{3\,\sigma} \quad \text{or} \quad \frac{\text{nominal} - \text{lower limit}}{3\,\sigma}$$

The difference between Cp and Cpk is analogous to the difference between precision and accuracy: a process is said to be accurate if the mean of its output conforms to the specified nominal value; a process is said to be precise if there is little variation in its output; the lower the standard deviation, the higher the precision.

For a process to be capable, both Cp and Cpk must be greater than one. If they are less than one; then less than 99.7 per cent of the output from the process will fall within the acceptable range, i.e. the process will not consistently produce conforming output. If Cp and Cpk equal 1 then just 99.7 per cent of output from the process will fall within the acceptable range; but any slight variation in the process will produce non-conforming product. In order to operate with a margin of safety and ensure the production of output within the required limits, then Cp and Cpk should approach 2.

Using process control charts for variables

Having established that the process is capable of meeting the output requirements, the process control charts illustrated in Fig. 7.2(a) may be used to plot actual output. Trends in the value of the output produced are monitored and actions taken if the process is seen to vary excessively as a result of assignable causes.

The charts show warning and action limits for the process. These are based on the 2σ and 3σ points from the normal distribution curve mentioned above. At intervals during the process the operator takes a sample (of at least four items) from the output and takes measurements. The results are plotted on the control chart. Adjustments to the process are made based on the results from the sample. Any variation in the process due to random causes should give a value within the action limits points (1–7). If the value plotted falls outside the warning limits (points 8 and 12) this may still be due to random variation (there is about a 1 in 40 chance of this happening), but it is grounds for suspicion that an assignable cause may be present. If this happens then a further sample is taken immediately and the result plotted. If this second result is within the warning limits then the process is allowed to continue (points 9 and 13). If the second sample is again outside the warning limits then action should be taken to adjust the process. If the value falls outside the action limits this indicates the presence of an assignable cause which should be investigated and the process adjusted.

The charts should be easy to understand and interpret. An experienced operator will frequently be able to tell the most likely cause of an error based on the characteristics of the process control plot.

Any changes to the process and additional samples should be recorded on the control chart when they take place. In practice coded marks are commonly used to mark changes in operator, materials or in the set-up of the equipment. This information helps identify causes of variation in the mean or range of output.

What types of control chart are there?
The most commonly used charts for variables are mean and range charts. Examples of mean charts are illustrated in Fig. 7.2(a) and (b)

For a mean chart the mean of the measurements taken from each sample is plotted on the control chart.

For a range chart, the difference between the highest and lowest value in each sample is plotted on the chart.

Using the process control charts for attributes
For attributes, the output follows a binomial distribution. In this case, number-defective or proportion-defective charts are commonly used to record variation. Warning and action limits may again be calculated and the control charts used in the same way as for variables. Other charts, such as moving average (or range), or cumulative sum (cusum) charts

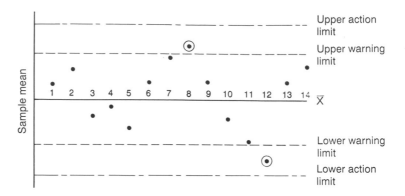

Figure 7.2 (a) Mean chart – stable process

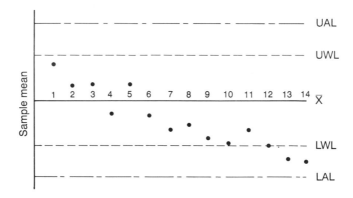

Figure 7.2 (b) Mean chart – drifting process

may also be valuable. Cumulative sum charts are powerful tools for detecting trends or changes in attributes.

What is the role of the operator?
SPC relies on the close control of the operating characteristics of processes. If a process starts to move out of control, it is necessary to implement prompt corrective action. To do this the operator should be given responsibility for ensuring that the process remains in control, producing output that conforms to requirements. To enable him to take this responsibility, he must be given the necessary training, procedures, tools, authority and information to do the job properly.

It is generally helpful to keep the information supplied to the operator to the minimum required to enable the process to be managed effectively. Providing too much information can create confusion.

Although control charts can be drawn manually, in organisations where they are routinely used to control a large number of processes, computer control of these charts is useful.

Modern computer driven process control systems may be programmed to present only those charts that are going out of control, and may issue operator instructions about how to bring them back under control.

Summary of steps to set up a control chart for variables

1. Take a minimum of twenty samples of the output; each sample should contain between 4 and 10 items.
2. Measure each item and record the results. Calculate the mean and range within each sample.
3. Calculate the average mean and range of all the samples.
4. Using look up tables draw the control charts, the action and warning limits.
5. Having plotted the control charts take at least 20 sample measurements, over a period of time, to determine whether the process is 'in control' i.e. the variation in the process is due solely to random causes.
6. If the process is 'out of control' then actions must be taken to eliminate the assignable causes.
7. If the process is 'in control', then determine whether the natural capability of the process is adequate consistently to produce conforming product. Calculate Cp and Cpk.
8. If the process is both 'in control' and capable, then the control charts can be used to monitor and adjust the process.

Within an organisation committed to Total Quality Management continuous improvement is a driving force. SPC can form an integral part of this process.

BENCHMARKING

A benchmark is a reference point against which to compare yourself. Leading businesses frequently use benchmarking to compare their performance in key areas against the results achieved by the best in the world. Benchmarking provides an insight into what is possible; an understanding of how it can be achieved; and a goal to aim for and exceed.

Why benchmark?

Trying to improve performance is generally difficult. The potential for improvement can be enormous, and to restrict yourself to incremental improvements based on existing performance limits your potential achievement. To become a world-class performer you must adopt world-class techniques. Only benchmarking provides information on what is required for world-class performance.

A recent study by McKinsey (reported in *McKinsey Quarterly*, 1991, no. 1) suggests that world class mechanical and electronic companies may introduce new products at less than half the cost, and in less than half the time it takes a typical company.

Data reported by the Massachusetts Institute of Technology and JD Power and Associates (Table 7.1) illustrates the significant differences between Japanese, American and European car assembly plants. According to this data, European car producers have tremendous opportunities for improvement. Incremental improvements in current performance will just not be enough. A 30 per cent improvement in

	Japanese in Japan	Japanese in the US	Americans in America	European Producers
Productivity (hours per vehicle)	16.8	21.2	25.1	36.2
Assembly defects per 100 vehicles	60	65	82	97
Repair area (% of assembly space)	4.1	4.9	12.9	14.4
Stocks (days) (*)	0.2	1.6	2.9	2.0
Training of new workers (hours)	380	370	46	173
Absenteeism (%)	5.0	4.8	11.7	12.1
(*) For eight sample parts				

Table 7.1 Car assembly plant characteristics – Averages for plants in each region in 1989

Source: Massachusetts Institute of Technology and JD Power & Associates. Reported in *The Economist* (10 August 1991).

productivity might appear to be an outstanding result; but this would still leave them a long way behind the best in the world. To survive in today's world markets requires world-class performance.

What are the benefits of benchmarking?

Businesses need to understand the skills and processes which are the keys to their success and to satisfying the requirements of their customers. Benchmarking can provide management with the necessary data to enable them to review critically their performance in these key areas against the best in the world. Benchmarking can produce the following benefits if performed effectively:

- an understanding of the activities and processes which are key to the success of the business and satisfying the requirements of its customers.
- alerting management to what is possible in a world class organisation.
- setting objective performance standards for key activities to match or surpass the best in the world.
- an insight into how other companies meet world-class standards.

Without benchmarking a company can become insular and complacent. It may set seemingly aggressive targets based on current performance but may not realise how far behind it is slipping compared with world-beating competitors.

What can you benchmark?

Almost any business characteristic can be benchmarked. The following examples illustrate the range of possibilities:

(i) Customer satisfaction – product conformance to requirements
– reliability
– on-time delivery
– lead times

(ii) Financial performance – sales per employee
– age of debts
– investment in R&D

(iii) Distribution – cost of distribution activities
– time in distribution cycle
– number of levels of distribution

(iv)	Purchasing	– number of suppliers
		– suppliers per buyer
		– buyers per 1000 transactions
		– late deliveries
		– rejection rate
		– shortages
(v)	Materials management	– warehouse space
		– inventory
		– cycle times
(vi)	Design	– time to introduce new products
		– number of engineering changes

(vii) Management practice. For example, the 'Best Practices' programme carried out by General Electric found that leading companies tend to focus on how departments work together as they perform processes rather than how they work in isolation. Their objective is to maximise efficiency as departments interact, leading to reduced lead times for product introduction, partnerships with suppliers, and reduced levels of stock (*Fortune*, 12 August 1991).

Identify key business activities

What are the driving forces behind your business? What activities directly influence customer satisfaction? What activities have an important impact on the bottom line? Which activities account for the largest proportion of your costs? These are all possible candidates for benchmarking.

Determining the key activities is essential because this drives the benchmarking programme. The team may identify the key activities using information from a variety of sources. These might include:

(i) Customer surveys. Carried out by the company to determine its performance and the requirements of its customers; and industry-wide surveys carried out by trade associations, newspapers or magazines may both be of value at this point. Table 7.2 illustrates the sort of information that is available. In this case, the 1991 Euromoney Business Travel Survey identifies the parameters people use when choosing airlines and hotels. These results may be used to determine areas where airlines and hotels might benchmark their performance against others.

(ii) Functional analysis identifies the purpose of the business and each of its functions in terms of satisfying the requirements of its external customers. The key activities identified by this process may be used as a starting point for a benchmarking programme.

(iii) Financial analysis indicates the activities which account for a large proportion of costs or where significant non-conformance costs occur. These activities may constitute key targets for benchmarking. Many manufacturing companies today buy components, with only final assembly carried out in-house. Here the internal value-added is relatively small. In this case supply management is a key business activity; possibly more important than the associated in-house manufacturing activity.

Reasons for choosing an airline

	Ranking	
	1991	*1990*
Safety	1	1
Punctuality	2	2
Scheduling	3	4
Cabin staff	4	5
Leg room	5	3
Route network	6	6
Price	7	10
Peace and quiet	8	9
Frequent flyers' programme	9	8
Connections	10	–

Reasons for choosing a hotel

	Ranking	
	1991	*1990*
Location	1	1
Quality of service	2	2
Comfort	3	3
Peace and quiet	4	4
Price	5	6
Room size	6	5
Quality of food	7	7
Sport and leisure	8	10
Business facilities	9	9
Prestige value	10	8

Table 7.2: Customer measures of performance

Source: Euromoney Magazine – The 1991 Business Travel Survey

Identify key parameters

Once the key business activities have been identified, the team should identify the key parameters driving performance for those activities. These are the parameters which should be benchmarked. In a programme described in *The McKinsey Quarterly* (1991 Number 1), one company considered that its purchasing function was one of the keys to its success. It then determined the following key parameters to benchmark:

- number of suppliers per buyer
- vendor lead times
- time to place orders
- late deliveries
- parts shortages
- instances of parts rejection
- the number of joint supplier quality assurance programmes to ensure quality of incoming parts
- number of buyers per unit value of purchases

Once the key parameters have been determined the company then needs to establish its performance against these parameters. The discipline of benchmarking frequently shows that companies do not know how they perform against their key business parameters.

Who to use as a benchmark?

Benchmarking will frequently incorporate competitor analysis. This involves analysing a company's performance and products against major competitors. Techniques such as reverse engineering and market analysis may be used. These techniques are useful when formulating a product or marketing strategy.

However, benchmarking is a much broader concept. It looks at the skills and processes necessary to create world-beating performance. Sophisticated businesses do not restrict their attention to their own industry. They frequently look at other industries where similar processes are employed. This enables you not just to equal the performance of your competitors but to leapfrog over them.

For example, a company such as ICL might analyse the products of its competitors to determine how they compare. It has also chosen to compare its distribution process against that of Marks and Spencer, a company for whom distribution is a key activity (as detailed in *The Economist*, 11 May 1991).

A variety of organisations may be used as a benchmark. These include:

(i) *Other parts of your own organisation; other departments, divisions or companies.* Here information is likely to be accessible, but this may produce insular 'safe' results.

(ii) *Competitors.* This is useful because it shows how you are performing against your direct competitors. These are the people who your customers could choose to buy from today if you fail to meet their requirements. Competitor analysis is a vital part of any business strategy. However, it has the disadvantage that it restricts you to performance standards currently achieved in your own industry. It is also generally difficult to get information from your direct competitors unless it is in the public domain.

(iii) *Other industries.* Companies which are in different industry sectors to your own may carry out similar activities in a totally different way. For example, one of the key activities in the fresh food industry is supply management. Here, it is vital to ensure the delivery of the correct quantities of food on a daily or hourly basis. Some companies have studied the lessons learned in the fresh food industry to identify techniques to streamline just-in-time manufacturing activities. The main advantage of this approach is that opportunities for dramatic improvement may be available as a result of adopting radically different techniques. It is also generally easier to develop a relationship with non-competitors so that information and visits can be exchanged. However it is important to be aware that not all techniques may be transferrable. An open mind is needed to see the possibilities which may be available. But do not underestimate the difficulties which may arise when trying to implement radical new ideas.

How can you get hold of appropriate information?

Two principal types of information are required for an effective benchmarking programme. These are:

(i) Who is a world-class performer at the activity you wish to benchmark? This information can be obtained from a number of sources, such as:

(a) customers and suppliers – they will often have information on your competitors and their performance in certain areas.

(b) journalists, academics, consultants and stockbrokers – they may often have a wider view of other industries.

(c) trade associations for your own or other industries.

(d) your employees – they may well have useful experience, especially of the retail and service industries.

(ii) How do you get the necessary information to use as a benchmark? In most cases it is only possible to obtain information on what has been achieved by a business. Information is not readily available to describe how successes have been achieved. The principal sources of information include:

(a) published accounts, market sector reports and business magazines.

(b) trade association reports are often a useful source of information on competitors who will not exchange information directly.

(c) customer surveys (by interview or questionnaire).

(d) approaching companies directly may be possible when the company is not a direct competitor and you can offer information in exchange. This is often the only way to gain access to *how* the performance standard was achieved in practice.

What have companies done in practice?

The principal objective of benchmarking is to throw light on opportunities to improve performance in key areas. It is a technique that is widely used by leading businesses.

For example, Rank Xerox regularly benchmarks a large number of parameters. Its guiding principle is 'Anything anyone else can do better, we should aim to do at least equally well'. After studying the distribution systems of a number of major companies, Rank Xerox found that:

● it operated an additional layer of stockholding which could be removed;

● information took a day longer to reach the centre from the field;

● other companies improved their warehousing through efficient manual methods, not necessarily through automation.

● 'first pick' availability of stock in the best warehouses was 90 per cent, in Rank Xerox it was 83 per cent.

Rank Xerox uses the results of its benchmarking programme to set targets for its Quality Management Programme.

ICL regularly compares its performance against that of its 20 leading competitors. This analysis covers a number of criteria relating to product and business performance, such as:

- debtors as a percentage of revenue
- expenditure on R & D as a percentage of revenue
- return on capital
- revenue per employee
- product reliability
- delivery time and delivery reliability

The information obtained for this benchmarking programme is analysed and distributed throughout the company so that everyone is aware of the performance gaps and the improvements which need to be made. (The information on Rank Xerox and ICL used in this chapter is from the DTI booklet 'Best Practice Benchmarking').

A continuous process: When should you use benchmarks?

Benchmarking can provide valuable information at all stages in the life of a business. One opportunity which is frequently overlooked is at the start of a new venture. It is at this time that key long term decisions may be taken which influence the way the business will develop. Establishing world-class performance measures for key activities at the outset will help ensure a firm foundation for future operations.

Having completed a benchmarking programme, it is important to continue to monitor performance. Benchmarking is a continuous process. Every business is seeking to improve its performance. As a result, last year's benchmarks are usually out of date. It is therefore important continuously to:

(i)   Check performance against benchmarks;
(ii) Update benchmarks for improvements in the performance of your competitors;
(iii) Review the activities being benchmarked to ensure they are still key to the success of the business; and
(iv) Seek to identify emerging key parameters which may provide a basis for future benchmarks.

Limitations of benchmarking

Benchmarking is only one of a range of tools which can help businesses to remain competitive. It is a very powerful technique for helping identify performance targets for key parameters. However, it is important to understand its principal limitations; these include:

(i)   Benchmarking alone will not tell you what customers actually want. If your product is obsolete, no amount of improvements in production processes will make it competitive.

(ii) Benchmarking can lead management to focus attention on existing competitive issues. By the time management has developed a response to these threats, the competition may have moved on. It is essential not to lose sight of the importance of forecasting emerging threats. Look to the future and try to identify the key competitive features that are likely to emerge over the next 5–10 years, and establish benchmarks for those activities.

(iii) Benchmarking is only the first step on the road to improvement. A company will only benefit if it implements improvements.

(iv) Benchmarking only identifies the performance levels. Little guidance may be given about how to achieve the desired improvements. Management must seek to understand how this level of performance was achieved. They must then try to identify how the same, or better, performance can be achieved in their own business.

How do you start?

As with all forms of analysis, it is important to start by planning the programme. Because almost any activity can be benchmarked, it is important to determine the activities which are key to the success of the business. The key parameters can then be identified and measured. These are the principal candidates for benchmarking. It is then necessary to find the best available company to act as a benchmark.

A successful benchmarking programme can be broken down into a number of key phases:

(i)   Form a benchmarking team. This should include key decision makers and process specialists. It will probably involve between six and twelve people.

(ii) Determine those activities which are the keys to the success of the business and where improvements need to be made.

(iii) Establish the performance measurements for your own company for these key activities.

(iv) Identify those companies which achieve world-class performance in these areas.

(v) Gather information on the performance standards of these companies. If possible, arrange with the company to talk to the managers and workers there to understand how their performance was achieved.

(vi) Identify lessons which can be learned from these companies and devise a way to implement them. Implement an improvement programme to achieve world class performance.

The following guidelines are useful when carrying out a benchmarking exercise:

(i) It is important to avoid gathering too much information. This can lead to 'analysis paralysis'. Focus on a few critical areas rather than too many at once.

(ii) Benchmarking is an expensive activity. If it is undertaken without an action plan to control, measure and improve performance, it is a waste of time and money.

(iii) Details of how world-class performance has been achieved can only be obtained by talking to the company personnel. A statement that a radical improvement in performance has been achieved by another company is of limited use unless there is accompanying information on how this was achieved. It will then be possible to determine how these methods can be adapted for use in your company. To this end it is important that the basis for comparison is valid, otherwise the results are only of limited value to your company.

(iv) It is usually only worth benchmarking those activities that improve customer satisfaction or have an impact on the bottom line.

(v) It is important to realise that benchmarking only shows what other companies are already achieving. The important issues change with time. It is important to devise a programme that is forward looking which provides information on the performance standards for the next generation.

QUALITY FUNCTION DEPLOYMENT

Quality Function Deployment (QFD) is a planning tool which is used to help businesses focus on the needs of their customers when setting design and manufacturing specifications. It draws together marketing, engineering and manufacturing skills from the moment the project is first conceived and ensures products are designed which reflect the needs and desires of customers.

The principal tool used in QFD is the 'House of Quality'. This is a matrix showing the relationship between customer requirements and engineering characteristics. An outline of the 'House of Quality' is illustrated in Fig. 7.3. Using this tool, companies are able to reconcile customer needs against design and manufacturing constraints. The model is very flexible and enables a company to record how important each characteristic is to its customers and how difficult it is to modify. This enables the trade-offs between characteristics to be made on the basis of objective criteria.

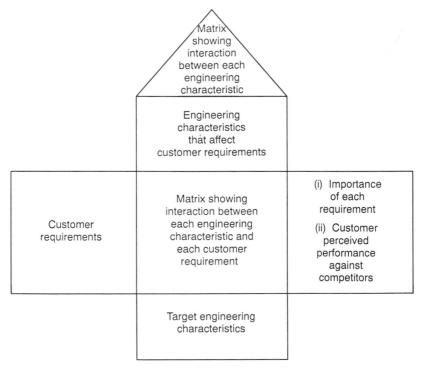

Figure 7.3   Basic outline for the house of quality

Who uses QFD?

QFD was first developed in Japan in 1972 by Mitsubishi, for use in its Kobe shipyard. The process has since been developed by Toyota and its suppliers who have used it in the design of motor cars. Today, the technique is used widely in Japan, and is beginning to be adopted in America and Europe by companies such as DEC, Hewlett Packard, AT&T, Ford and General Motors.

In Japan, the tool has been used successfully for controlling the design and manufacturing of a wide range of products, including:

- consumer electronics;
- motor cars;
- domestic appliances;
- integrated circuits;
- clothing; and
- the design of local amenities, retail outlets and housing.

Companies are naturally reluctant to talk about how they utilise QFD in practice because of the commercial sensitivity surrounding the product development cycle. Being first in the market with a successful new product provides companies with a significant competitive advantage. Companies are therefore naturally keen to retain this advantage.

What are the benefits of QFD?

QFD ensures that a company focuses on understanding the customer's requirements *before* any design work is carried out. This may lengthen the planning phase of design projects but it generally reduces both the overall length of the design phase and the number of post-release design changes.

The tremendous impact QFD has on streamlining the introduction of new models is illustrated by Fig. 7.4 which shows a comparison between the number and phasing of design changes introduced by a Japanese car maker which uses QFD with that of an American car maker which does not.

The key benefits of QFD are as follows:

(i)   It focuses the design of new products and services on customer requirements. It ensures that customer requirements are understood and that the design process is driven by objective customer needs rather than by technology.

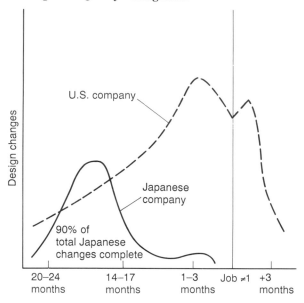

Figure 7.4 Japanese automaker with QFD made fewer changes than US company without QFD

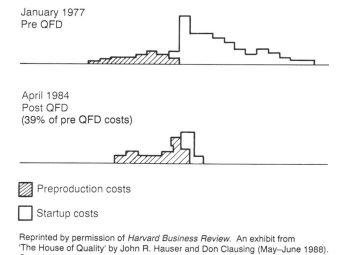

Figure 7.5 Start-up and pre-production costs at Toyota Auto Body before and after QFD

(ii)   It prioritises design activities. This ensures that the design process is focused on the most significant customer requirements.

(iii) It analyses the performance of the company's products against those of its principal competitors for key customer requirements.

(iv)   By focusing the design effort, it reduces the overall length of the design cycle and hence reduces the time to market for new products. Current estimates put this saving at between one third and one half of the pre-QFD cycle time.

(v)   It reduces the number of post-release design changes, by ensuring focused effort is put into the planning phase. This significantly reduces the cost of introducing new designs. Fig. 7.5 illustrates the impact of QFD on start-up and pre-production costs at Toyota Auto Body.

(vi)   It promotes teamwork, and breaks down barriers between departments by involving marketing, engineering and manufacturing from the outset of each project. Each team member is of equal importance and has something to contribute to the process.

(vii) It provides a means of documenting the process, and a sound basis on which design decisions can be taken. This helps guard the project against unforeseen changes in personnel.

How does QFD work?

The concept behind QFD is quite simple and represents a common sense approach to designing new products. In practice it relies on the constructive interaction between design, marketing, production and engineering departments. It may be necessary to overcome organisational problems in companies which are not geared up to operate cross-functional teams.

Using the example of one customer attribute for a car door to illustrate the flow of information, QFD works as follows. The flow of information is illustrated graphically in Fig. 7.6, and was first discussed in 'The House of Quality' by John R. Hauser and Don Clausing (*Harvard Business Review*, May–June 1988, pp. 63–72).

1. Details of customer requirements (termed 'attributes') are collected and weighted in terms of importance by the marketing department. The customer attribute here is 'Does not leak in rain'.

2. These customer attributes are translated into key engineering characteristics, such as 'water resistance in pounds per square inch'.

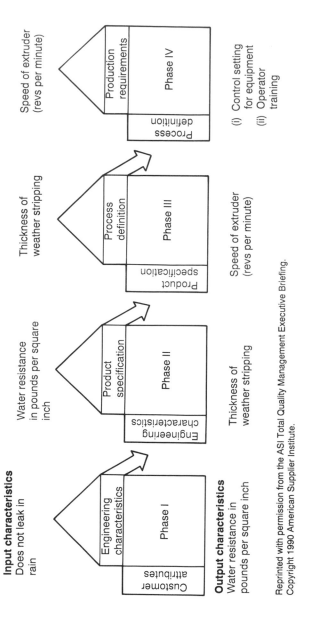

Figure 7.6 The translation of customer requirements into production planning using 'The House of Quality'.

3. At this stage it is possible to compare the performance of the product against customer preferences, and against competitors' products. This process identifies key areas demanding improvement.
4. It is then possible to assess objectively the impact of engineering changes on:

   (i) Customer attributes; and
   (ii) Other engineering characteristics. For example, increasing the resistance to water penetration may make the door more difficult to close.

5. By assessing factors such as the technical difficulty of introducing engineering changes; the importance of characteristics to customers; and the estimated cost of making the changes, the target outcome for each engineering characteristic can be determined. For example, water resistance has been specified at 70 psi.
6. Engineering characteristics may be translated into a product specification in terms of, for example, the thickness of the weather stripping required around the door (Phase II).
7. The process requirements for producing the required weather stripping can then be defined (Phase III) in terms of, for example, the speed of the extruder used to make it.
8. Production requirements (such as control settings and operator training) can then be defined (Phase IV).

An outline of the House of Quality

In practice the 'House of Quality' provides a very powerful tool, but it can appear quite complex at first sight. The basic components of the House are illustrated in Fig. 7.3.

1. Customer attributes are detailed along the left hand side of the House.
2. These are then prioritised. The performance of the company and its competitors against these attributes is detailed along the right hand side of the House.
3. Engineering characteristics which may affect one or more customer attributes are listed along the top of the House.
4. A matrix showing the relationship between the engineering characteristics and the customer requirements completes the body of the house. A number, or symbol, is used to show the strength of this relationship and whether it is positive or negative. This matrix shows

the impact of changes in engineering characteristics on customer attributes. Changing an engineering characteristic may reduce its ability to meet a particular customer attribute (a negative relationship); or it may increase it (a positive relationship)

5. The roof of the House shows the interaction between different engineering characteristics. It demonstrates how a change in one characteristic may positively or negatively affect another. Again, a number or symbol is used to show the strength of the relationship.

6. The measured performance of each engineering characteristic of the product is then compared with its principal competitors along the bottom of the matrix. The bottom of the matrix may also be used to list any other information which the team needs to consider when setting targets for engineering characteristics. This might include, for example, the cost to implement changes or the technical difficulty of the change.

7. Finally, the team records the design targets for each engineering characteristic along the bottom of the matrix. This is the result of intensive discussions between the members of the multidisciplinary team.

QFD in practice

When undertaking a QFD project, more than 100 customer requirements may be identified for an individual product. The QFD matrix enables these requirements, and the engineering characteristics which cause them to be met, to be displayed in such a way that rational, informed decisions can be taken.

Building a House of Quality

The following example, showing a small part of a QFD matrix, is adapted and reprinted by permission of Harvard Business Review. An excerpt from *The House of Quality*, by John R. Hauser and Don Clausing (May–June 1988). Copyright © 1988 by the President and Fellows of Harvard College; all rights reserved.

The following commentary refers to Fig. 7.7. The steps necessary to build the House of Quality are as follows:

1. The marketing department identifies the customer attributes for the product. In this case we are considering five requirements for a car door:

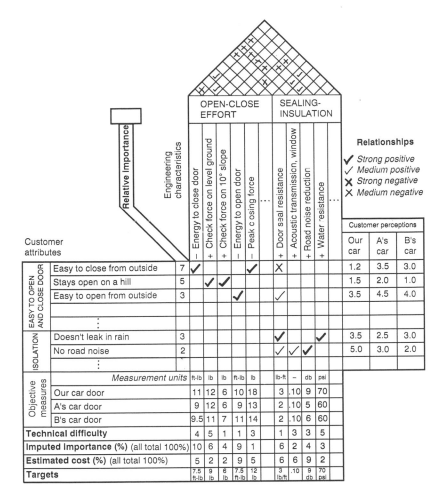

The figure shows a House of Quality matrix with the following data:

Customer attributes		Relative Importance	Energy to close door	Check force on level ground	Check force on 10° slope	Energy to open door	Peak closing force		Door seal resistance	Acoustic transmission, window	Road noise reduction	Water resistance		Our car	A's car	B's car
			‒	+	+	‒	‒	...	+	+	+	+	...			
EASY TO OPEN AND CLOSE DOOR	Easy to close from outside	7	✔				✓		✗					1.2	3.5	3.0
	Stays open on a hill	5		✓	✓									1.5	2.0	1.0
	Easy to open from outside	3				✓			✓					3.5	4.5	4.0
	⋮															
ISOLATION	Doesn't leak in rain	3							✔			✔		3.5	2.5	3.0
	No road noise	2							✓	✓	✔			5.0	3.0	2.0
	⋮															

OPEN-CLOSE EFFORT; SEALING-INSULATION

Relationships
✔ Strong positive
✓ Medium positive
✗ Strong negative
✗ Medium negative

Customer perceptions

Measurement units	ft-lb	lb	lb	ft-lb	lb		lb-ft	–	db	psi
Our car door	11	12	6	10	18		3	.10	9	70
A's car door	9	12	6	9	13		2	.10	5	60
B's car door	9.5	11	7	11	14		2	.10	6	60
Technical difficulty	4	5	1	1	3		1	3	3	5
Imputed importance (%) (all total 100%)	10	6	4	9	1		6	2	4	3
Estimated cost (%) (all total 100%)	5	2	2	9	5		6	6	9	2
Targets	7.5 ft-lb	9 lb	6 lb	7.5 ft-lb	12 lb		3 lb/ft	.10	9 db	70 psi

Objective measures

Figure 7.7 House of quality

- easy to close from outside
- stays open on a hill
- easy to open from outside
- does not leak in the rain
- no road noise

These attributes are listed on the left hand side of the house.

2. The importance of each of these requirements is then assessed. In complex cases, the least important attributes may be excluded from the matrix. The weighting given to attributes may be obtained directly

from customers (for example during surveys), or it may be based on the opinions and experience of the group.

3. Customer perceptions of the relative performance of the company's products, compared with that of its principal competitors, is recorded on the right hand side of the House. In this case we are interested in two competitor products, A and B.

4. The engineering characteristics which affect customer attributes are recorded across the top of the matrix. These characteristics should be capable of being measured (for example, the force required to close a door in lbf or Newtons). Each characteristic is pre-fixed by a + or −. This indicates whether an increase or decrease in the value of the characteristic is likely to be desirable. For example, the + in front of 'door seal resistance' indicates that an increase in the value of the seal resistance is likely to be an objective of the team. The − in front of 'energy to close the door' indicates that reducing the energy required to close the door is likely to be an objective of the team.

5. The team discusses the impact of each engineering characteristic on each customer attribute. The consensus view is marked on the matrix. The strength of the effect, and whether it is positive or negative, is recorded. In this case, the group decided that the energy required to close the door had a strong positive influence on the customer attribute 'easy to close', i.e. a reduction in the energy required to close the door would make it easier to close the door.

The group also decided that 'door seal resistance' had a strong negative influence on the ease of closing the door, i.e. an increase in door seal resistance, although it would reduce leakage, would also make it harder to close.

We can begin to see from this example the trade-offs which the group need to make when setting design criteria.

6. The group then completes the roof matrix. Here the impact of changing one engineering characteristic on all the other characteristics is recorded. Symbols are again used to indicate the strength of the relationship. In this case, increasing the door seal resistance helps reduce road noise and improve water resistance, but means that more energy is required to close the door.

7. Actual performance for each engineering characteristic is then compared with the product's principal competitors at the base of the house. This part of the house is often customised to give additional information which the team should take into account when making its decisions.

In this case the company has recorded a measure of the technical difficulty; cost to implement; and its assessment of the importance of making an improvement, against each engineering characteristic.

8. Finally, the group uses all the information on the matrix, together with its own judgement, to set target values for each characteristic.

In this case, the most important customer attribute was felt to be 'easy to close door from the outside'. Here, the company's product performs poorly against those of its competitors. The group therefore decides to look in detail at improving the ability of the door to meet this attribute. The key engineering characteristics which affect this customer attribute are:

a) energy to close door;
b) peak closing force; and
c) door seal resistance.

Both a) and b) are positively related to the customer attribute, so the group decides to investigate these further.

The roof of the house indicates that reducing the energy to close the door has a positive effect on:

- door opening energy; and
- peak closing force.

but a negative effect on:

- check force on level ground;
- window acoustic transmission; and
- road noise.

The group then needs to balance the benefits arising from improving the door's ability to close easily with the impact on other customer attributes. The relative importance of the customer attributes; current performance against competitors and the cost of making the improvement are all taken into account at this stage.

In this case the group decided that improvements had to be made in the ease of closing the door from outside. Customers perceive this attribute to be important and the company's existing doors perform poorly. Target levels for the key engineering characteristics are then set. Here the target level of energy to close the door is set at 7.5 ft lb; the aim in this case being to become better than the competitors.

Looking at the customer attribute 'doesn't leak in rain', two engineering characteristics have an impact here:

(a) door seal resistance; and
(b) water resistance.

These are positively related. An improvement in door seal resistance would improve water resistance; and both would improve the overall water resistance of the door.

Looking at the roof matrix, however, we see that these engineering characteristics have a strong negative impact on the energy required to open and close the door. Improving door seal resistance and water resistance would make it more difficult to reduce the energy required to open and close the door.

As the company's existing door is perceived by customers to have better water resistance than those of its competitors it is decided not to adjust the target for these characteristics because any change would make it more difficult to close the door.

These examples demonstrate the complex interactions which exist between engineering characteristics and customer attributes. QFD enables all the available information to be presented in a straightforward manner so that the impact of making trade-offs can be determined. This enables sound, complex decisions to be taken.

The next steps

Having specified the target engineering characteristics, the team is able to develop the detailed product specification (Phase II); design the production processes (Phase III); and define the production requirements such as operator training and machine settings (Phase IV).

What are the requirements for carrying out QFD?

QFD requires commitment from both the project team and management if it is to be successful. The key factors which help companies ensure QFD yields significant results are set out below:

1. Most importantly, the project team must have the demonstrated, active support of management. QFD is a time-consuming activity. However, it can become the core of an effective design strategy and so the investment can be well rewarded.
2. The team requires time to pull together the necessary information, identify the key parameters and draw up the House of Quality matrix.

An experienced team may take some 16–20 hours to draw the first matrix if all the necessary information is available. In companies where this information is not available, the project will take considerably longer to complete.

Experienced teams may choose to draw up the matrix during a two-day workshop. This may be necessary where team members are located some distance apart and all the information can be made available at one site. If there are no travelling problems teams tend to meet for a series of two hour sessions. Each session allows one part of the matrix to be completed, although an extended session may be required for the final decision matrix. This approach allows team members time to think about each part of the matrix, and to gather additional information as the House is constructed.

3. Members of the team should be carefully selected. A representative should be drawn from the marketing, engineering, manufacturing and quality functions. Team members should be chosen for their ability to contribute to a team project and their ability to approach new ideas with an open mind.

4. The scope of the project and the team's objective should be clearly defined at the outset.

5. A team leader should be appointed who understands the project and can lead a team. He is responsible for ensuring that each team member contributes, and the project meets its objectives.

6. A facilitator who understands the QFD process can help the team to use the House of Quality approach.

7. A relatively easy project should be chosen for the first matrix so the team can learn how to use the House of Quality. A project involving the re-designing of an existing part may be a good starting point.

8. The team should make a formal presentation of their conclusions to management. A reasoned decision to accept or reject the conclusions should then be made quickly.

Where does the customer information come from?

QFD is driven by customer requirements. As a result, it is essential that their requirements are fully understood. In many cases there are a number of customers in a supply chain for any given product or service. A manufacturer may sell to a wholesaler who supplies a number of retail outlets. The retail outlets make sales to the final consumer. Each of these customers is likely to have different requirements.

Take, for example, the case of a kettle. The final customer buys the kettle to boil water. The retailer is likely to be looking for a product which is easy to display, robust during storage and handling and easy to repair. It is important that all customers are identified so that their requirements can be established and taken into account during the design phase.

There are a number of sources of customer information. Some information is actively sought by many companies through:

- Customer surveys and trials
- Trade surveys and trials
- Working with selected, important customers
- Competitor analysis
- Focus groups.

In these cases the company is usually able to structure the request for information so that it receives the information it wants.

There are also other sources of information which, although not actively sought by the company, have an important bearing on understanding customer requirements. These include:

- Customer complaints
- Legal standards and guidelines
- Lawsuits against the company or against companies producing similar products or services
- Informal customer, or potential customer comments received from sources such as the sales force after customer visits; feedback from other employees; comments heard at conferences, training courses and trade exhibitions

This information is usually received in a variety of forms. Although it is generally more difficult to interpret and use this type of information, it represents a vital source of information on customer requirements.

QUALITY AWARDS

Introduction

A number of quality awards are made each year around the world. Each award is managed by a different organisation, each using its own judging criteria. The awards generally command a high profile in their own country, and sometimes around the world. The award programmes can play a significant role in raising the profile of Quality in the business community and so, as a result, may have an important role to play in a Programme of continuous quality improvement. In broad terms, the awards have the following benefits:

(i) They raise the profile of the continuous improvement of quality within the companies which apply for them. The publicity given to the award winners about their successful introduction of quality improvements gives an important signal to their customers and employees; and may also serve to generate interest in Total Quality amongst other companies.

(ii) The application for an award can add a feeling of excitement to the improvement process. It may also lead to the recognition of the whole company's achievement if the company wins an award.

(iii) The award criteria sometimes offer useful guidelines to companies wishing to implement a programme of continuous quality improvement. This is particularly true for the US Malcolm Baldridge National Quality Award where detailed selection criteria are published in the application guidelines.

It is, however, important to keep the value of the awards in perspective. There are a number of potential pitfalls with award programmes which persist despite the best efforts of the awarding bodies. The following issues should be borne in mind:

(i) Companies should not adopt the formal assessment criteria slavishly as a model for success. These criteria may not be appropriate for all businesses. The award criteria should only be used as guidelines, which may be adapted to suit an individual organisation.

(ii) The application for an award should be the result, not the aim, of any continuous improvement programme. Companies should focus on the continuous improvement and not on winning a quality award. The key reward for a successful programme of continuous improvement of quality is commercial success and improved customer satisfaction.

(iii) The application for an award can be very time-consuming and expensive. It is reported in the July 1991 edition of Fortune magazine that the Corning telecommunications division spent some 7,000 man-hours just applying for the Malcolm Baldridge Award in 1989; and they did not win! Resources should not be diverted from the programme of continuous quality improvement in order to apply for an award.

In summary, an application for a quality award can provide excitement and renewed focus for an established quality improvement programme. The award criteria may also provide useful guidelines to companies which are in the process of introducing, or wish to re-focus, an improvement programme. There is, however, a danger that winning an award can become the goal rather than a consequence of the company's continuous quality improvement programme.

The Quality Awards

Brief details of the principal quality awards from around the world are set out below, focusing on:

(i)   How they are run; and
(ii) Details of the selection criteria, where available. A description of the key concepts underlying the 1991 Malcolm Baldridge National Quality Award is included because these offer useful guidance in a number of areas which an improvement programme needs to cover.

The British Quality Award

This award was founded in 1984 and is administered by the British Quality Association (BQA). The BQA is an association of member companies which are committed to Quality improvement. One or more awards may be made each year. Special commendations are also made for finalists which have achieved significant quality improvements.

The judging of entries is carried out by a panel of 10 individuals with extensive practical experience of quality management. The selection of these judges appears to be by nomination rather than by open application. No specific training is given to the judges about the selection criteria for the awards.

The BQA states that its principal criterion for judging the competition is evidence of significant, sustained improvement in quality over a period of at least four years. This improvement can be associated with the following activities:

- product design or manufacture;
- the planning or operation of a service;
- the development or operation of a process.

The judges are looking for a process of continuous improvement. The key features which the judges look for are:

- satisfying customer requirements at competitive cost
- improved product or service performance
- technological innovation to improve product quality
- measurable commercial and operational success
- motivation and education of personnel to improve quality
- a substantially higher quality standard than that prevalent within the industry as a whole.

No further information has been published to explain these criteria, although it is understood that the BQA is considering issuing guidelines.

An application for an award is made by the company in the form of a report addressing the above criteria. The judges study the reports and select approximately a dozen finalists for a site visit. The judges do not give a feedback report to the companies at any stage in the competition. If they were to do this, it would be of considerable benefit to the applicants. No charge is currently made to applicants.

The Digital Scotland Quality Award
Digital Equipment Scotland Ltd administers the Digital Scotland Quality Award. This award is open to any group or individual operating in Scotland. The selection criteria for winners are similar to those for applicants for the BQA award.

The Irish Quality Award
This award is administered by the Irish Quality Organisation. This is the equivalent body to the BQA in The Republic of Ireland. The award is supported by the Confederation of Irish Industries, the Training and Employment Authority and the Irish Congress of Trade Unions. Three major awards are made annually:

(i) Any company can apply for the 'Quality Mark'. This award is given on the basis of answers to a written questionnaire and a site visit. Here, the company is effectively assessed against a slightly expanded version of ISO9000. The assessment criteria include, for example, training, quality costs and personnel appraisal, in addition to the ISO9000 requirements. Each criterion is given a weighting. Any company which scores higher than 80 per cent receives the 'Quality Mark'. All companies are informed of their score and receive a feedback report.

(ii) At the end of each year, the highest scoring companies within each industrial sector receive the 'Irish Quality Award'. The winners are selected on the basis of:

- the highest overall result in their sector;
- consistently high ratings in all areas;
- exceptionally high ratings in a few areas;
- an emphasis on quality planning; and
- improvement since the previous audit.

(iii) An overall winner is selected annually, drawn from all the industry winners.

The administration of the award is well planned, with clear selection criteria and feedback reports. However, the criteria are based very much on ISO9000 and are not closely linked to business performance.

The Deming Prizes

There are three categories of Deming Prizes: the Deming Prize which is awarded to individuals, the Deming Application Prize, which is awarded to companies, and the Deming Factory Prize. These awards have been operated by the Japanese Union of Scientists and Engineers (JUSE) for over thirty years. In 1970, a further award was established; the Japan Quality Control Award. This is awarded to companies which have demonstrated a sustained commitment to Total Quality Control at least five years after receiving a Deming prize.

These awards focus heavily on Statistical Quality Control (i.e. the improvement in quality through the control of processes) as the basis of a Total Quality Control (TQC) environment. The audit checklist for the Deming prizes covers the following criteria:

(i)   Corporate policy;
(ii) Organisation and administration;
(iii) Education;
(iv) Implementation in specific departments;
(v)   The effects of TQC on product quality and other key parameters, such as profits, delivery, safety and costs; and
(vi) How the company intends to carry the TQC programme forward.

The Malcolm Baldridge National Quality Award

The Malcolm Baldridge National Quality Award is an American award for excellence in Quality achievement and management which is made annually. The award was established by the US Congress in 1987 to commemorate a former Secretary of Commerce, Malcolm Baldridge, and to encourage Quality improvement throughout American industry. Although funded by application fees, responsibility for the award lies with the US Department of Commerce and it is widely supported by Government, as witnessed by the following two quotes.

George Bush is reported prominently on the front cover of the 1991 Application guidelines for the Malcolm Baldridge National Quality Award as saying: 'The improvement of quality in products and the improvement of quality in service – these are national priorities as never before'.

Robert Mossbacher, Secretary of Commerce, is quoted as saying: 'The winners of this award have made quality improvement a way of life. Quality is their bottom line, and that kind of can-do attitude makes for world-class products and services.'

There are three categories of award:

(i)   Manufacturing industry;
(ii) Service industry;
(iii) Small business – less than 500 employees.

Up to two awards can be made annually in each category. However, since 1988 when the first award was made, only nine awards have been given. The award winners are listed below.

1988 Award winners
   Globe Metallurgical
   Motorola
   Westinghouse – Commercial Nuclear Fuel Division

1989 Award winners
   Milliken and Company
   Xerox Business Products and Systems

1990 Award winners
   General Motors – Cadillac Motor Car
   IBM – Rochester
   Federal Express Corporation
   Wallace Co Inc

The awards are only open to 'for-profit organisations' located in the United States of America or its territories.

The administrators of the Baldridge Award issue a detailed set of guidelines each year to prospective applicants. In addition to instructions on how to apply for the award, the guidelines include a comprehensive list of criteria against which applicants will be judged. This lists seven categories and thirty-two items which the company must address in its submission. The guidelines also include details of the weightings given to each of the selection criteria.

To apply for the award, a company must submit a report setting out its achievements against the award criteria (maximum 75 pages!) for judging. A panel of judges considers each report and awards a score for each item. These are then totalled to give an overall score. Those companies which score highly on the written submission are then subject to a 3–4 day visit by a panel of judges, to ensure the submission is accurate. All the judges used for the Baldridge Award receive training on how to assess applicants against the selection criteria. Judges stand for re-election each year.

At the end of the judging process, each company receives a feedback report on its performance.

In addition to capturing business imagination and raising the profile of Quality, the major strengths of the Baldridge Award are:

(i)   The clear guidelines on continuous improvement; and
(ii) The feedback report which every applicant receives.

There are, however, some potential weaknesses in the system. These include:

(i)   The whole process takes a lot of time and money. This may divert resources away from the principal objectives of the improvement process itself. For example, Corning Telecommunications Division estimate that they spent some 7,000 man-hours applying for the award (*Fortune* magazine, July 1991);
(ii)   Some essential business objectives are missing from the criteria. These include innovation, long-term planning, financial performance and the ability to change rapidly;
(iii) The award does not seem to focus attention on profitable businesses. IBM, Motorola and Xerox have all seen profits fall since winning the award. A brief review of the award winners so far suggests that the award seems to favour blue-chip companies. Perhaps these are the only ones which can afford the necessary time and money to apply for the award?
(iv)   Companies nominate themselves. The award might be more meaningful if companies were nominated by their customers. Customers

are usually in the best position to verify the success, or otherwise, of quality improvements made by a supplier.

Details of the Malcolm Baldridge National Quality Award criteria
The selection criteria for the Malcolm Baldridge National Quality Award provide some very useful ideas for companies committed to the concept of continuous quality improvement although the relevance of each point to individual businesses should be assessed.

The key concepts underlying the Malcolm Baldridge National Quality Award criteria are:

(i)   Quality is defined by the customer.
(ii)   The senior leadership of the business needs to create clear quality values and build the values into the way the company operates.
(iii)   Quality excellence derives from well-designed and well-executed systems and processes.
(iv)   Continuous improvement must be part of the management of all systems and processes.
(v)   Companies need to develop goals, as well as strategic and operational plans to achieve quality leadership.
(vi)   Shortening the response time of all operations and processes of the company needs to be part of the quality improvement effort.
(vii)   Operations and decisions of the company need to be based on facts and data.
(viii) All employees must be suitably trained and developed and involved in quality activities.
(ix)   Design quality and defect and error prevention should be major elements of the quality system.
(x)   Companies need to communicate quality requirements to suppliers and work to elevate supplier quality performance.

These concepts form part of the 1991 Award guidelines published by the American National Institute of Standards and Technology, part of the Department of Commerce.

TEAMWORK FOR QUALITY

The objective of Quality Improvement is to increase the effectiveness and profitability of the organisation by improving its ability to meet external customers' requirements at minimum cost. This requires:

(i)   A clear understanding of external customer requirements; and
(ii) Internal processes which work effectively to produce the required output.

A Quality Improvement Programme (QIP) is a planned and structured approach to resolving problems which cause non-conforming output. Three principal types of team may be set up to achieve specific objectives as part of a QIP:

(i)   A Quality Improvement Team (QIT) plans and directs the QIP.
(ii) Corrective Action Task Forces resolve complex problems and typically include representatives from a number of departments.
(iii) Progress groups are small problem-solving groups drawn from one department.

Further details about the activities of these teams, and guidelines for effective teamwork are set out below.

Quality Improvement Team

In most companies, significant changes are required when implementing a Quality Improvement Programme. In order to plan and direct the implementation of the Programme, most companies form a Quality Improvement Team. This Team should be composed of a chairman, an administrator, and a representative from each department.

Selection of the chairman and administrator is important since they will become deeply involved in the Programme and will direct the running of the Quality Improvement Team (QIT). The following are the key requirements for the members of the QIT:

1. The chairman should be selected by the general manager and management team. It is essential that senior management have confidence in the person chosen.
2. The chairman should be a senior member of management who understands and enthusiastically supports the need for Quality Improvement and is committed to defect prevention. The chairman may be from any department within the company. In view of the importance of this role, he needs to be able to devote approximately 20 per cent of his time to the QIP. Ideally the chairman should not be the Quality Manager because this reinforces the myth that Quality is really the

responsibility of the Quality department. Quality is everyone's responsibility!

3. Having been appointed, the chairman selects the rest of his team in conjunction with the department heads. As all departments are involved in the QIP, they must all be represented on the QIT.

4. The appointment of the administrator generally needs to be approved by the general manager since he will need to devote approximately 50 per cent of his time to the QIP.

5. At the start of the Programme, it is often useful for the Team to consist of the senior management team. This ensures the QIP receives sufficient management attention to get it off the ground, and demonstrates the commitment of senior management to the QIP. It is not essential for each QIT member to be the head of a department, but each team member must have the full support of the head of his department. The team member from each department represents their department on the team, and represents the QIT to the department.

6. Once the need for a QIP has been accepted by the general manager and management team, it is important that, where present, union support for the Programme is established. It may be desirable to include a union representative on the QIT.

The purpose of the QIT is to plan and direct the implementation of the Quality Improvement Programme. It is the responsibility of the head of each department to implement the Programme in their area.

The QIT should meet regularly. Its first objective is to develop the action plan for the Quality Improvement Programme. Once completed, this should be presented to the general manager and management team for approval and support. Firm dates should be set to accomplish each activity.

The general manager should regularly monitor progress of the QIP with the chairman and administrator. This helps ensure the QIP is kept on track, and provides assurance to the Team that it has the support of the general manager and management team at all times.

Corrective action groups

An effective system to recognise and eliminate problems which prevent Quality Improvement and the performance of error-free work is an essential part of any QIP. To achieve this, it is generally necessary to consider introducing formal problem solving groups.

1. Progress Groups (also known as Quality Circles)

Progress groups generally include a small number of individuals from within one department, who carry out similar work. The group meets regularly to identify, implement and monitor the progress of actions taken to resolve problems arising within their work area. It may sometimes be necessary to involve other departments in discussions where they are affected by a particular problem.

It is essential that the members of the progress groups are trained so they understand the objectives of the QIP, and the role they have to play in Quality Improvement. It is also important that they understand how to investigate problems and implement effective solutions. Without adequate training, the group will find it difficult to implement effective solutions. This may well lead to the group losing interest and disbanding.

It is an unfortunate fact that the concept of Quality Circles has a poor reputation in the UK. Many Quality Circle initiatives were introduced in the 1970s and 1980s and failed. The principal reason for this seems to be that they were introduced as an isolated measure in the hope that they would improve quality. Quality Circles were rarely given sufficient authority or training to resolve significant problems. As a result of this, they were unable to make much impact; the team members lost interest, and the teams disbanded.

The key problem here was that management was not prepared to invest sufficient resources to make the scheme work. Quality Circles do not have the influence to change the culture of a business on their own. That step requires the complete commitment of all employees; and the general manager must play a key role in this.

Quality circles do have an important role to play in businesses. Implemented as one element in a Total Quality Improvement Programme, they allow employees to play an active role in resolving the many problems they face on a day-to-day basis.

However, the well-publicised failure of Quality Circles in the past may lead to some resistance to their use. This may be overcome by using an alternative name (such as progress group).

2. Corrective Action Task Force

Complex problems frequently arise during the course of a Quality Improvement Programme. Sometimes these problems are particularly complex, contentious, or may involve a number of departments. To solve these problems it may be necessary to form a Corrective Action Task Force. A Task Force is established with the sole objective of identifying and eliminating the cause of a specific problem. A member from each department affected by the problem is appointed to the team. Because a Task Force may involve a substantial commitment from a number of people, it is essential that only a small number operate at any one time. Accordingly, the authority to form a Task Force is typically restricted to the QIT.

The problem the Task Force is tasked to resolve should be clearly defined, and progress should be carefully monitored by the QIT. Once the objectives of the Task Force have been achieved, it should be disbanded. Typical problems which may require the setting up of a Task Force include the following:

- Problems identified by the management team when formulating the strategic business objectives for the company.
- Problems identified during the education sessions.
- Problems identified by progress groups which they are unable to resolve.
- Complex problems identified by the Error Cause Removal (ECR) system.

Team Work

Effective teams can develop plans and solutions to problems which could not be resolved by individuals working on their own. Managing a team to work effectively and get the best out of each team member can be a very complex operation. Its success depends on the personal strengths and commitment of each individual team member.

This section describes a number of practical ideas to help ensure teams run smoothly.

Team dynamics

Teams are formed to find solutions to problems. If this simply involved applying problem solving techniques (identifying the problem and potential causes, gathering data, recommending and implementing a solution) life would be easy. However, when people get into groups, hidden concerns may get in the way of progress and prevent a team from working effectively. By being aware of the potential pitfalls, these problems may be avoided.

When individuals are chosen to work in a team they will inevitably have a number of potential concerns. These may fall into two principal categories:

(i)   Identity in the team: it is important to help individuals feel they are an active member of the team who can influence the collective decisions; and that all team members are pulling together to find a solution to the common problem.
(ii) Identity in the organisation: individuals will generally retain responsibilities in their departments and will want to know that their duties for the team will not result in any conflict with departmental objectives. It will usually be the team project that suffers if conflict does arise. It is therefore important to ensure that the team objectives do not conflict with the departmental objectives of the team members.

The identity of the team within the organisation is also important. For the team to succeed it is essential that the team and its objectives are fully supported by management. This helps attract people to the team and ensure their commitment to the project. It may also help ensure that the solutions proposed by the team are implemented.

Setting up a successful team

Before the team is set up it is important to lay the groundwork for success. The success or failure of a team can often be determined by the level of preparation before it is established. The key features of a successful team are:

- A well defined objective or purpose;
- Appropriate team members; and
- Management support for the activities of the team.

Objectives of the team

A formal objective should be established for the team prior to beginning any investigation. The objective may be set by the team itself, in the case of a Quality Circle; or by management, in the case of a Corrective Action Task Force. For example, an accounts department which has been monitoring the time taken for customers to settle their accounts in order to improve cash flow might set itself the following objective: 'To analyse the reasons for the late payment (defined as after 90 days) of accounts by customers and to identify recommended solutions for consideration by the Finance Director'.

Appropriate team members
Team members should be chosen carefully on the basis of the skills and experience they can bring to resolving the problem.

In the case of Quality Circles, all employees who carry out similar activities in a department should be encouraged to join the team, since everyone involved has something to contribute. If the team gets too large, with more than 15 people in it, then it may be appropriate to split it into two circles.

Having set up a team, it may evolve as further issues require consideration. For example, the team set up to resolve the problem of outstanding debts may initially consist only of accounting staff. Once more information is gathered about the causes of the problem it might be necessary to invite personnel from other departments (perhaps from sales or service) to join the team.

Teams generally include the following principal members:

Team leader. The team leader is responsible for the smooth running of the team. Their success will generally be measured in terms of the success the team has in identifying the cause and implementing an effective solution to a problem. The team leader guides the group through the problem solving process, ensuring the appropriate steps are taken and using the skills of each member to the full. This is a very difficult role which requires organisational skill, tact, the ability to get people to work together, and often some inspiration to succeed!

The role of team leader may be rotated amongst the team members in a quality circle. Usually this change in team leader occurs after one problem is solved and the group looks for a new problem to tackle. This avoids disturbing the flow of the problem solving process.

Secretary. The secretary is responsible for the administration relating to the team. This includes notifying members of meetings, preparing minutes and action plans following meetings, and ensuring assignments are completed according to schedule.

Members. Team members are part of the team because their skills and experience may be necessary to help identify the causes of a problem. Their role is to find a solution to the problem and help implement the proposed solution. Individual team members have a responsibility to ensure their departments understand and support the work of the team.

Specialists. Specialists attend a limited number of meetings to give the team the benefit of their experience on specific issues.

It is important that at least some members of each team have been trained in problem solving techniques. As a minimum the team leader should be trained in these skills. The team may then provide a means of teaching these problem solving skills to the other team members. Further details of problem solving techniques are set out in chapter 8.

Management support is critical to the success of all teams. Before agreeing to set up and lead a problem solving team, it is important for the team leader to ensure the team has the full support of management. The level of support necessary depends on the nature of the problem to be resolved. Problems which involve a number of departments and are complex or contentious are likely to require a considerable level of support. These problems are usually addressed by a Corrective Action Task Force, which requires the support of the whole Quality Improvement Team to set up. A local team looking at a local problem might only require the support of their departmental manager.

Running a team

Teams are set up to help resolve problems and effect solutions. As a result, their work is often challenging and may not progress smoothly. Sometimes progress will be rapid; at other times progress may be slow or (hopefully not too often) things will seem to go backwards.

The success a team has in making progress will frequently have an important impact on morale and hence the smooth running of the team. It is important that the team leader monitors carefully the running of the team and helps ensure all members are working effectively towards the common goal by:

- building a team spirit within the group.
- ensuring basic ground rules are established and followed.
- taking an interest in individual team members.
- informally helping individual team members to resolve problems.
- smoothing resistance to suggestions by holding informal discussions between meetings and laying the groundwork for a consensus view.
- developing a sense of cohesion and common purpose for the team.
- resolving tensions between group members.
- ensuring each member is involved in every meeting and that their views are treated with consideration by the rest of the team.

During the problem solving process the team may meet many times to discuss the problem and decide on the actions necessary to resolve it. Since the team will spend a lot of time and effort at meetings it is important that they are run effectively and efficiently. Each team member is responsible for ensuring that meetings are positive and make progress. The team leader is responsible for ensuring that objectives are set for each meeting and that they run smoothly.

Running meetings

At the start of a meeting (especially the first one) the team leader should welcome all the participants and remind them of the objectives of the meeting. It is useful to ask each member of the team to introduce themselves and describe their roles. The team leader should then outline the proposed plan to identify and implement a solution to the problem.

Having opened the meeting the team leader is responsible for directing the flow of the meeting. Important points to watch out for are:

- ensure everyone knows in advance the purpose of the meeting and any preparation they are required to do for the meeting.
- keep the meeting running to schedule.
- ensure discussion is focused on the points at issue. It is easy for meetings to be sidetracked and achieve very little.
- ensure basic courtesies are followed, and that everyone has the opportunity to express their ideas.
- dynamise the team if it starts to flag and maintain a positive attitude among members. It is frequently useful to have a board to record ideas and help focus discussion during meetings.
- ensure everyone understands and follows the ground rules for meetings.

At the end of a meeting the team leader should summarise the points raised and progress made at the meeting. He should also agree with the secretary the date the minutes and action plan will be released. This should be shortly after the meeting, within 48 hours if possible.

The other team members should be prepared to undertake actions between meetings to progress the problem solving activity. Responsibility for specific actions should be recorded in the action plan drawn up by the team secretary. Team members are responsible for ensuring individuals in their department are kept informed of the progress made by the team.

Meetings – ground rules
(i)   Members should attend all meetings of the team if at all possible.

The secretary should be informed in advance if a member will be absent from a scheduled meeting. Members should not leave during the meeting.

(ii)   Team meetings should start and end on time. Everyone has other things that need to be done. Arriving late for a meeting wastes everyone's time; it is a cost of non-conformance!

(iii)   The team secretary should find a date which is convenient for all the members required at the next meeting and then confirm it in a Notice of Meeting. This should include the date, start time, location, agenda, end time, and details of preparation required of members. It is useful if team members keep the secretary informed of progress in preparing material. The secretary should ensure that all assignments are completed to schedule. Prepared material may be circulated prior to the meeting to enable members to read it in advance; or it may be handed out at the meeting.

(iv)   All meetings should have a stated objective. The role of the team leader is to ensure the objective is met.

(v)   Each member has an obligation to the rest of the team to contribute to the meeting to the best of his ability. Each team member should be given the opportunity to express his ideas; these should be treated with respect by the rest of the team.

(vi)   The effectiveness of each meeting should be evaluated to identify any improvements necessary for the next meeting.

(vii)   A record should be kept for future reference of discussions and decisions taken at each meeting in a set of minutes.

(viii) It is frequently necessary for a team member to complete assignments between meetings (perhaps gathering or analysing data or preparing a report on a specific aspect of the problem). The secretary should prepare an action plan following each meeting to record the actions and timescales agreed.

8 PROBLEM SOLVING

INTRODUCTION – WHY PROBLEM SOLVING IS IMPORTANT

A Quality Improvement Programme is designed to increase the ability of a company to compete in the marketplace. This demands that a company fulfils the needs of its customers at minimum cost. This can only be achieved by ensuring the company understands its customers' needs; ensuring the company is organised to fulfil those needs; and enabling each individual within the company to carry out their job in the most efficient way possible. This requires the elimination of rework and checking activities and the introduction of means to prevent errors arising.

One key means of eliminating rework and checking is by tackling all the problems which prevent people from performing their jobs right first time. The ability of employees to recognise problems, trace their root causes, and implement effective corrective actions is fundamental to the success of a Quality Improvement Programme.

Many problems facing modern businesses are complicated or involve more than one group of employees. Design teams should work with marketing teams to develop products that customers will want. They should also work with production to ensure the product can be produced cost effectively. The sales and production teams should work together to ensure the right product is delivered to the customer at the right time. In all these tasks, especially where a number of departments are involved, problems may arise which prevent employees from performing every task right first time. These problems must be tackled and eliminated. Failure to do this may result in dissatisfied customers and increased costs. These may include excessive after sales and warranty costs, delayed payment or bad debts, excess inventory, lost customers or legal action.

To resolve problems effectively, it is generally necessary to set up dedicated groups to investigate and eliminate them. This requires management support to ensure they have the correct tools and training to enable them to identify the root cause of problems and implement corrective actions to eliminate them.

PROBLEM SOLVING GROUPS

Problems principally arise because of a failure in a process to produce conforming output. Problem solving groups, therefore, focus on analysis and investigation of processes. Problems in business can broadly be divided into two categories:

(i)   Those involving only one department; and
(ii) Those affecting more than one department.

As a result two principal types of 'problem solving' team may be recognised: Progress Groups (also called Quality Circles), and Corrective Action Task Forces. A Task Force is a team formed to solve a particularly difficult problem affecting more than one department. A Task Force is disbanded as soon as the problem is solved. Progress Groups are formed within a department to solve problems which affect only that department. Progress Groups do not generally disband once a problem is resolved but turn their attention to another problem within the department.

PROBLEM SOLVING METHODOLOGY

For a problem solving team to be effective it needs to understand how to investigate a problem, find its root cause, and implement a solution. To do this, groups need to understand a range of problem solving techniques. This chapter describes an effective methodology for solving a problem from identification to the implementation of the final solution. It is important to understand each of the problem solving tools and how it can be used in the problem solving process. It is also important to understand how the tools link together to provide a simple, powerful, proven method for investigating and resolving problems at all levels within an organisation.

The flowchart in Fig. 8.1 illustrates the principal steps in this problem solving methodology.

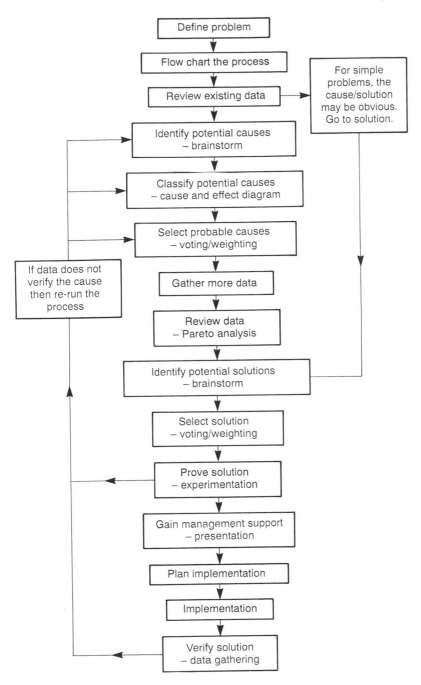

Figure 8.1 Flowchart of problem solving methodology

Define the problem

Purpose of this Section:

Before starting to investigate a problem it is essential to ensure it is fully understood. This involves defining the symptoms of the problem and understanding the process which gives rise to the problem. This helps to avoid wasting effort in the problem solving process. A problem which is fully understood and defined is well on the way to being solved.

The two tools commonly used to help define a problem are checklists and flowcharting.

Checklist Method

To define a problem effectively it is necessary to understand as much as possible about it. Answering the following questions as fully as possible helps ensure the problem is thoroughly understood.

What?	What is the problem?
	What has been observed?
Who?	Who is involved in the problem?
	Who is upstream/downstream of the problem?
Where?	Where does it show up?
	Where does it originate?
When?	On what occasion does it appear?
	At what time and for how long?
How?	How does it show itself?
	How often does it occur?
	How important is the problem – time wasted?
	– cost?
	– frequency?
Why?	Why does the problem occur? This is the key question we are seeking to answer.

This approach focuses attention on the problem and helps weld together newly formed problem solving groups. At the first meeting, groups often find that they do not know the answers to all these questions. If this is so, it is necessary to find out more about the problem. Only then will it be possible to try and solve it. This is essential to avoid wasted effort later in the problem solving process.

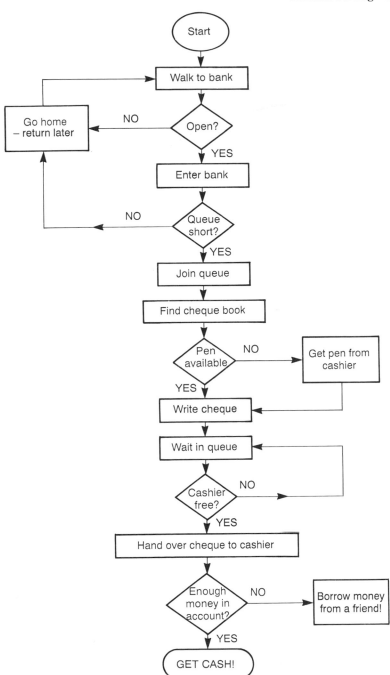

Figure 8.2 Simple flowchart of the process of cashing a cheque

Flowcharting

Having fully defined a problem it is important to understand the process giving rise to it before attempting to identify the cause. Flowcharting provides a means to ensure that every stage in the process and its links to the next stage are understood. A flowchart is basically a picture which describes the process as a series of activities, each linked to the next. The cause of a problem may lie in any one or more of the activities associated with the process. It is essential to understand the interaction between activities before trying to look for potential causes of the problem. A simple flowchart describing the process of cashing a cheque at the bank is illustrated in Fig. 8.2.

Constructing a flowchart

When drawing a flowchart the following guidelines are useful:

(i)   The right people must be involved in drawing the chart. The people involved in the activity, their suppliers and their customers should generally all be involved. If other people are identified as being involved in the activity when drawing the chart, a decision should be taken as to how these people should be involved in the flowcharting process.

(ii)   All members of the team should be involved in drawing the flowchart. A clear understanding of how the process works will be key to the successful resolution of a problem.

(iii) If the flowchart is prepared at a meeting it should be visible to all members of the group at all times.

(iv)   Flowcharting usually takes more time than initially anticipated. More than one session is often required. This may be useful as it enables group members to find out more about the process between sessions.

(v)   Before beginning the flowchart, the group should decide how detailed the flowchart needs to be. A very detailed flowchart is time consuming to construct and may not always be required.

(vi)   Questions are the key to a successful flowchart. A good team leader will ensure the group asks questions throughout the process. Some useful questions are:

- What is the first thing that happens?
- What happens next?
- Where does the service/material come from?
- How does it get there?

- When a decision is required within the process who makes it?
- What happens if the decision is yes/no?
- Where does the product/service go to next?
- What tests are performed on the product/service?

The following symbols are generally used when drawing a flowchart:

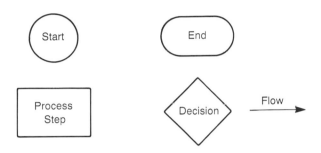

Figure 8.3 Flowchart symbols

Identify and classify potential causes

Purpose of this section:
Once a problem and the process giving rise to it has been fully understood and defined, the group needs to decide on the most likely cause(s) of the problem. To avoid jumping to conclusions, which may later prove incorrect, it is necessary to adopt a systematic approach to first identify all the potential causes and then home in on the most likely cause. The following steps may be used to achieve this:

(i) Identify potential causes through:
  - reviewing existing data
  - brainstorming
(ii) Classify and select probable causes by using:
  - cause and effect diagrams
  - voting and weighting techniques

Review existing data
When investigating a problem, it is frequently possible to find that some relevant data already exists within the organisation. It is important to review this data since it might prove useful as a guide for subsequent steps

in the problem solving process. Occasionally, for simple problems, the existing data may be sufficient to identify the cause of the problem, and the group can then move directly to identifying a solution. However, it is more likely that insufficient data is available, or the data is not directly relevant, to enable the cause of the problem to be identified. Perhaps the existing data only provides circumstantial evidence to indicate potential causes of the problem. These can be considered during subsequent stages of the problem solving process.

When reviewing existing data, it is useful to look for threads of (dis)similarity. Consider the problem of incorrect sales orders. An analysis of existing data may reveal that:

(i)   The problem occurs whoever enters the order in the sales office (similarity);

(ii) It also occurs with orders received from one salesman, Joe, but not from Elizabeth (dissimilarity); and

(iii) Errors occur on orders entered directly by the salesman (who usually uses a printed product listing as a database) but not on orders entered directly by the sales office (who use an on-line computer database) (dissimilarity).

This data does not identify a definite cause of the problem but it does provide useful information about the potential cause. In this example, analysing the data in this way would lead you to look more closely at differences between the printed product listing and the computer database, and what Elizabeth does differently to Joe. But it does not directly identify the cause of the problem. To display the threads of similarity within data it is often useful to use a matrix such as that illustrated in Fig. 8.4. To get as much information as possible from the data it is useful to ask the questions detailed in the checklist in the section on defining the problem (above).

Brainstorming

The objective of brainstorming is to ensure that all potential causes of a problem are identified at the beginning of the problem solving process. It can be used to supplement existing data or to generate ideas when no data is available. It is a creative process which uses each member's knowledge of the problem, their creativity and any data already available to generate as many ideas as possible about the possible causes of the problem. Brainstorming should be fun to do and may be used to build a relaxed and familiar atmosphere within the group right at the start of the project.

	Problem occurs	Problem does not occur
Who		
Where		
When		
How		

Figure 8.4 Matrix for recording threads of similarity data

The brainstorming technique

Brainstorming is a means of generating as many ideas as possible by allowing the creative thought process of each person in the group to freewheel. It is vital to allow all ideas to come to the surface and be expressed. This will only happen if the atmosphere is relaxed and all ideas are accepted without criticism. To help develop a relaxed atmosphere, and keep some structure to such a freewheeling process, the following steps should generally be followed:

(i) A group leader should be appointed to ensure everyone understands the problem. He/she then ensures all the brainstorming ideas are written down where everyone can see them and that the brainstorming rules are followed.

(ii) Everyone spends five to ten minutes, in silence, thinking about the problem and jotting down their ideas.

(iii) Each group member, in turn, then calls out an idea. At this stage all the ideas are written down. No comments or criticism are allowed. Only the person calling out the idea and the person writing down the idea should be allowed to speak during this stage.

(iv) The leader should move quickly from one idea to the next, passing over anyone who is short of a suggestion. All ideas should be welcomed and encouraged.

(v) Fig. 8.5 shows a typical cycle for the generation of ideas during a brainstorming session. The initial stage where ideas flow thick and fast usually lasts about 20 minutes. There is generally then a lull, followed by a second peak after about 25 minutes. It is important to continue brainstorming through this lull since the second peak often produces the most creative ideas. These will frequently have been built on ideas generated earlier in the session. For this reason it is important to keep all the ideas in front of everyone during the brainstorming session.

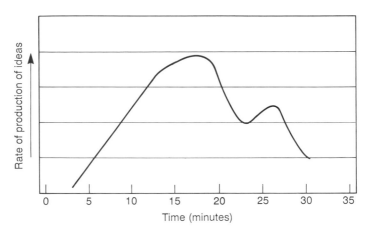

Figure 8.5 Typical cycle of ideas generated during brainstorming

(vi) After about 30 minutes, when ideas have started to dry up, the group should review and discuss their list. Duplicated and related ideas can be grouped together and unrealistic ideas eliminated. It is important to handle this phase sensitively to ensure ideas are not criticised. The person who proposed the idea may withdraw it, or the group may vote to accept or reject the ideas presented.

Classify the potential causes – cause and effect diagram

Once a list of potential causes has been generated it is necessary to whittle these down into a working list of probable causes. The '80/20' (or Pareto) rule suggests that most of the problem (perhaps 80 per cent) will be caused by a few of the causes (perhaps 20 per cent). Effort needs to be directed at finding these 20 per cent, and so maximise the return on effort. Once the most likely causes have been identified these may be used to guide the data gathering exercise when trying to prove the actual cause of the problem.

In order to analyse the ideas generated during brainstorming it is generally useful to group ideas together under appropriate headings. Thi can help identify the major potential causes of a problem. A cause and effect diagram (also called an Ishikawa, or fishbone, diagram) is often used at this stage because it provides a clear visual picture of the problem, showing potential causes and the links which may exist between indivi- dual causes.

Generating a cause and effect diagram

The following steps describe how to generate a cause and effect diagram:

(i)   The group agrees on the problem (or effect) being investigated. This is written in the box on the right hand side of the page. An outline cause and effect diagram is illustrated in Fig. 8.6.

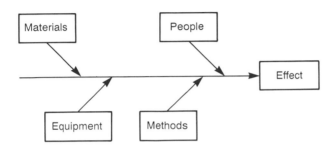

Figure 8.6 Outline of cause and effect diagram

(ii)   A long arrow is drawn from left to right. This is the central branch or 'fishbone'.

(iii)   The group identifies the principal categories of potential causes of the problem being investigated. These major cause categories are drawn as arrows pointing towards the main branch. Fig. 8.7 illustrates the categories chosen for the problem of persistent car breakdown. If no obvious categories come to mind at this stage, then it is useful to consider the key factors which affect processes, namely: Machines (Equipment), Materials, Methods (Procedures), and People. These are useful general headings to start the process rolling.

(iv)   The potential causes identified during brainstorming can then be listed under the appropriate headings.

(v)   In some cases, the group may brainstorm directly onto the cause and effect diagram by asking the question 'What would contribute to

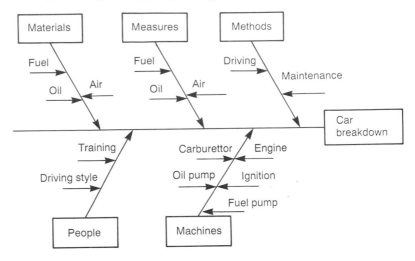

Figure 8.7 Cause and effect diagram to study the problem of car breakdown

each of the main causes?' Having identified sub-causes, the question can then be asked again to determine possible causes of each sub-cause. This structured form of brainstorming generally requires skilful team leading to execute successfully.

(vi) Sometimes a cause may fit into more than one category. In this case the cause can either be listed more than once, or the group will vote on which particular category to list it under.

(vii) The cause and effect diagram can be built up over a number of sessions, especially if the problem is complex.

Fig. 8.8 illustrates the potential causes of dissatisfied customers for one company. In this example, the major cause categories are shown together with a more detailed analysis of one of the major categories, service. This shows a number of levels of cause and demonstrates that the diagram can be quite complex when drawn up in detail.

The cause and effect diagram is a powerful, visual means of displaying the potential causes of a problem in such a way that related causes are linked together.

From this diagram the group may select the most probable causes to guide the data gathering activity.

Voting and weighting
Having identified all the potential causes of a problem, the group needs to select probable causes in order to focus the data gathering exercise.

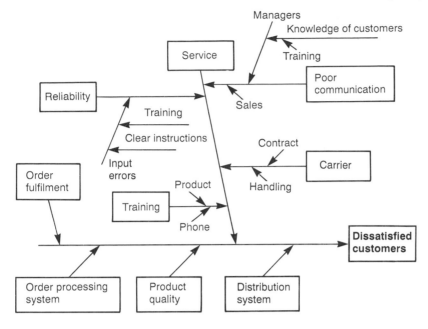

Figure 8.8 Cause and effect diagram showing detailed analysis of one major category

Reviewing the cause and effect diagram directly may lead the group to decide to investigate a particular area further. For example, a cause which has a large number of sub-causes may well indicate a complex area requiring further investigation. However, it is more usual for the group to select the area on which to focus attention as a result of voting on each cause in turn.

Voting
When there are a large number of potential causes, many of these are unlikely to be the cause of the problem and can be eliminated fairly quickly and simply by the process of multivoting. This will quickly reduce a list of potential causes to a manageable number of likely causes which the group can discuss and analyse more carefully.

Multivoting
This method eliminates the least likely causes without requiring a great deal of discussion and analysis. Each round of multivoting reduces the list by approximately one half. The principal steps are as follows:

(i)   Number each cause.

(ii)   Each member should write down the numbers of the causes which they feel the group should investigate further. Each member should only be allowed to vote for about one third of the total number of potential causes. For example, if there are 100 potential causes, each individual should have 34 votes. For 48 items each should have 16 votes.

(iii) The team leader should tally the total number of votes for each choice.

(iv) Once the voting is complete, those items with fewest votes are eliminated. The size of the group influences the analysis of votes. For groups with fewer than five members, cross off items with fewer than two votes. For groups with 6–15 members eliminate those with fewer than three votes. For groups with more than 15 members eliminate those with fewer than four votes.

(v)   Repeat steps (ii) to (iv) reducing the number of votes each time until 10 or fewer choices remain.

Once the least likely causes have been eliminated, the group can spend more time considering the causes which remain. Because it is difficult for an individual to decide amongst the remaining 10 possible causes of a problem, a technique such as paired comparison, where only two choices are compared at one time, is frequently used.

Paired comparison

This technique proceeds as follows:

(i)   List and number the remaining potential causes (10 or fewer).

(ii)   Each member of the group then completes a voting chart. An outline of the voting chart is illustrated in Fig. 8.9. Each member compares item 1 with item 2 and decides which of the two is the most likely cause of the problem and rings this number. The process is repeated by comparing item 1 with item 3 through to item 10. Item 2 is then compared with item 3 through to item 10, and so on, until the chart is complete.

(iii) The number of times a choice has been ringed is then tallied for each individual.

(iv) The scores for each team member are then added together. The choice with the highest score represents the consensus view of the group as to the most likely cause of the problem.

Fig. 8.10 illustrates the use of the paired comparison technique to identify the likely causes of poor telephone answering on a company switchboard. In this case only five choices remained.

Weighting

Another means of selecting the most likely cause of a problem, once the number of potential causes has been reduced to 10 or fewer, is for the group to score each potential cause against a number of criteria.

Choice	Descriptions	Voting chart								
1		1 2	1 3	1 4	1 5	1 6	1 7	1 8	1 9	1 10
2		2 3	2 4	2 5	2 6	2 7	2 8	2 9	2 10	
3		3 4	3 5	3 6	3 7	3 8	3 9	3 10		
4		4 5	4 6	4 7	4 8	4 9	4 10			
5		5 6	5 7	5 8	5 9	5 10				
6		6 7	6 8	6 9	6 10					
7		7 8	7 9	7 10						
8		8 9	8 10							
9		9 10								
10										

Figure 8.9 Voting chart

						Tally
1	Lack of training	①2	①3	①4	①5	4
2	Equipment breakdown	2③	2④	②5		1
3	Not enough staff	3④	③5			2
4	Poor morale	④5				3
5	Doing other work					0

[The most likely cause is lack of training]

Figure 8.10 Paired comparison on likely causes of poor telephone answering

Having decided that each of the remaining causes may contribute towards the problem, now try to determine which contributes the most. For example, each choice may be evaluated and given a score between 1 and 10 against a selection of the following criteria:

Urgency
Frequency of occurrence   Each cause is usually
Risk of non-detection   evaluated against 2 or 3
Importance of the effects   of these criteria.
Influence on CONC

The scores may be selected as follows:

Very low	1–2
Low	3–4
Medium	5–6
High	7–8
Unacceptable	9–10

Having evaluated each cause against the selected criteria, the scores should be multiplied together to determine the significance of each cause. The most significant cause is the one with the highest score.

Fig. 8.11 illustrates the evaluation of three causes A, B, C, against three criteria, urgency, frequency and risk of non-detection. The total significance is calculated for each cause. The one with the highest score (cause B in this example) is the most important potential cause.

Criteria \ Cause	A	B	C
Urgency	4	8	3
Frequency	4	6	8
Risk of non-detection	2	9	6
Total significance	32	432	144

Cause B is selected as the most significant cause. For 3 criteria:
minimum = 1 × 1 × 1 = 1 maximum = 10 × 10 × 10 = 1000

Figure 8.11 Weighting of causes

Data gathering and analysis

Once the number of potential causes has been narrowed down to the one or two most likely causes of the problem, it is necessary to gather data to verify the actual cause of the problem.

Data gathering methods

There are a number of standard methods for gathering data. It is important to ensure that the data gathering methods, in addition to providing relevant and meaningful data, are simple to use, clear and unambiguous.

Data can generally be gathered in three forms:

(i)   A tally sheet or data sheet: here data is logged onto a data sheet. Once the data has been gathered, further analysis is required before a decision can be made.

(ii) A check sheet: here, information collected by the operator is recorded on the sheet in the form of a graph, so that any trends can be assessed directly, and decisions taken without further analysis of the data. This method is widely used in the application of SPC.

(iii) A location plot (sometimes called a concentration diagram or measles chart): this is a very useful, simple method for plotting the location of errors on a chart.

Fig. 8.12 illustrates a location plot for missing components on a printed circuit board.

The method of recording data depends on the nature and complexity of data being gathered, and the degree of analysis required. Data sheets are

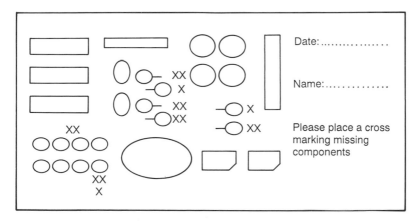

Figure 8.12 Measles chart showing missing components on a printed circuit board

useful when a lot of complex raw data needs to be gathered which may need to be analysed in a number of ways. Check sheets avoid the need for further analysis. Location plots provide a readily understandable picture of the data. However, it only has a limited number of applications, where for example the location of a defect may be significant.

Before deciding on how to collect data, the following questions need to be answered by the group:

(i) What is the purpose of collecting the data? What are you trying to prove/disprove?
(ii) What data needs to be collected?
(iii) Where in the process should data be collected? Try to choose an area which will cause a minimum amount of disruption, provided it will enable you to answer the key questions.
(iv) Who will collect the data? Select people close to the process who can be trained to collect reliable, unbiased data.
(v) When, and how much data should be collected? Determine the frequency and duration of data collection.

Having considered all the above, the group can decide how the data will be collected. It is then necessary to devise a means to gather the data effectively and reliably. The following steps are a useful guide to setting up the data gathering activity:

(i) Write down a clear description of how the data will be gathered. Define what is to be measured or counted; how the measurement/ count should be made; how many measurements should be taken; what equipment should be used; what accuracy is required, and what constitutes an error.
(ii) Devise a clear, simple form on which the information can to be recorded.
(iii) Agree the contents of the form and the method for gathering data with those who will actually gather the data, before finalising them.
(iv) Once arrangements have been agreed by all concerned, train those individuals who will be gathering the data so they know why the data is being gathered, how to gather and record the data, when the recording will start and end, and how soon the results will be available.
(v) Once the data has been analysed, ensure those who gathered the data are informed of the findings and what will happen next. This is important to enable the data gathering team to understand the significance of its work.

Analysing the data

It is generally difficult to make a decision based on masses of data from tally sheets or tables. It is therefore necessary to analyse raw data and present it in a way that is easy to understand and from which decisions can be made.

Data may be analysed and displayed in a number of different ways:

Bar graphs

A bar chart, such as that illustrated in Fig. 8.13, provides a graphic summary of data, making it easy to absorb and understand.

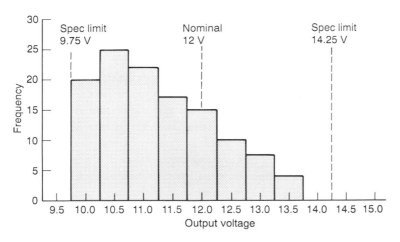

Figure 8.13 Bar chart of power supply voltage output

This shows immediately that, although all the units are within the specification, very few are rated at 12 volts and most are at the lower end of the allowed range, between 9.75 and 11.75 volts. This provides a pointer as to where the problem may lie and where the group should investigate further.

Analysing data in this way makes patterns easier to spot. Once a pattern can be seen in the data, likely causes may be identified for further investigation.

Pareto analysis

This is another way of looking at data. Problems are frequently the result of a number of factors. Pareto analysis is designed to help identify the principal causes of a problem. It is then possible to focus attention on removing these principal causes and have a significant impact on resolving the problem.

This method of analysis is a result of a finding of an Italian economist, Vilfredo Pareto, during the 19th century. He discovered that 80 per cent of the wealth in Italy was in the hands of some 20 per cent of the population. Looking more broadly, this type of distribution is found to apply to many other situations. For example, 80 per cent of the contributions to charity apparently come from some 20 per cent of the possible sources: 80 per cent of telephone calls made from work typically come from 20 per cent of the employees. This principle has become known as the Pareto principle.

In industry, this principle has been applied to help analyse the principal causes of problems. The proposition is as follows: a small number (perhaps 20 per cent) of the causes of a problem are likely to account for a large proportion (perhaps 80 per cent) of the problem.

If we can identify the principal causes of a problem, we can direct our attention towards removing those causes. This enables a solution to be identified which achieves the maximum impact with the minimum resource. The contribution made by each cause to the overall problem may be analysed using a variety of measures. Typical measures include:

- frequency of occurrence
- length of down-time
- cost of non-conformance
- measure of customer dissatisfaction
- number of defects

The contribution made by each factor is represented on a bar graph by the length of the bar.

Having established the appropriate measure to use and gathered the necessary data, the bars should be arranged in descending order from the largest on the left. This form of analysis will usually highlight the two or three principal causes of the problem under investigation.

An outline of a typical Pareto chart is illustrated in Fig. 8.14. A chart of the causes of delay in sending a fax is illustrated in Fig. 8.15.

Multiple levels of Pareto analysis
Sometimes it is necessary to use a second level of Pareto analysis to break down a problem into manageable portions before a solution can be readily identified. For example, a finance department trying to reduce the time it takes for debtors to settle their accounts (measured as debtor days)

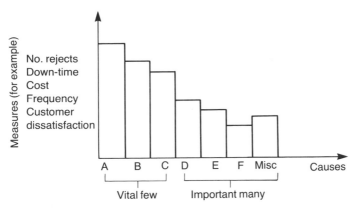

Figure 8.14 Typical Pareto chart

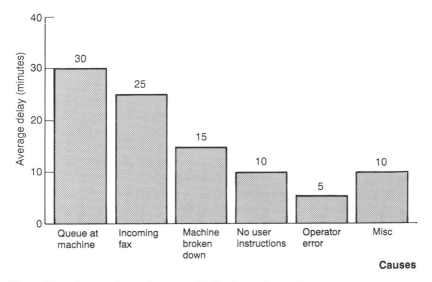

Figure 8.15 Pareto chart of causes of delay in sending a fax

identified the causes put forward to explain why customers took over 120 days to pay their accounts. These are illustrated in Fig. 8.16.

From this analysis, it was decided to gather data on the reasons for incorrect invoices. The second Pareto chart is illustrated in Fig. 8.17.

On the basis of this information it was discovered that the person responsible for raising the invoices did not always have access to all the information required to enable correct invoicing. The information came from a variety of different sources. No one source contained all the

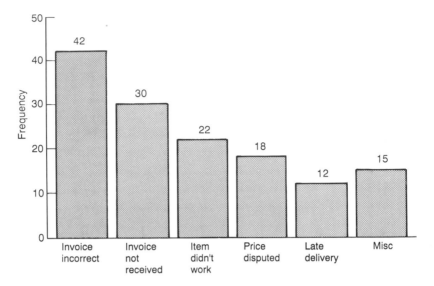

Figure 8.16 Pareto chart of causes of excess debtor days

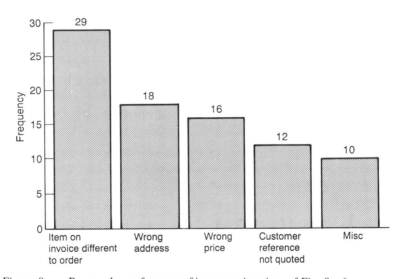

Figure 8.17 Pareto chart of causes of incorrect invoices of Fig. 8.16

necessary information. This problem was solved by changing the method of raising invoices, and holding a training session for the employees concerned.

Monitoring improvements using Pareto analysis
Pareto analysis is a very useful means for monitoring improvements resulting from corrective actions. Data can be compared before and after implementation to identify the impact of corrective actions which have been taken.

Scatter diagrams
Scatter diagrams are a simple means for comparing two characteristics to see if a relationship exists. For example it is possible to assess whether or not the number of typing errors made by a secretary might be related to the backlog of work. Fig. 8.18 illustrates a series of data which would tend to support this suggestion.

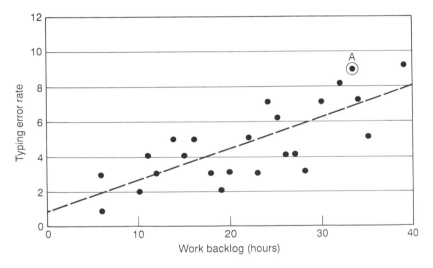

Figure 8.18 Scatter diagram showing relationship between typing error rate and work backlog

The independent variable (backlog of work) is drawn along the x-axis and the alleged dependent variable (the error rate measured as errors per page) is plotted along the y-axis. For each measurement, a cross is marked on the graph where the x and y values meet. For example, point A shows that when the secretary had 32 hours' backlog, the typing error rate was nine per page. Completing the diagram suggests a positive relationship between backlog and typing errors in this case. The longer the backlog, the greater the number of typing errors made. In some cases the relationship might be inverse, as for example the relationship between the shelf life for dairy produce and temperature. Or there may be no relationship at all. The scatter diagram is a useful practical tool helping to show whether or not a relationship might exist between two parameters.

But scatter diagrams do suffer from two principal drawbacks. A fairly large amount of data is required before a meaningful diagram can be drawn; and scatter diagrams can suggest a correlation between two parameters even if they are not related. One well known example of a spurious relationship is between the level of Lake Superior and the Dow Jones index! A scatter diagram of these shows that as the level of the lake rises so does the Dow Jones index. It is therefore important to screen results to ensure such spurious relationships are eliminated before implementing potential solutions based on this type of analysis.

It is also important to be aware that, although a simple scatter diagram may provide some useful indicative evidence, it is not sufficient to support quantitative conclusions. Regression analysis is a technique which can be used to identify the line that provides the best fit for the data in a scatter diagram. However this is a complex technique and requires expert input.

Pie charts

Pie charts take the form of a round chart, or pie, in which each cause of a problem is shown as a slice. The size of each slice represents the proportion each cause contributes to the problem.

A pie chart is particularly useful as a means of illustrating data for presentations. Pie charts are not so useful for analysing data as the methods described above, although they provide a clear visual picture to aid the understanding of data, and demonstrate particular points.

The data on the causes of delay in sending faxes shown in Fig. 8.15 is illustrated in Fig. 8.19 in the form of a pie chart.

Establish the root cause

Having reached this stage in the process it is important to step back and assess whether or not the root cause of the problem has been identified. Implementing a solution may be expensive both in terms of management time and necessary resources. If we have not eliminated the root cause of the problem, it will represent an expensive mistake. It is therefore worth critically reassessing the results of the previous steps to get to the root cause of the problem. This is particularly important if the problem is complex and involves a number of departments. The following errors

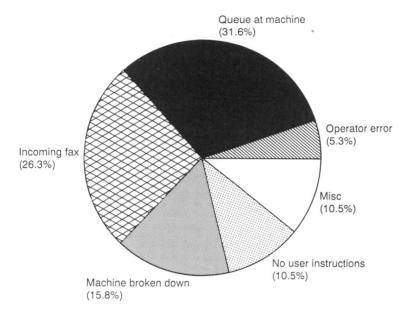

Queue at machine
(31.6%)

Operator error
(5.3%)

Incoming fax
(26.3%)

Misc
(10.5%)

No user instructions
(10.5%)

Machine broken down
(15.8%)

Figure 8.19 Pie chart showing causes of delay in sending faxes

may be identified as a result of a critical re-evaluation of the results of the previous steps:

(i)   The cause identified was not the root cause. With complex prob-lems, especially where only limited data is available, it is frequently very difficult to identify the root cause at the first attempt. It may be necessary to repeat the data gathering process in order to identify the cause of the cause. This is rather like peeling the skin from an onion until the cause is found.

(ii) The probable cause turns out not to be the real one. In this case it is necessary to go back to the cause and effect diagram and see if an alternative cause can be identified. It may also be necessary to re-run the brainstorming activity.

(iii) There is insufficient data to enable a cause to be identified. Deciding on the appropriate data to gather is a skilled task which takes experience. With new or inexperienced problem solving teams, it is possible that there is insufficient data to enable the root cause to be identified. In this case, it is necessary to repeat the data gathering exercise.

Implementation

Purpose of this section

Once the root cause of a problem has been identified it is necessary to identify, gain support for and implement a solution which successfully eliminates it once and for all. In practice it is possible that more than one potential solution may be proposed. It is then necessary to identify the most cost effective solution which has the best chance of succeeding. It is also important that the solution prevents the problem recurring again in the future. To introduce inspection and correction activities would merely add to the costs borne by the company and not solve the root cause of the problem.

The following steps provide a useful practical approach to implement corrective actions cost effectively.

Devise potential solutions

By this time a great deal will be known about the problem and its causes. This accumulated knowledge will frequently enable a number of potential solutions to be identified.

It is frequently useful to hold a brainstorming session to identify all of the possible solutions, particularly if there are only a few obvious alternatives. Recording some basic information on each solution at this stage (the table illustrated in Fig. 8.20 is a useful outline for this) will form a useful basis for the selection process.

At this stage it is important to take account of the whole range of possible solutions and avoid the danger of jumping to one superficially attractive solution.

All potential solutions should be ruled out unless they are prevention activities designed to eliminate the cause of the problem once and for all. A short-term inspection and rectification activity should only be considered as an interim measure pending implementation of a final solution. The danger of pursuing this course of action is that the interim solution may become a permanent fixture!

Select one solution

Once a number of potential solutions have been proposed, it is necessary to select one solution to implement. A number of selection criteria may be important when evaluating each solution. These include:

(i)   Cost of implementation. The costs of implementing a solution can be

PROBLEM:

Possible solutions	Resources to implement	Cost to implement	Reduction in CONC if implemented	Time to achieve results	Probability of achieving result	Comments

Figure 8.20 Table to analyse possible solutions

calculated. These include the one-off start-up costs such as training personnel, writing procedures and the additional ongoing operating costs (equipment, materials and labour) resulting from changes in procedures.

(ii) Reduction in the cost of non-conformance (CONC). Each solution may resolve the whole or only part of the problem. The problem is likely to cause some non-conformance costs associated with errors and rectification. These costs can be estimated. The reduction in the CONC can be measured for each proposed solution. It is often useful to compare (i) and (ii) in terms of a cost benefit analysis. For each solution the ratio of benefits/costs can be calculated.

(iii) Time taken to implement the solution and achieve the results: in some cases it is essential to implement a solution fairly rapidly and so it may be important to know how long each of the proposed solutions will take to yield results. In some cases, especially if the existing CONC is high, it might be appropriate to implement a quick interim solution followed by a more permanent solution at a later date.

(iv) Risk of solution not being effective through lack of support.

However beneficial a solution might appear it will not succeed unless it is supported by the people who have to implement it. Sometimes a financially less attractive solution may actually yield a better result because it is more likely to be accepted by the organisation. It is important to be aware of the forces working for and against each solution before the selection is made. This will help when selecting and implementing the optimum solution.

The ideal solution is one that:

- fully eliminates the root cause of the problem;
- is the most cost effective;
- has the support of everyone;
- is certain to succeed; and
- takes only a short time to implement.

It is not often that a solution meets all these criteria and so the relative merits of the alternative solutions should be compared and the most appropriate solution selected. There are a number of approaches to assessing the relative merits of alternative solutions; one important technique is described below.

It is frequently possible to split the selection criteria into two types: those which the solution MUST meet and those which the group WANT the solution to meet. For any given problem the MUSTS and WANTS will differ. For instance, in a company where cash flow is tight, it may be necessary to limit the cash outlay for implementing the solution – 'It must cost less than £10,000 to implement in the first year'. In another company other criteria assume greater importance – 'It must be implemented within three months, before peak production starts'.

Each solution can be evaluated according to the musts and any solution that does not meet these key criteria is eliminated. The remaining solutions can then be assessed against the wants. Wants may be weighted according to their importance as illustrated in the following example:

(i)   The group may consider it important that the solution is widely supported within a number of departments or it just will not work. This criterion might be given a weighting of nine.

(ii) The group might consider it important that the solution is implemented quickly. If the solution is not implemented before the beginning of the busy season, in four months time, then it will not be implemented this year. As a result the group assigns a weighting of seven to this criterion.

(iii) The group wants the solution to be cheap to implement. This is given a weighting of six.

The potential solutions should then be evaluated according to these predetermined criteria. Fig. 8.21 illustrates the weighted evaluation of the following three potential solutions to a given problem: solution A is quick to implement, is well supported but expensive; solution B is cheap and quick to implement but is not well supported; and solution C is well supported but will take a long time to implement and is expensive.

The higher the score the more closely the potential solution meets the selection criteria. In this case, solution A was selected as it met the selection criteria most closely.

Addressing internal obstacles to change

At this stage it is important to ensure that any forces acting against the solution are addressed and appropriate action is taken to ensure the problem is effectively resolved.

A useful technique to assist in this process is force field analysis. Here the solution is drawn in a box on the right hand side of a piece of paper (see Fig 8.22). The forces helping the solution to succeed are drawn below the line pointing upward. These are known as driving forces. Forces working against the solution are drawn pointing downwards to the line. These are restraining forces. The length of the line, or the thickness of the line, indicates the size of the force.

Solutions / Criteria + weighting	A		B		C	
	Score	Score × weight	Score	Score × weight	Score	Score × weight
Well supported 9	8	72	2	18	8	72
Quick to implement 7	9	63	9	63	2	14
Cheap to implement 6	3	18	8	48	3	18
Total		153		129		104

Figure 8.21 Weighting solutions

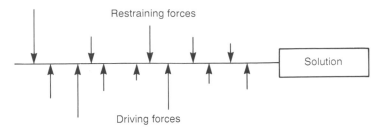

Figure 8.22　Diagram of force field analysis

Restraining forces may include:

- factions, rivalries or vested interests
- increased complexity of a process
- inertia.

Restraining forces must be addressed as part of any plan for implementing potential solutions to the problem. These forces might be so powerful that they influence the group against a given solution, or it may be possible to overcome them by appropriate action when implementing a solution.

Experiment

Once a solution has been chosen, it is important to verify that it does eliminate the problem when implemented. It is also important that the solution does not cause new problems to arise, or just cause the old problem to reappear elsewhere in the process. It is frequently useful to carry out a series of experiments to demonstrate this. If the experiments yield satisfactory results, then it is time to gain management approval to implement the solution.

Gain support

Once a solution has been chosen and proven, it is necessary to convince management to give its authority to implement the solution. This may require a formal presentation to the Quality Improvement Team or an informal presentation to the departmental manager depending on the nature of the problem. In either case this represents a milestone in the group's efforts and is very important. The following steps should form part of the team's presentation, supported by data and diagrams to stress important points:

- the team objective
- the original problem
- the investigation carried out by the group
- the cause of the problem supported by the data gathered
- the proposed solution
- the expected results and how these will be measured
- the proposed plan to implement the solution and achieve the results.

A formal presentation may typically last about 30 minutes, and the group will be closely questioned on the data gathered and the decisions which they made. In addition to the material presented, the group may need to refer to additional data to support their case and answer questions.

The aim during the presentation is to persuade the audience to commit its support to implementing the proposed solution. It is important that the team leader ensures a decision is made before the meeting is closed.

Implementing the solution

Once the solution has been agreed upon, and the team has been given the go-ahead to implement it, it is important to plan thoroughly the implementation before proceeding. In most cases it is advisable first to implement a pilot scheme to prove the solution and the implementation plan. Where possible, the pilot should be restricted to a small part of the business, such as one product line or one secretary, and strictly controlled by the group. The pilot scheme demonstrates whether or not the solution is feasible, and eliminates the problem. It also enables the group to determine if any changes are necessary before full scale implementation of the solution.

The following guidelines are helpful when planning to implement a solution to a problem:

(i)   Define the sequence of key steps required to implement the solution. Then break this down into sub-steps.
(ii) Define who will be directly involved in each step; who will be affected; and who will need to be consulted.
(iii) Define the changes that will be required in work methods. How will these be documented? What training will be required and who will carry this out?
(iv) How long will it take to implement each step?
(v)   How will you know when each step is complete? What milestones will be used to measure progress?

(vi) How will you check the success in implementing the solution? What data will need to be gathered?

It is frequently useful to draw a GANTT chart at this stage, to plan and monitor progress. This is a time chart showing the proposed start and finish date for each of the necessary actions. An example of a GANTT chart is illustrated in Fig. 8.23. Progress can be monitored against this plan and actions taken if the schedule slips. Other techniques, such as PERT, may be employed if the solution is complex or will take a long time to implement.

Having planned the implementation phase, the team can then go ahead. Possibly the most important aspect of implementation is communicating what is going on to everyone affected by the changes. It is important to gain their support and incorporate their suggestions where possible. Useful groundwork for this should have been laid down during the data gathering exercise. If people were consulted and involved then, they will be more likely to accept changes now.

Once the procedures have been written, the training carried out and the solution implemented, it is important to gather data to ensure that the problem has been eliminated and does not recur.

Generalise the solution

Once the solution has been implemented and proven to work, it is important to see if it can be applied elsewhere in the organisation. This can be done in a number of ways:

(i) The method used to resolve the problem and identify the solution should be documented. This material can be made available to other problem solving groups which may find it useful.

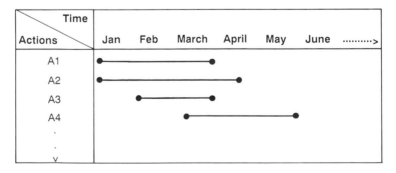

Figure 8.23 GANTT chart

(ii) The success achieved by the group should be publicised throughout the organisation to encourage other people to become involved in problem solving, and identify problems in their own area where the solution could be applied.

(iii) The group might be tasked with looking for other areas where the solution might be applied (other product lines, departments, sites etc).

9 SUCCESS STORIES

THE ICL EXPERIENCE – SUCCESSFUL IMPLEMENTATION

Background

ICL was formed in 1968 as a result of the merger of two leading UK computer suppliers: English Electric Computers and ICT. In 1984, ICL was acquired by STC. In November 1990, the Japanese company Fujitsu took an 80 per cent shareholding in ICL.

Following its recent merger with Nokia Data Systems, ICL has some 26,000 employees in over 70 countries. ICL concentrates on the provision of information systems and services in four key market segments:

(i)   retailing;
(ii) manufacturing;
(iii) financial services; and
(iv) public administration.

ICL develops, manufactures, sells and supports products ranging from notebooks to mainframes. It provides customers with a complete range of related services including:

● hardware maintenance;
● systems design;
● software design; and
● customer training and consultancy services.

A summary of the group's financial results for the period from 1986 to 1990 is set out in Table 9.1.

Product development takes place in Bracknell, Manchester, Reading and Stevenage in the UK, and at Santa Clara in the United States. Manufacturing takes place primarily in Kidsgrove (printed circuit board

	1990	1989	1988	1987	1986
Turnover	1,611.8	1,632.3	1,353.1	1,307.6	1,194.2
Pre-tax profit	110.1	148.6	139.0	112.2	81.2
(All figures in £Million)					

Table 9.1 Summary of ICL results 1986–1990

production) and Ashton-under-Lyne (product assembly) in the UK, and also in Denmark (UNIX systems) and Irvine, USA (retail and office systems).

Total Quality – The Decision

In the mid-1980s, ICL undertook a complete overhaul of its business strategy. It set its objective as becoming customer driven; focusing on providing systems, products and services which meet the customer requirements in its four key markets.

This mission relies upon getting close to customers, to understand their wants and requirements, and to understand how current performance levels could be improved. To support this change in the culture of the company, the Chief Executive, Peter Bonfield, and the Board decided in 1986 to implement a programme of continuous Quality improvement. This programme is designed to ensure that all employees recognise and fulfil their role in providing an outstanding customer service. Employees arc responsible for understanding the needs of their customers and ensuring those needs are satisfied. The voice of the customer must drive every activity, at every level within ICL.

To underline the commitment by senior management to the Improvement Programme, and ensure all employees recognise its importance to the success of the group as a whole, Joe Goasdoué was appointed to the Main Board as Director of Quality. This commitment is also demonstrated by the investment, both in terms of time and money, in the programme. ICL estimates that it spends £1Million each year to ensure the success of its improvement programme. In excess of 100,000 man-days have been invested so far in the training programme.

Implementing Total Quality

The steps taken by ICL illustrate how one company has achieved considerable success as a result of implementing a programme of continuous quality improvement. The key steps taken by ICL are described below:

Phase 1: Planning

ICL recognised early on that planning is one of the keys to success in the drive for the continuous improvement of quality. Its first action was to form a central team, chaired by the Quality Director, to investigate the methodologies available, generate ideas about how to implement the programme at ICL and formulate its basic strategy. This team started with some 30 members and stayed together, although with the number of members gradually diminishing, for a period of almost 12 months. This team developed the blueprint for quality improvement within ICL, known as 'Quality – The ICL Way', which would be followed by each Quality Improvement Team throughout ICL. Responsibility for implementing the Programme, within the blueprint, lies with the management of each unit.

In order to focus attention on the key objectives of the Quality Improvement Programme, the central team stresses four underlying principles:

1. Quality is defined as conformance to requirements
2. The system for causing Quality is prevention
3. The performance standard is Zero Defects
4. The measurement of Quality is the price of non-conformance

(These are basically the 'four absolutes' propounded by Philip Crosby.)

To ensure each employee understands the company's commitment to these principles, the Board adopted the following statement of its Quality Policy. This sets out the key objectives of the group in relation to its service to customers:

> To provide competitive systems, products and services which fully meet the customers' requirements first time, on time and every time.

In order to translate these basic principles into practice, the team produced a step-by-step guide for use by the Quality Improvement Team (QIT) in each operating unit. The QIT handbook sets out the Quality blueprint to be implemented by the QIT; each step is described, the objectives, the benefits, who needs to be involved and guidelines on how it can be implemented. The QIT then adapts each step to fit its own organisation before implementation. The handbook provides structure and commonality to the Programme without restricting the creativity of each unit. Each unit is responsible for implementing a Programme which fits its organisation. This is felt to be particularly important in such a diverse, multi-national organisation.

Phase 2: Identifying Quality costs

One of the key elements when persuading management and employees that the 'right first time' approach is in their interests, and that of the company, is to calculate what it costs the company to keep doing things wrong and then correcting them afterwards (the price of non-conformance).

Rather than collect the price of non-conformance (PONC) for every activity, ICL decided to nominate eight key areas, 'The Big Eight', for which the PONC would be collected throughout the group. Although by no means the only areas in which improvements could be made, they were areas where a reduction in PONC would lead to a significant improvement in business performance. The ICL Big Eight are:

- Support
- Bug-fixing
- Avoidable service visits
- Rework
- Performance concessions
- Overdue accounts
- Delivery to time/spec
- Inventory

These eight areas were identified following the review of the total PONC for a pilot site. The Big Eight were those areas with the highest PONC during the pilot study.

This illustrates the intensely pragmatic approach taken by ICL to the improvement of Quality. They have not become bogged down in detailed calculations of PONC for all activities at the start of the programme. They have, instead, focused on the areas giving rise to the largest PONC. This has enabled them to gather the necessary information quickly and set improvement targets.

The real significance of the QIP to the success of ICL was underlined in 1987 when it was announced to the Board that the total PONC in the Big Eight for the group as a whole amounted to some £160 million. This represented 13 per cent of turnover. In the same year, ICL achieved a pre-tax profit of £112.2 million! By tolerating non-conformance, ICL severely impaired its ability to compete effectively in an ever more competitive market.

As a result of this study, ICL determined to eliminate non-conformance in the Big Eight areas over a five year period. The means utilised to achieve this ambitious objective are set out below.

Phase 3: Training and communication

For most companies, implementing a programme of continuous quality improvement means a permanent change in the way it is run. This was true for ICL.

A key to making the necessary changes lies in educating all employees, throughout the company. By starting at the top and working down and across the organisation, the training message was cascaded through the company. The objective is to teach management and employees that errors and problems are not a fact of life. By insisting that errors and problems are eliminated at source, once and for all, it becomes unnecessary to work around them by providing temporary fixes. Each employee is also encouraged to plan to do all their work right first time, and to try and identify means of preventing errors and problems once they have been identified.

To date 22,000 employees have attended a basic Quality training course. A further 1,500 have attended additional specialist courses. In total, more than 100,000 man days have been invested so far in the training programme.

The purpose of this type of comprehensive training programme is twofold:

(i) To lay the foundations necessary to enable every employee to fulfil their commitment to Total Quality and change the way the company operates; and
(ii) To indicate to every employee the importance of TQM and the commitment which the company is making to ensure its success.

Phase 4 – Measuring success

When introducing the continuous quality improvement programme, ICL decided that it would measure the overall success of the programme in three key areas:

(i) Improvement in the opinions held by customers about the quality of the overall service provided by ICL and its ability to satisfy its customers' requirements.

(ii) Improvement in the opinions held by ICL employees of the quality of the service provided by ICL to its customers and of their satisfaction with the company as an employer.

(iii) Reduction in the PONC.

Customer opinion

The ability of a business to meet its customers' requirements better than its competitors is the only reason a company survives and prospers. In order to survive in today's market, it is essential that businesses understand their customers' requirements; how well these requirements are being met by the company; how well they are being met by competitors; and how the business can improve its performance in key service areas.

ICL has been very careful to avoid falling into the potential trap of becoming introspective and concentrating so much on improving internal processes, procedures and practices in an effort to reduce PONC, that the needs of external customers are forgotten. External customers are the ones which pay the bills. All improvement activities at ICL are designed to improve the ability of the company to meet its customers' needs. This element of the programme cannot be over-emphasised.

Since introducing the continuous quality improvement programme, ICL has monitored the opinions of its customers directly and by means of independent surveys in an effort to gauge the success of the programme, with the following results:

(i) A survey carried out by Datapro in France showed that the ICL mainframe series 39 gave the greatest overall level of customer satisfaction of any comparable mainframe product. It was rated top in eight of the twelve categories surveyed.

(ii) ICL's own surveys show a significant change in the perception held by its customers of the quality of the service provided by ICL. Since the implementation of the programme of continuous quality improvement, ICL is perceived as a company committed to quality improvement and to meeting its customers' requirements.

Employee opinion

ICL surveys its employees annually to determine their views on how the company is run; how well each individual is treated; and the opportunities they have to develop within the company. The key results from the surveys in 1987 and 1989 are set out in Table 9.2. This data illustrates the improvement in the perception held by employees since the programme of continuous quality improvement was launched. Employees are generally much happier in their work, the company and their development within the company. This is a common finding among companies which are serious about quality improvement and has important implications for staff recruitment and retention.

	Negative comments (per cent)	
	1987	*1989*
View on your work	24.4	18.7
Objectives & Performance Appraisal	21.4	17.0
Training & Career Development	40.3	29.5
Planning	39.8	32.4
Organisation Style & Standards	25.8	16.6
Communication	30.2	20.1
Pay, Benefits, Conditions & Work Environment	21.4	21.2
Quality	29.8	18.5
Overall satisfaction with ICL	31.4	21.4

Table 9.2 Results of employee survey

The Price of Non-Conformance

In 1987, it was estimated that the annual PONC for the Big Eight areas amounted to £160 million. In order to reduce this tremendous burden, each operating unit was allocated target savings required over the next five years. ICL has since tracked the reduction in the PONC by measuring the savings achieved by each operating unit. Provided they deliver the savings they have met their PONC targets. ICL chose this method rather than to re-run the PONC calculation annually.

One of the key successes achieved by ICL has been the achievement of the £160 million savings targeted in 1987 in the first five years of the programme.

The group has continued to set demanding targets for reducing waste as a result of the quality improvement programme. Overall, the group seeks to achieve a saving of £25 million in each year. In order to achieve this, each operating unit is allocated a proportion of the target for the year. The ability of management to achieve the required savings and the other Quality improvement goals, is an important part in the performance appraisal for each unit and its senior management at the end of each year. These criteria are taken into account in the management bonus scheme.

Phase 5: Prevention and improvement

ICL has implemented a comprehensive programme of prevention and improvement to ensure it continues to become more competitive. The key features of this programme are:

(i) Setting goals for improvement. The key financial goals which are targeted have already been discussed. The group also targets operational goals. Benchmarking, which is one of the keys to the successes achieved by the group, is discussed further below.

(ii) Corrective action teams and Quality Circles. In the five years since the programme of continuous Quality Improvement was implemented within ICL, several hundred corrective action teams have been formed to tackle specific problems affecting a large number of people or departments. Members of these teams are drawn from the affected departments.

Quality Circles are formed to tackle quality problems which only affect a specific work area.

Benchmarking

ICL makes extensive use of benchmarking techniques. As part of the training process, every employee is encouraged to examine critically how activities are currently performed and suggest how these can be improved. This informal benchmarking is encouraged throughout the company, at every level and for every activity. Formal benchmarking teams are set up periodically to identify the best practices in particular activities throughout the world. ICL then examines the techniques to identify whether or not they can be adapted for use within ICL to improve performance and competitiveness.

Examples of the parameters ICL has chosen to benchmark recently include:

(i) The time it takes to get a personal computer from the feasibility study to launch. A comparison with the best in the market showed that ICL was taking too long to be competitive. As a result of the benchmarking study, a time to market target of nine months was set. This target was beaten for the ICL DRS model 95; here the time to market was eight months.

(ii) The ICL distribution activity was benchmarked against those of

Harrods and Marks and Spencer: companies for whom distribution is one of the keys to survival.
(iii) ICL is now benchmarking its level of overheads.

The ability to study the best in the world, understand how their performance is achieved; and then take the lessons on board and apply them within ICL is a key feature of ICL's competitive strategy.

Phase 6: Recognition

Implementing a programme of continuous quality improvement requires the commitment of all employees. The excerpt from the Quality Improvement Status Report for the Ashton manufacturing plant, shown in Table 9.3, illustrates how employees have become involved at one ICL facility.

Out of a total workforce of some 610 people, some 60 per cent were involved directly in Corrective Action Teams (CATS) or Quality Circles in 1989.

Quality improvement status report	*1988*	*1989*
Measurement		
Charts in use		214
Charts with goals		137
Charts with PONC		54
Big 8 PONC (£ million)		4.24
Forecast PONC saving (£ thousand)		400
Corrective action		
ECRs raised	178	445
ECRs cleared	16	325
Corrective action teams (CAT)	3	32
Quality circle teams (QC)	15	34
Recognition		
Number of awards	17	69
Employee involvement		
Number in QCs or CATs	124	385
% in QCs or CATs	20	63

Table 9.3 Quality involvement at the Ashton manufacturing facility

Active involvement in TQM gives employees the ability to change how things are done, utilises more of their skills and makes them feel more involved in the way the company is run. This in turn frequently improves morale and loyalty to the company. This can have a significant impact on the performance of employees and, as a result, on the performance of the business as a whole.

In view of the extra efforts required from employees, it is important that management considers means of rewarding exceptional perform-ance. At the Ashton plant, quality awards were made to some 69 employees in 1989; this demonstrates the level of commitment made by employees.

Reaping the Rewards

In the five years since ICL became committed to the continuous improve-ment of quality, it has made significant improvements to its busi-ness. The following key performance indicators illustrate the measure of its success:

1. It has eliminated £160 million in wasted time, effort and other resources. In some instances this has resulted in direct savings and improved the bottom line. An example of this is the reduction of inventory. In other cases it has released time to enable individuals to improve both their own personal, and the company performance. This has resulted in improved employee satisfaction and improved business performance.
2. It has significantly improved its level of customer service. ICL is now perceived as a company committed to Quality and to satisfying customer needs.
3. Commitment to the continuous improvement of quality has taken hold throughout the organisation. Over 60 Quality Improvement Teams and several hundred corrective action teams and quality circles have been formed. Some examples of the improvements achieved by these groups are given at the end of this section.
4. ICL has won National Training Awards for its Quality training in both 1988 and 1989.
5. ICL's factory at Ashton-under-Lyne was chosen as one of the five 'Best British Factories' in 1989 judged by 'Management Today' and A. T. Kearney, consultants, against quality, productivity, cost and cus-tomer satisfaction criteria.
6. ICL won one of only three British Quality Awards presented by the British Quality Association in 1990. The BQA looks for evidence of the total commitment to Quality throughout an organisation over a number of years, resulting in sustained improvement in Quality across all activities.

Words of Warning

Every organisation is unique. As a result, every business should adopt a methodology for introducing continuous improvement in quality which is tailored to fit its organisation and culture. ICL has had five years of experience and come across many of the pitfalls. The ICL experience has resulted in the following guidelines and words of warning!

1. A quality improvement programme will only succeed if it fits the organisation. Individuals must want to be part of the improvement activity and not feel threatened by it.
2. Quality Improvement will only succeed if top management is committed to making it happen and communicate this commitment to the whole workforce. Management must state clearly the purpose and aims of the Improvement Programme. Management commitment is necessary at every level, every day, in every activity. Lack of management commitment is probably the most significant obstacle to success.

    There is, unfortunately, no easy solution. It requires continuous effort and hard work to convince managers of the benefits to be gained from the continuous improvement of quality, and their personal involvement. Fortunately it does become easier as managers and employees become more committed to Quality, and improvements and successes are achieved.
3. Careful planning of the Programme is essential and takes time. It is important not to set unrealistic expectations for the Programme over short periods of time.
4. The needs of the external customer are paramount. It is essential to ensure the quality improvement process does not become introverted, focusing on improving processes and reducing the PONC at the expense of the needs of the external customer.
5. Training is the key to changing the way the organisation works. Without an adequate training programme, Quality Improvement will not succeed.
6. It is important to ensure the Quality Improvement Programme is implemented through the normal management channels for each unit. Managers must own and accept responsibility for the Programme.
7. To ensure that Quality Improvement is seen as the key to improving business performance, it should be near the top of the agenda in all business reviews and reports.
8. In order to gain commitment to the Programme, pay and performance bonuses should be linked to the achievement of Quality Improvement

goals. It is no use telling people Quality Improvement is important and then incentivising them to perform against some other goals.

9. Every means possible should be used to stimulate and maintain interest in the Programme. Posters, newsletters, policies, videos, certificates, ongoing education and above all the communication and recognition of successes are important parts of this process.

EXAMPLES OF IMPROVEMENT ACHIEVED BY ICL

The following are examples of the improvements which have been made at ICL since 1987:

1. The world-wide spares organisation took action to address the reasons for the large number of complaints about deliveries of spare parts. Many deliveries were late, included the wrong items, or were badly packaged. In order to gauge the scope of the problem, ICL encouraged customers to record errors and complaints on a standard form which was analysed by the group. Applying problem solving techniques to complaints, the group defines the problem, responds to the customer and arranges a replacement of the part within 24 hours. The group then seeks to identify the root cause of the problem and introduce corrective action. This programme is achieving a saving of £500,000 a year.

2. The ICL Services Division calculated that the annual cost associated with people not turning up to training courses, or cancelling at short notice, amounted to £650,000. A corrective action team introduced a central tracking system and improved the processes for booking, confirmation, waitlisting, cancelling, and informing attendees of the benefits of courses. This has resulted in a saving of £580,000 per year.

3. A corrective action team was formed by a number of secretaries to look at how they could save the time and effort associated with looking for standard information. The time wasted was estimated at an hour a day per secretary, and equated with some £1 million per year. An information file has been introduced for every secretary which contains the most frequently used information.

4. In December 1989, a team was formed to improve the time taken to repair client equipment. At that time, the call-to-fix time was 13 hours. During 1990 this was reduced to five hours by measuring the call-to-fix times for each repair and implementing corrective actions in all areas

where this exceeded five hours. One of the reasons for the long call-to-fix times was the number of wasted service visits. These might result from the failure of the operator to read the manual, or the service engineer not having the correct parts when making a site visit. A range of corrective actions was introduced to reduce the number of these visits. The success of these measures is illustrated in Fig. 9.1.

Figure 9.1 Reduction in costs of unnecessary service visits

5. At the Ashton facility, over 90 per cent of product cost is represented by materials. The effective management of materials is therefore a key to the success of the business. With a manufacturing programme that can change significantly each month, manufacturing flexibility must be achieved with the minimum investment in inventory. The materials management activity is responsible for ensuring that the right materials are in the right place at the right time. This requires accurate data on inventory levels and production requirements. The materials management department undertook the following steps to introduce a Just-in-Time (JIT) method of working to improve its performance: by thoroughly re-examining its role, it determined the key service measures to enable it to achieve maximum flexibility and service to the customer whilst, at the same time, minimising inventory levels. It then introduced actions to improve performance in all areas. The success of the measures undertaken at Ashton are illustrated in Fig. 9.2.

6. In 1985 the approach taken by the purchasing department was to buy on price. They would be prepared to switch suppliers frequently and accept any supplier which came 'close enough' to the required quality standards. As a result of the change to a JIT method of material control, the purchasing department recognised that they needed to

	1980	1985	1986	1987	1988	1989
Programme cycle time (days)	50	40	30	26	15	14
Goods-in process time (hours)	60	40	16	8	2	0.5
Manufacturing cycle time (days)	50	40	29	22	15	13
Automatic data capture (%)	0	0	5	10	60	80
Stock service level (%)	90	92	95	98	99	99
Data accuracy (%)	90	90	94	98	99	99
Output service level (%)	93	94	94	95	95	96
Inventory turns (No)	2.5	3.2	6.6	7.1	11.2	12.2

Figure 9.2 Improvement in materials management

change their buying philosophy and their relationship with suppliers. They implemented a policy focusing on long-term partnerships with suppliers. Before entering into this commitment, they had to ensure every supplier provided a world-class service in terms of quality, service and total cost. This meant taking account of the overall service from their supplier, and not just the price of goods purchased. In order to achieve these improvements, the following series of measures was introduced:

- by agreeing a specific time slot for deliveries by major suppliers, ICL is able to ensure delivery of goods to the production line and minimise inventory levels. This is one of the features of a 'just-in-time' regime
- the Ashton plant regularly reports on the quality of incoming materials to the supplier. This has a salutary effect on the conformance of these goods to requirements.
- Ashton regularly reviews the procedures, methods and performance of each supplier and agrees quality improvement targets in these areas. The resulting improvement in quality has enabled a significant reduction in the level of goods inwards inspection, and an increase in the number of suppliers on 'ship-to-stock' rating. This initiative has developed into a formal vendor rating system, and Ashton makes awards to suppliers who achieve consistent, high levels of performance quality, delivery and service.
- on-site inspection is carried out at the supplier's premises, by Ashton employees, before shipment of any new part is permitted. This ensures the supplier remains responsible for any non-conforming

products, is made aware of the importance Ashton attaches to quality, and enables the Ashton goods-inwards inspection facility to be minimised.

- The purchasing department organises periodic conferences with suppliers to discuss improvements which could be made on both sides to improve supplier performance.

The significant impact these measures have had on the purchasing department at Ashton is illustrated in Fig. 9.3.

	1985	1989
Number of suppliers	180	240
Number of parts	1500	4000
Orders per month	1000	2500
95% Requisition clearance	20 days	8 days
Lead times less than 6 weeks	10%	60%
Daily deliveries	NIL	25%
Daily pick-up	NIL	20%
EDI – Suppliers EDI – Parts	NIL NIL	50 (12.5% of total) 1500 (35% of total)

Figure 9.3 Improvement in supplier management

PLANNING FOR THE CONTINUOUS IMPROVEMENT OF QUALITY IN NATIONAL HEALTH SERVICE HOSPITALS

Introduction

Health Services are big business. The National Health Service (NHS) in the UK accounted for expenditure amounting to £20,000 million in 1989/90. This represented some 5.8 per cent of the Gross Domestic Product in the UK in 1989. A larger proportion of GDP is spent on health services in many overseas countries, for example 8.8 per cent in Sweden, 8.2 per cent in Germany and 8.7 per cent in France.

The UK National Health Service

The NHS is the subject of continuing public scrutiny. It is regularly the centre of political attention, and subject to changes imposed from outside. It is currently undergoing its most radical reform since its creation in 1948. The cornerstone of this revolution is the 1990 NHS and Community Care Act which has separated for the first time the roles of 'provider' and 'purchaser' for health services.

The role of the key elements in the NHS are:

(i)   The Department of Health is responsible for:

- securing national funding for the health service.
- determining the national strategy for the health service.
- researching and implementing health care initiatives on a national scale in co-ordination with District Health Authorities (DHAs).
- providing funding for DHAs.
- setting target levels of performance for DHAs.
- monitoring the performance of DHAs.

(ii) DHAs are responsible for:

- defining the health needs of their residents.
- purchasing the health care necessary to meet those needs.
- securing funding for the health care of the district.
- determining the district health care strategy; and developing a comprehensive plan to control the implementation of the agreed strategy.
- negotiating service agreements, frequently incorporating target levels for the quality of performance, with health care providers.

(iii) Family Health Services Authorities are responsible for:

- assessing the health needs of the population, particularly in respect of primary health care.
- ensuring the development of high quality General Practitioner services to meet those needs.
- they have also been heavily involved in the activities surrounding the introduction of the new General Practitioner Contract, in which great emphasis is placed on health promotion.

(iv) General practitioners (GPs) remain as the first port of call for patients. They are responsible for:

- meeting the needs of the patients on their list.
- GP fund holders have their own budgets to purchase outpatient appointments, a wide range of non-urgent surgical procedures, domiciliary consultant visits and pathology services.

(v) Health care provider units (such as general hospitals, ambulance, mental health care and community services; whether NHS Trusts or not) are responsible for providing the services agreed with the DHAs.

A national strategy for the health service

The Department of Health has published details of the broad objectives of the National Health Service in the UK. These were set out in the Department of Health paper 'Working for patients' (HMSO, London, 1989), in the following terms:

> The prime role of the NHS is to improve the health of the population by providing healthcare for individuals and, through programmes of health promotion and disease prevention, the population as a whole

The Government Green Paper, 'The Health of the Nation' published in 1991, stresses the need for a health strategy to ensure everyone with a role to play in health care is heading in the same direction. This strategy will:

● identify the major health priorities;
● set specific targets and objectives;
● suggest how the targets can be met;
● suggest how improvements can be measured.

What are the constraints on the NHS?

However, the NHS faces a complex series of problems in trying to achieve its ambitious objective of improving the health of the population in the UK. The three principal problems are:

(i)   the ageing population;
(ii) limited resources; and
(iii) the absence of a co-ordinated national strategy to promote a healthy life-style and avoid preventable health problems.

The ageing population

The population in the UK is gradually ageing, and as individuals age they are likely to require more regular and more serious medical intervention in order to remain fit and healthy. The Public Health Review included in the 1990 Annual Report of the Central Nottinghamshire Health Authority (CNHA) records that by 1995 almost one in five CNHA residents will be a pensioner.

Limited resources

Modern technology is expensive, and modern techniques allow doctors to undertake treatments which would not have been possible only a few years ago. All these factors conspire to escalate demands on the health service budget, and yet it is not possible to grant unlimited resources to the NHS. As a result, health service providers have to allocate their resources where they can do the most good.

The 1991 Annual Report of the Director of Public Health, Southern Derbyshire, illustrates the problem graphically.

> When all the resources available to the District Health Authority (DHA), the Family Health Services Authority (FHSA), the GP Fund holders, and the Social Services Department (ie all those concerned with purchasing services necessary to meet the health and social needs of the population) are combined, there is £510 per capita to spend on all health and social care needs of Southern Derbyshire residents (Fig. 9.4).

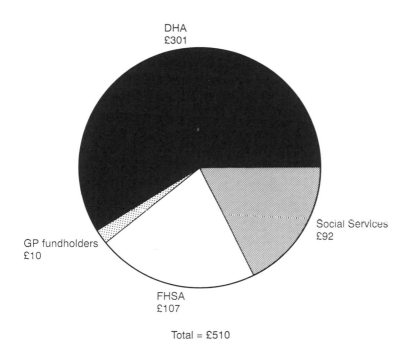

Total = £510

Figure 9.4 Per capita expenditure on health in South Derbyshire Health Authority

This emphasises the need for joint purchasing specifications to be developed from the health programmes, clarifying the contribution to be made by different professionals, agencies and also voluntary groups involved in the long-term management of patients. The aim should be to produce integrated care of good quality to ensure that the most appropriate intervention is made at the appropriate time and making best use of combined resources.

Preventable health problems

A considerable amount of the work of hospitals stems from the failure to adequately promote a healthy lifestyle. The abuse of smoking, alcohol and cars are major causes of preventable health problems and deaths in the UK:

(i) John Appleby and Beverley Adams (from the National Association of Health Authorities and Trusts central policy unit) reported in *The Health Service Journal* (10 January 1991) that alcohol is implicated, either directly or indirectly, in 28,000 premature deaths each year; one-quarter of all male acute admissions to hospital; 17,500 psychiatric admissions; and one-fifth of all industrial accidents. Alcohol is also associated with absenteeism from work, criminal damage, assault, domestic violence, child abuse, divorce and road accidents.

(ii) Almost 20,000 years of life were lost in 1989 because of people dying before reaching 75 in the area managed by the Central Nottingham-shire Health Authority. Almost 1,500 years were lost by accident victims, including more than 800 years lost because of traffic accidents. Other major causes of death were strokes, bronchitis and lung cancer; all smoking related. And lung cancer alone, usually caused by smoking and an almost wholly preventable disease, robbed local people of 1,095 years of life (from the *'Public Health Review'*, included with the annual report of the Director of Public Health, Central Nottinghamshire Health Authority, 1990).

These statistics indicate that many of our current health problems are preventable. The costs associated with problems such as alcohol abuse are costs arising from the failure of public policy in this area. They are failure costs.

The factors giving rise to these failures should be identified and, where possible, eliminated by implementing preventive actions such as effective health education and progressive taxation measures. Implementing effective measures to eliminate this type of problem may well provide the single most important means of reducing the need for acute health treatment in the UK, and so free significant health service resources to treat other problems. In many cases, efforts are required on a national scale in order to make a significant impact on these problems. The 1991 Report of the Director of Public Health, Southern Derbyshire supports random breath testing, higher taxation on alcohol and tobacco, and a ban on tobacco advertising as measures which will help to improve public health.

A number of DHAs are starting to address the preventable causes of health problems on a local basis, although in many cases these plans are at an early stage in their development. The 1991 Annual Report of the Director of Public Health, Southern Derbyshire illustrates the direction of their strategy in this area:

> Many of the causes of premature mortality in the District are to a large extent preventable. Currently there is no comprehensive strategy for health promotion in the District which clarifies the contributions that different agencies are making, or intend to make, in promoting good health. Such a strategy will ensure maximum benefit is obtained from the variety of resources that are put into health promotion in the District and should be jointly developed.

Other districts are already taking an active role in helping people to adopt a healthier lifestyle. The objective of these initiatives is twofold:

(i) It helps people attain a healthy and fulfilling lifestyle; and
(ii) It may reduce the number of health problems suffered by residents. By preventing health problems from arising, the District will release resources to help resolve other deserving problems. The following example looks briefly at one such initiative taken in Hull.

The healthy cities initiative – Hull

There is an increasing body of evidence that links health problems to the long-term consumption of an unhealthy diet. This problem particularly affects poor and elderly households because they may not have access to healthy foods, either because they are unable to get to shops which stock healthy food, or they cannot afford to buy these foods.

During 1990, the Hull Health Authority initiated a project to improve the range of healthy foods readily available to everyone within the area. A working party, chaired by their Health Authority dietician, began a project to improve the range of healthy foods available at competitive prices from inner city and local shops.

Having drawn up a list of the basic foods required for a healthy diet, they approached a local chain of stores to ensure these products were available. Any store which stocked the range of products at competitive prices would be permitted to display the project logo and would be provided with a stock of health education leaflets, and recipes for healthy meals. It is hoped that continued investment in this type of prevention activity may ultimately reduce the incidence of health problems in the area. (From *The Health Service Journal*, December 1990, 'Healthy Eating in Hull', by Lynn Holdridge and Jo Lancaster.)

The position of hospitals

In the face of restricted resources in the past, Health Authorities have implicitly 'rationed' access to health services by the lengthy waiting periods for treatment. Waiting lists are now regarded as a major indicator of how health services are performing, and Health Authorities have been working to ensure no patient needs to wait for more than two years for treatment.

If the population wants a comprehensive health service in which treatment is available at short notice then it may be necessary to increase Health Authority budgets. This is a political issue.

If budgetary constraints mean that services continue to be restricted, then it is important to focus the available resources on those with the greatest clinical need. Some Health Authorities are considering whether some of their existing services should continue to be provided at all. For example, the Nottingham Health Authority has recently taken the decision that it will no longer purchase vasectomy reversals or the removal of minor lumps, bumps and tattoos (reported in the 1991 Annual Report of the Director of Public Health for Southern Derbyshire). It is only possible to take this kind of decision once the authority has defined its health strategy, based on the needs of its patients and the resources available.

But have health service provider units fully explored the opportunities available from adopting a TQM approach to their activities? Ensuring each hospital provides the best possible service within the allocated budget is a Quality issue that can be tackled now.

Surveys within the Health Service show that the costs arising from inefficiency, waste, and unnecessary procedures may account for 25 per cent of health service expenditure. By improving performance in this area, NHS service providers may be able to release resources to care for more patients, and improve the service provided.

Saving these costs could free resources to reduce waiting lists; reduce waiting times at clinics; reduce pressure on staff; increase the time each doctor and nurse can spend with patients; and generally improve the service offered to patients. This is what the drive for continuous Quality improvement within hospitals is trying to achieve.

Hospitals already apply a range of monitoring systems linked to quality standards. These include professional, regulatory, legal, and informal or local procedures. However the monitoring systems are frequently unco-ordinated, and the absence of a structured approach significantly reduces the effectiveness of existing initiatives.

During 1989 a team from the York University Centre for Health Economics undertook a survey of quality initiatives in England and Wales. The results were reported in 'Questions of Quality' by Dr Roy Carr-Hill and Gillian Dalley (*The Health Service Journal*, 2 August 1990).

This survey showed that a number of District Health Authorities have promoted Quality initiatives in recent years. In a majority of instances these initiatives are directed by people with a nursing background. A wide range of professional groups was reported to be undertaking some quality related activities, with nurses and paramedics the most heavily involved categories. Relatively few doctors and senior managers appear to be involved. This is perhaps surprising in view of the fundamental importance of the active commitment by senior management to the success of continuous quality improvement programmes in industry. This may need to change if the full benefits of continuous quality improvement are to be realised.

Quality initiatives

In order to increase the application of quality management methods within the Health Service, the NHS management executive has introduced a programme of special funding to support a programme of quality initiatives. For example, it is making a total of £4 million available in 1991/2. The money has been allocated to four key areas:

- Total Quality Management (existing sites)
- primary health care

- accident and emergency services
- day case units

(*NHS Management Executive News*, April 1991)

A national award system has also been established for the benefit of the Health Service. The Hewlett Packard Healthcare Quality Award was announced in July 1991 by Bill Darling, NAHAT (National Association of Health Authorities and Trusts) chairman. This new award, which is open to all NHS staff, aims to encourage and reward measurable quality improvement projects in the NHS. Projects will be assessed by advisory panels. A national board will agree award criteria and present the prize of £10,000.

What do patients want from general medical hospitals?

A typical general hospital offers a wide range of health services to patients. These include:

(i)   Accident and emergency – treating the victims of accidents, or individuals requiring emergency treatment.
(ii) Medical treatment – applying tests to identify the causes of illness and providing appropriate treatment.
(iii) Surgical treatment – applying surgical procedures to treat health problems.

Patients may be treated as outpatients, admitted for day surgery, or they may require admission for a period of time for medical observations and treatment, or to enable the necessary surgical procedures to be performed.

In each of the above cases, patients have similar requirements of the NHS. Patients generally have realistic expectations of the NHS. They are generally prepared to:

(i)   Wait a reasonable period of time for an appointment to be arranged. The length of time a patient is prepared to wait depends on their problem;
(ii) Wait for a short period of time once they turn up at the clinic for their appointment (perhaps as long as half an hour), provided they are kept informed;
(iii) Accept that gourmet food is not served. But they do expect their food to be hot, what they ordered, nutritious and eatable! They also

expect a reasonably comfortable stay in hospitable surroundings and to be treated with respect as individuals whilst in hospital;

(iv) Accept that doctors and nurses cannot spend hours with each patient, provided they receive the appropriate medication and treatment. Many patients do expect medical staff to tell them about the problem they suffer from and to discuss the treatment they propose. This helps the patient to feel involved in these important decisions.

Patients are the principal consumers of the services provided by hospitals, but they are not the only customers whose requirements must be met. Other requirements which hospitals must satisfy include:

(i) An obligation to GPs to provide effective medical treatment for their patients;

(ii) A reasonable provision for visitors; and

(iii) A cost effective treatment from the perspective of the DHA.

As Quality standards in other industries improve, customers of the health service are increasingly expressing their requirements and expecting them to be met. In order to ensure they satisfy their customers, hospitals need to obtain reliable information on the requirements of their patients. There are two principal sources of this information:

(i) Patient surveys

Health Authorities may survey the opinions of the general public in a district, or of individual patients who have received treatment in a hospital.

Each of these types of survey can provide useful information for health service providers.

(a) A general survey in a district may identify requirements to guide health strategy. For example, a Mori poll in the Trent Region revealed the following key requirements for the health service locally:

- quicker access to GPs when they think they need it;
- more and better information on diagnosis and treatment choices;
- shorter waiting times; and
- less time wasted in outpatient departments.

(*NHS Management Executive News*, July 1991. 'Setting our sights on quality')

(b) Patient surveys may help determine the level of patient satisfaction with the service they have received. Patient surveys in Wandsworth revealed the lowest levels of satisfaction were for domestic services, information and parking facilities. The highest levels were recorded for medical and nursing staff and for clinical treatment and care ('Satisfaction guaranteed?', by James Raftery and Gerry Zarb, published in *The Health Service Journal*, 15 November 1990).

(ii) Analysis of patient complaints.

An interesting analysis of patient complaints is reported by Morris ('Aspects of Quality in Health Care' by B. Morris, *International Journal of Health Care Quality Assurance*, Vol. 2, No. 4, 1989, published by MCB University Press Ltd.). Here patient complaints received by one Health Authority over a period of 14 months have been analysed. The greatest number of complaints were recorded for the adequacy of treatment received. By applying Pareto analysis, Morris identified the Vital Few causes of patient complaint. These are illustrated in Table 9.4.

Type of complaint	Total Number	Percentage	Cumulative Percentage
Inadequate treatment	75	25.25	25.25
Unsatisfactory staff attitude	44	14.81	40.07
Unsatisfactory care	25	8.42	48.48
Poor/inadequate communications	19	6.40	54.88
Errors in procedure – discharge	15	5.05	59.93
Errors in procedure – communications	12	4.04	63.97
Failure to keep appointment time	11	3.70	67.68
Inadequate resource availability	10	3.37	71.04
Length of wait for treatment	9	3.03	74.07
Cancellations	7	2.36	76.43

Table 9.4 The Vital Few Causes of Patient Complaint

Each type of survey is important as it can provide a different type of information:

(i) Responses to a patient survey may focus on how patients were treated in hospital; typically highlighting administrative and domestic problems (as in the Wandsworth survey).
(ii) Customer complaints tend to focus on key areas of patient concern. Here, the quality of medical and nursing treatment is likely to be top of the list.

Using just one type of survey can produce a distorted picture of customer requirements and how well they are being met. A small number of cases of unsatisfactory medical treatment may not show up in a general customer survey for a number of reasons. However, this is the most important service requirement for most customers.

Continuous Quality Improvement – The Way Forward

The following sections describe how health service organisations can move forward by ensuring the continued improvement of performance. This can lead to improved customer satisfaction, reduced costs and greater employee morale.

Functional analysis – Understanding customer requirements and how to meet them

The first step towards quality improvement is to understand the requirements of every customer. Each customer will have different requirements.

It is then important to understand the role of each function within the hospital in terms of satisfying customer requirements, and how well these requirements are currently being met.

It is then possible to measure performance and set targets for improvement in key areas. This may involve a radical re-think of how tasks are carried out.

One recurrent complaint about the Health Service is the waiting time before treatment is available in hospitals. The waiting time may be caused by a number of factors, which include:

(i)   an inadequate number of bed spaces;
(ii)   insufficient theatre time; and
(iii) insufficient qualified medical staff.

A number of studies have identified means by which hospitals can assess whether or not they are achieving the most from the resources available to them. Some of the principal opportunities for improvement include:

Improving operating theatre usage time: At present, NHS hospitals frequently only schedule theatres for use on weekdays between 8.30am and 5.30pm. This leaves a scarce resource unused for considerable periods of time. This is not the case in the private sector where extended hours are part of the normal schedule. The scheduling for operations is frequently not co-ordinated centrally. As a result up to one third of regular sessions may not be used in some hospitals. Improvement in this area could greatly increase the number of patients operated on.

Improving bed utilisation: The national figure for bed occupancy rates is 75 per cent. Some nursed wards (ie wards which have not been closed) have an occupancy rate as low as 30 per cent. This inefficient use of available beds may be the result of having a fixed number of beds allocated to certain specialities or consultants. This can only be overcome by increasing flexibility and enabling beds to be used by the people who need them.

(Information taken from an article by Donald Light published in *The Health Service Journal*, 18 October 1990, 'Labelling waste as inefficiency'.)

Health Service hospitals can achieve a dramatic reduction in their waiting lists by applying a concerted effort. For example, Wexham Park Hospital, Slough, achieved a 25 per cent reduction in its waiting lists in 1990 by implementing a number of measures. Although some patients were taken off the lists after proper validation, the principal improvements stemmed from extra surgery sessions:

- Surgery sessions were regularly extended until seven o'clock and extra sessions took place on alternate Saturdays and statutory holidays.
- The number of day cases was increased. Gynaecology increased the number of day cases from 69 to 234 in a single year.
- Orthopaedics had a 'bunion' initiative dealing with all kinds of minor foot problems that might not otherwise have been treated for months.

The General Manager, Nigel Crisp, paid tribute to the support from all the staff at the hospital. Everyone was involved – consultants, medical records, secretaries and the central sterilising supplies department. In fact, the initiative could only succeed because staff wanted to do it. The initiative had a good effect on staff morale and social events were combined with some of the Saturday events. However he stressed that this level of activity is not something that can continue for ever because of the strains imposed on staff.

(*NHS Management Executive*, Issue 36, August 1990. 'No gimmicks-just sheer hard work')

Analyse the cost of quality
(i) Failure costs
Failure costs are incurred as a result of repeating activities, correcting

errors, and dealing with dissatisfied patients. These costs would not arise if the right activities were carried out right first time. Examples of failure costs include:

The time, expenses and overheads associated with:

- preventable health problems
- resolving customer complaints
- unnecessary, inaccurate or lost lab and X-ray tests
- absence of medical records, X-ray or test results during appointments
- malfunctioning or outdated equipment
- unnecessary medication
- medication and prescription errors
- correction of purchase orders
- time wasted by patients waiting for appointments
- patient failure to attend clinics
- high staff turnover and stress related illness/absence from work
- correcting incorrect treatment
- patient litigation

An analysis of failure costs is critical to the successful implementation of a quality improvement programme. However, the collection of failure costs is hampered by the belief that this information may be used by management as a basis for apportioning blame. The following quote from Juran (Juran, JM, 'Juran on Planning for Quality', *New York, NY, Free Press*, 1988) illustrates the negative impact this concern may have on attempts to collect failure costs, and the importance of making people aware of the positive reasons for collecting this data:

For years the hospital industry had only the vaguest idea of the extent of errors in the process of giving medication to patients. All hospitals posted rules requiring nurses to report medication errors promptly . . . however, in many hospitals the nurses had learned that when they made such reports they were often subject to unwarranted blame. Hence they stopped making such reports. In due course a classic study made by a qualified outsider showed that (1) about 7 percent of the medications involved errors, some quite serious, and (2) the bulk of the errors were management-controlled, not worker-controllable.

(ii) Prevention costs

Activities which lead to a better understanding of customer requirements, and ensuring these requirements are met right first time, are prevention activities. These activities are designed to eliminate errors and waste. Costs associated with prevention activities include:

The time and expenses associated with:

- health education – a focused programme making people aware of the health consequences of their lifestyle;
- education and training of employees;
- staff appraisal; and
- development of standard procedures for support services.

Having identified activities associated with high failure costs, it is possible to identify measures to prevent errors from arising in future. For example, the incidence of patients suffering from health problems arising from preventable causes might be targeted for long term reduction as a result of health education, progressive taxation measures and, for example, random breath testing for drivers.

Performance may also be improved by benchmarking the best practice for particular activities. Benchmarking techniques may usefully be applied to a number of activities undertaken by health service organisations, including:

(i)   The cost of specific surgical treatments;
(ii) Theatre usage time as a percentage of the seven day week;
(iii) Bed utilisation as a percentage of the seven day week;
(iv) The ratio between administration costs and total costs;
(v)   The length of stay in hospital for specific categories of patient. This information should be considered in the light of subsequent patient performance to ensure no adverse effects are suffered by patients.

The implementation of TQM in practice

A number of NHS organisations have taken steps to implement Quality Improvement Initiatives. Reports are published regularly in professional journals, and organisations are frequently willing to share their experiences. Here, two examples are given of Quality Management initiatives within the National Health Service:

(i) East Birmingham Hospital outpatients department; and
(ii) Initial steps taken by the Doncaster Royal Infirmary and Montagu Hospital Trust.

East Birmingham Hospital outpatients department

Outpatients departments have been a major source of patient dissatisfaction for many years. Patients frequently experience long delays in busy, noisy waiting rooms, and short consultations with a series of doctors and/or other clinical staff. Clinicians have been concerned that the unwieldy clinic sizes and varied case mix requires more professional attention than is feasible.

In 1989 the East Birmingham Hospital established an Outpatient Services Project Team to tackle these problems by introducing a Quality Management approach. By developing a mission statement, the team set out the agreed purpose of the department. Its next step was to define the principal functions of the department. These statements are recorded below.

East Birmingham Hospital outpatients department – mission statement

To provide the highest quality outpatient service to the patients of East Birmingham Hospital within the resources available. High quality services are appropriate, efficient and effective and are delivered through a partnership between clinical staff, support staff, managers and patients. The provision of relevant, accurate and timely information is a key to effective service provision. Specific objectives of the outpatients department are:

1. To facilitate specialist medical consultations, provide diagnostic and treatment procedures and advice to patients, their carers and general practitioners.
2. To recognise every patient attending the Department as a unique person with their own personality, cultural background, social responsibilities and physical and/or psychological problems. These facets together make up an individual, who is entitled to the highest standards of appropriate multi-disciplinary care to promote and maintain all aspects of his/her well-being.
3. To fully involve the patients in the giving and evaluation of care, enabling them to leave the Department with the knowledge and confidence to enhance/ resume their previous lifestyle or adapt to new circumstances.
4. To expand knowledge and to enhance practice and the environment of care by encouraging innovation and learning at every level.
5. To promote an atmosphere conducive to good performance by encouraging shared ownership and responsibility for quality assurance and by monitoring and evaluating locally supported service quality standards.

East Birmingham Hospital outpatients department – principal functions

1. The organisation of the service (resources; systems, staff) to provide safe and effective care to outpatients, reflecting the objectives of the Department and the needs of the people served.
2. The efficient and effective operation of the service by the provision of appropriate and safe facilities and equipment.
3. The provision of specialist consultation and advice to patients, their carers and the general practitioner or other source of referral.
4. The provision of in-service and continuing education programmes to all levels of staff to encourage training and development on issues relevant to the needs of the individual and the objectives of the service.

The team developed a co-ordinated approach to tackling its problems:

- Clinics were streamlined by altering their case mix to facilitate multi-disciplinary input.
- The mix of skills in the department was reviewed to enhance the roles of key nurses and ensure effective and efficient use of skills in clinics.
- Signposts, toilet facilities and other environmental improvements were implemented.
- The roles of support services and clinicians were defined and an interpreter service was developed.
- Staff training and appraisal procedures were established on a firm footing.

The project team knew that it was performing the principal functions outlined above. However, it did not have standards against which to measure its performance. As a result, the team developed a series of performance standards together with criteria for assessment of performance. An example of the performance standards (and associated performance criteria) relating to Principal Function One is illustrated below. These criteria can be progressively tightened up in order to achieve a steady increase in the overall quality of service provided to patients. Each of the performance criteria is measurable. Where necessary, monitoring systems have been introduced to enable staff to monitor progress.

Example of outpatient performance standards and the criteria for measurement

Principal Function 1: Standard 7
Patient appointments are individualised and offer choice and reliability to patients
Criteria:

7.1 All patients are given – individual appointment
                                          – choice of time of appointment

7.2 All patients seen in appointment order (except where patient's condition demands urgent attention)

7.3 Patients are seen in clinic by a doctor or other clinical staff within 15 minutes of the appointment time allocated.

7.4 Where in-clinic waiting times exceed 30 minutes beyond planned appointment times patients are informed of the reason for delay and expected projected waiting time.

(Information on Birmingham Outpatients department, based on research funded by the Institute of Health Service Management, as reported in *Health Services Management*, October 1991. Quality Assurance in Outpatient Departments by Angela Hopper.)

DONCASTER ROYAL INFIRMARY AND MONTAGU HOSPITAL TRUST
A CASE STUDY

Background

The Doncaster Royal Infirmary and Montagu Hospital Trust was formed in April 1991 to serve a large part of South Yorkshire. The Trust incorporates two hospitals: the large, modern Doncaster Royal Infirmary; and the smaller Montagu Hospital which has close links with the local community of Mexborough. The Trust employs some 3,500 staff: approximately 3,000 within the Doncaster Royal Infirmary, and 500 at the Montagu.

Each speciality within the trust has its own clinical directorate, with a clinical director who reports to the main Trust Board.

The Quest for Quality

David Nicholson, now Chief Executive, initiated the study into

Continuous Quality Improvement in November 1989, long before the Trust was formed. The impetus for this decision was twofold:

(i)   a number of staff were interested in the application of Quality principles to their activities; and
(ii) the NHS was showing an interest in how Quality could be applied to the Health Service and was looking for pilot sites.

David formed a steering committee to consider how to introduce Quality Improvements in the Doncaster hospitals. At the time they had no 'Quality experts' within the hospital and so they sought advice and assistance from external consultants, whilst ensuring the whole process was not taken over by an outside consultant.

The drive for the continuous improvement of Quality

The Trust has adopted a step-by-step approach to implement the Continuous Quality Improvement Programme. They felt a strong, structured framework was important as a foundation for the Quality Improvement Programme (QIP). This would enable them to keep a firm control over the process and help establish a feeling of ownership among hospital staff. The framework would also help guide their actions. Each step has been carefully planned in order to ensure it is fully owned by the clinical directorates.

The organisation for improvement

A steering committee meets regularly to oversee the Programme throughout the Trust. This committee determines the framework for the Improvement Programme; implements activities which are common to all Directorates (for example education); monitors the activities in each Directorate to ensure they stay on track; provides advice; and communicates information on successes and activities.

A QIT has been established in each Directorate to introduce quality improvements. The role of the QIT is to plan and implement the QIP within its Directorate. The clinical Director is responsible for the success of QIP within his Directorate. In some cases the Director is a member of the QIT. In others, the Director oversees the QIT by means of strong links with the QIT chairman.

A Programme Manager and a Project Co-ordinator have been employed by the Trust on a full-time basis to facilitate the Improvement

Programme. They have received an intensive 8-day external course on the Quality improvement process. They now act as advisors, facilitators and trainers to all the QITs and to the steering committee.

With only a small number of people who really understand the Improvement Process, the Trust recognised that it would be very difficult to move every QIT forward at the same pace. It therefore decided to use the Montagu as a pilot site. By investing resources in the early stages at the Montagu, it accelerated progress. It is now able to use the lessons learned, and the enthusiasm gained following early successes, to give extra impetus to the Improvement Programme at the larger Doncaster Royal Infirmary.

The Montagu is an ideal pilot site as it is relatively small and closely linked to the local community, with a strong commitment to customer service. It is led by Dr Richard Leigh who is actively committed to the continuous improvement of Quality.

Awareness – generating enthusiasm for Quality

In order to stimulate people's interest and generate a buzz of excitement about the Quality Improvement Process, the Steering Committee released a trickle of information in the few weeks prior to the 'Awareness week' which was used to launch the Programme. The awareness week incorporated:

- the launch of the Montagu Quality policy (see below)
- the publication of the Quality slogan and logo.
- a series of short seminars (45 minutes) to introduce people to the Programme. Although entirely voluntary, more than 95 per cent of staff attended this programme.

A varied programme of awareness measures has since been introduced in order to keep staff informed about developments. A Quality noticeboard has been sited just outside the dining area, with photographs of people who have been trained, and details of processes being improved, including measurements before and after the improvement process started. The hospital newspaper is used to reinforce the message of the Quality Improvement Programme. All communications on Quality use the Quality logo to ensure a common theme.

The mission statement: Doncaster's quality policy

We will provide an individual service which meets the patient's requirements and is timely, accurate and appropriate to personal and medical needs. Therefore activities of the whole service will be organised to fulfil this requirement. We will aim to promote an organisation culture that values staff by helping them to be confident, knowledgeable and in control.

Cost of non-conformance – counting the cost of error

One of the first activities undertaken as part of the Quality Improvement Programme was to estimate the costs being incurred as a result of errors and repeating activities. This was in line with other studies made in the Health Service and gives an idea of the scope for improvement in patient care and service as a result of more effective use of resources. A further estimate of Quality costs will be made once the programme has been under way for a significant period of time.

The cost of non-conformance (CONC) within the Health Service is a very sensitive issue, especially at a time when public spending is being tightly squeezed. To ensure staff become actively involved in improving Quality the organisation must state clearly why it wishes to gather the CONC. If hospitals use it to highlight errors and waste, and utilise the resources saved to improve the service which is provided to customers then the QIP is likely to flourish, even if this means some reorganisation of roles, activities and staff. If the CONC is used merely to identify areas where staff cuts can be made, with no thought for improvement in customer service, then the Quality initiative may wither and die.

Training – the bedrock for improvement

Having formed a QIT within each Directorate, the process really began to get underway with a one-day awareness seminar for all clinical directors. This made sure each Director understood the objectives of the Programme, how it would be implemented, and what was required from each of them to ensure its success.

QIT members and one additional person from each department have also been trained. These personnel are then responsible for planning, piloting and implementing the Programme within their Directorate. Each Directorate has formed an education team, which includes the Project manager and co-ordinator, which is responsible for training everyone else in the Directorate. This cascading of the education and training messages forms an important part of the team building programme, and helps everyone to understand and become actively involved in the Improvement Programme.

For most people this is the first time they have been on a training course with people from other disciplines (nurses, doctors, porters, catering staff). This has given them the opportunity to sit down and talk about problems which affect them all and which can only be solved by working together. It also represents the first time management has given them the power and opportunity to resolve problems and make improvements. The refreshing openness of discussions and willingness to change that comes from these training sessions is already beginning to yield improvements.

Measurement – monitoring the gains

The training sessions have been carefully tailored to be directly relevant to the activities at the hospitals concerned. Discussion sessions are used to identify areas where patients receive poor service, errors are made, and time or money is wasted. These problems are investigated and suggestions made for improvement. By introducing measurement charts, each group can evaluate the importance of problems and monitor the impact of corrective actions.

In some cases, problems are identified which the group cannot solve either because they are too contentious or too complex. These types of problem are referred directly to the QIT which prioritises them and forms action teams to investigate them and introduce corrective actions to eliminate them. Figs. 9.5–9.7 illustrate a few of the measurements which have been introduced. In some areas corrective actions have been introduced and improvements can be seen (for example, a reduction in the number of faulty water/saline bottles; see Fig. 9.7). In other cases, the measurements are being used to investigate the process in order to identify where errors or breakdown in performance occur so that corrective actions can be introduced.

Early successes

Until recently, activities requiring improvement have generally been identified by individuals and training groups rather than by management,

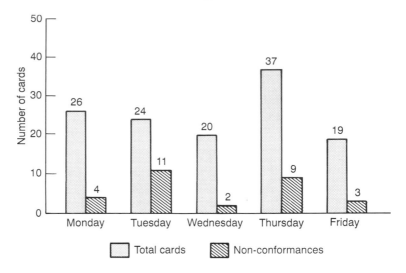

Figure 9.5 Non conformances: patient identification cards

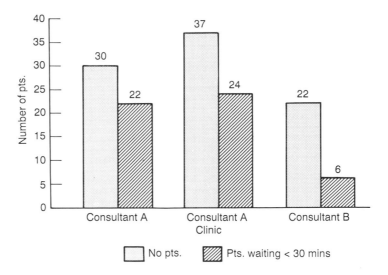

Figure 9.6 Clinics: waiting time

the Steering Committee, or by departmental QITs. The Project manager and co-ordinator are now focusing on identifying customer requirements. They intend to use this information as the driving force for the next phase of the improvement programme. The need to do this is already being seen as new contracts with their DHA and GP fund holding practices include

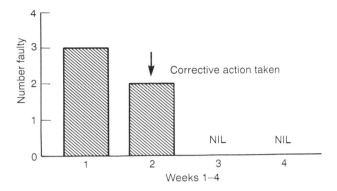

Figure 9.7 Sterile water/saline: numbers of faulty bottles

performance requirements. It is important that individual hospitals and Directorates understand these contractual requirements, are capable of meeting them, and can demonstrate, through measurement, that they have been met.

Two examples illustrate the range of problems addressed during the early stages of the QIP:

(i) *The number of incorrect meals delivered to patients:* this is a problem which seems to affect every ward within the hospital. The group has just begun to gather information to enable it to understand when, where and how often the problem arises; and who is involved in the processes giving rise to the problem. Any improvement in this area would directly improve the service provided to patients and would save the costs associated with chasing round to find the correct meals, throwing unwanted meals away and soothing upset patients!

(ii) *Elderly patients' knowledge about their treatment before discharge:* a number of the staff felt that some elderly patients were readmitted because they had not correctly taken their medication following an earlier visit. Improvements in this area would mean that patients would not require readmittance to hospital. This would improve the health of the patient, relieve pressure on bed space and save money which could be used to treat someone else. This action team is undertaking a survey of patients to determine how well they understand their medication so that this can be compared with subsequent readmission records.

Successes

Although the programme of Quality Improvement is still in its early stages at Doncaster, a number of improvements have already been made:

1. Attitudes have changed. Individuals now feel that if they work together they can change the way things are done and make improvements. Autocratic management styles are beginning to disappear, having been replaced by teamwork.
2. Clinical directors and consultants are becoming committed to the improvement of all activities which affect customers. They are responsible for success or failure of the Quality improvement process in the areas they control. All staff are developing an understanding and enthusiasm for Quality Improvement. The process of continuous quality improvement is gradually building up a momentum of its own.
3. Individuals now have the skills and the desire to talk to each other to solve problems. Everyone is starting to talk the same language, without recriminations and finger-pointing.
4. Communication between departments has improved. Departments are less insular and more aware of their dependence on others.
5. Measurements are being implemented and improvements made.
6. Internal customer requirements are being established.

Concerns

1. Achieving the active, demonstrated commitment of staff and management is a constant problem. They frequently want improvements in the Quality of services but do not have time to do anything themselves. The Quality Improvement process needs to be implemented from the top and cascade downwards if it is to achieve real, lasting success.
2. The need to understand and satisfy the requirements of external customers is paramount. External customer requirements must be fully understood. The role of each department must be established in terms of meeting external customer requirements if the Programme is to fulfil its full potential. Improvements in internal processes will yield some benefits; but all internal processes should be directed towards meeting external customer requirements.
3. The initial stages of introducing a Quality Improvement Process take a long time. It takes time to build a team of people who understand the process.
4. It is important to guard against unrealistic expectations about the speed in which benefits will be realised from a QIP.

5. Education and training is essential for all employees. The education programme should be realistic and directly relevant to the people being trained.
6. It is essential that the process does not become too dependent on a small number of experts. It is important to spread the knowledge about the process as widely as possible.

The way forward

The Quality Improvement Programme has now been established, and is beginning to yield results, particularly in improving relationships between functions. However, the improvements introduced so far have been driven, and implemented by nursing and support staff. These improvements can play an important role in improving the service provided to the patient, and reducing the hassles suffered by staff. They do not, however, tackle some of the big issues which could have dramatic impact on quality. These issues can only be addressed with the commitment and active support from the top. Issues which are receiving attention include, for example:

(i)   Understanding customer requirements for all the services provided by the hospital. Patients, GP's, visitors and the District Health Authority are all important customers for this purpose;
(ii) Defining the role each function in the hospital plays in terms of meeting those customer needs;
(iii) Assessing how well customer needs are being met, and identifying where improvements could be made. This will help the hospitals to set objectives for each of its functions.

A QUALITY REVOLUTION IN RETAIL BANKING

Introduction

The market for retail banking services is becoming ever more competitive. In this environment, the quality of customer service is becoming increasingly important as a factor in attracting and retaining customers. With the opening of the Single European Market in 1992, UK banks must move quickly if they are not to lose out to the increased competition from overseas. They must also seek to take advantage of the significant opportunities available in mainland Europe.

The importance of retail banking to major banks in the UK

Retail banking is one of the principal sources of profit for high street clearing banks in the UK. For example, TSB Group PLC recorded a profit of £353 million in the year ended on 31 October 1990. The retail banking division contributed 73.1 per cent of this amount. A summary of the group's results for this period is shown in Table 9.5(a).

Summary of results for the year ended 31 October 1990

	£ million	%
Profit/(loss) earned by:		
Retail banking	258	73.1
Insurance and investment services	114	32.3
Corporate banking	(40)	(11.3)
Commercial activities	21	5.9
	353	100.0

Table 9.5(a) TSB Group PLC

It is not always possible to identify the results of the UK retail banking activity for other major UK banks. However, it may be possible to gauge the relative importance of activities by identifying the proportion of total assets employed. Table 9.5(b) illustrates the assets employed in different activities by Lloyds Bank PLC at 31st December 1990. This shows that Lloyds Bank PLC employed 48.9 per cent of its total assets in retail banking in the UK market at that date.

Total assets employed at business units at 31st December 1990 (after deducting provisions for bad and doubtful debts)

	£ billion	%
UK retail banking	27.0	48.9
Corporate banking and treasury	14.4	26.1
International banking	6.7	12.1
Other	7.1	12.9
	55.2	100.0

Table 9.5(b) Lloyds Bank PLC

The UK retail banking market represents the principal activity for both of these major banking businesses.

Competition for the services traditionally offered by these banks in the UK is increasing rapidly from a number of directions:

- Building societies are increasingly offering banking services
- Department stores are offering credit cards
- Oil companies are offering petrol cards
- Banks which are authorised to provide services in one Member State may provide services in all the other EC Member States without further authorisation after 1992.

In view of the increasingly competitive nature of the retail banking market, it is vital for banks continuously to improve the quality of their service to customers.

UK banks must respond positively to the challenges imposed by increasing competition. They must identify the requirements of their customers, and provide a service which satisfies those requirements first time, every time. In order to minimise penetration by EC banks into the UK market, it will be necessary for the UK banks to provide services at a comparable price to those available from their EC competitors. This may involve a reappraisal of the cost of services provided to customers.

The Cecchini Report ('The cost of Non-Europe – Basic findings') found that there are significant differences in the cost of consumer finance between different EC Member States. For example, they reported that:

(i) Consumer credit was more expensive in the UK than in other EC countries (Table 9.5(c)); and

(ii) The UK was cheapest for the provision of mortgages (Table 9.5(d)). UK mortgages are also more widely available, with 100 per cent mortgages available, than in many EC Member States, where only 60 per cent mortgages are available. (In both Tables, the costs are measured as the average yearly rate of interest charged above market rates.)

Country	Cost
Belgium	2.3
Denmark	9.2
Spain	5.4
France	8.0
Luxembourg	2.8
Netherlands	5.1
UK	8.6

Table 9.5(c) Consumer credit costs by country.
Source: 'The UK banking industry and the Single Market', by Rob Dixon, *The Single Market Monitor*, September 1991.

Country	Cost
Belgium	1.92
Denmark	2.30
Spain	3.20
France	2.61
Italy	1.40
Netherlands	1.37
UK	1.16

Table 9.5(d) Mortgage costs by country.
Source: 'The UK banking industry and the Single Market', by Rob Dixon, *The Single Market Monitor*, September 1991.

Because of the freedom of access for foreign banks, and the lack of exchange controls, the domestic retail banking market in the UK is already highly competitive. By identifying opportunities for trading profitably in other EC Member States, UK banks may be able to expand their operations significantly. UK banks may be susceptible to competition from EC banks in some areas, and they may be in a strong position to compete in other areas. It is up to each individual bank to develop its strategy to take account of its strengths and weaknesses.

If they are to be successful in this venture, the UK banks will have to:

(i) Develop a strategy to enable penetration into selected markets in which the bank may trade profitably.
(ii) Understand the trading conditions in the overseas markets. There is considerable variation in the sophistication of the financial markets in different Member States. An interesting analysis of the payment systems and services available in EC Member States is set out in 'The UK banking industry and the Single Market' in *Single Market Monitor*, September 1991.
(iii) Develop a strategy to gain access to customers in the market sectors chosen as a vehicle for penetration. A comprehensive retail banking operation requires an extensive network of branches or offices. Other services, such as consumer credit services, do not require an extensive branch network, and so can be established without the same level of capital expenditure.
(iv) Identify and pursue opportunities for establishing relationships with overseas banks where these are advantageous.

Bank products and services

Retail banks provide a wide range of services to customers, including:

- current accounts;
- credit cards;
- deposit accounts;
- loans for major purchases such as cars and houses; and
- other services such as foreign exchange.

For each of these services, customers have a number of key requirements. The issues which may affect a customer's decision whether or not to do business with a particular bank may be summarised as follows:

Products – the terms attached to the current account, deposit account, loans, credit card, trust and other services banks provide for customers.

Customer service – the additional help banks provide their customers including account and other enquiries, customer references and resolving problems.

Service facilities – the physical environment banks provide for customers to access the bank's services, including the branch network, Automatic Teller Machines and electronic banking facilities.

Service manner – The behaviour of the bank's personnel towards customers when they visit the branch or telephone in. Considerations include friendliness, courtesy, promptness and patience.

Each of these characteristics may influence the customer's decision to open a new account.

What are the key objectives for a successful retail bank?

The key objective of any business is to maximise its profitability. For a successful retail bank, this strategy may be achieved by:

- retaining existing profitable business from existing customers;
- cross-selling products to existing customers; and
- winning profitable business from new customers.

Although customers are becoming increasingly sophisticated, these objectives are unlikely to change. However, banks are likely to find customers are more discerning and will shop around for the best deal when entering major transactions such as home loans. If they find another bank which offers a better service than their existing bank then they may well transfer all their accounts to it.

How do banks win new customers?

Until recently, customers have frequently only held accounts with one bank. In many cases, customers open their first account when they start work or further education. As a result, they may only take a short term view about the services they require from a bank.

In practice, customers may not invest much time deciding with whom they will open their first bank account. Frequently customers will open an account with the same bank as their parents; the bank around the corner because it is convenient; or with a bank recommended by a friend.

Having chosen a bank, customers may be reluctant to change to another, although they may change branches. This is not necessarily because they have great loyalty to the bank, or believe they get a better service than they would elsewhere. One of the principal reasons for not changing banks is the hassle associated with the change. The barriers confronting a customer who seeks to change their bank include:

(i)   surveying the market for a better package deal;
(ii)   closing the existing account and cancelling existing arrangements (such as direct debits and loans);
(iii) negotiating new loan and overdraft arrangements;
(iv)   opening a new account;
(v)   reinstating direct debit arrangements; and
(vi)   informing employers and other interested parties of the change.

As a rule, people do not generally change banks at present unless they have suffered a very poor level of service, or if they can secure a better package deal from another bank for the services they require. If a bank could reduce the effort required to move bank accounts, then it might receive an increased inflow of customers, provided it offered a better overall service level.

Once a bank has secured a new customer, it has been traditionally quite difficult for another bank to attract them away. However, a number of customers now hold more than one account. Banks may increasingly use this as a basis to help prise further work from customers. As customers become more sophisticated and discerning about the quality of service they require they may become more inclined to change banks if they are not satisfied with the service from their existing bank. As a result, banks must work increasingly hard to keep their existing customers. Providing the services their existing customers require is the key to success. Servicing their existing customers and attracting profitable new lines of business from them may well represent the bulk of the continuing businesses for many banks.

However, it is also important for banks to try and attract profitable new business from new customers. There are generally two sources from which a bank can gain customers:

1. Attracting new customers who have never previously held a bank account; and
2. Attracting customers dissatisfied with the service from other banks.

The most effective form of communication with potential new customers is through an existing customer. Word-of-mouth communications are more likely to increase bank patronage than an advertisement (Skern and Gould, 'The Consumer as Financial Leader', *Journal of Retail Banking*, Vol X No. 2, 1988). A positive message will only be given if the customer receives outstanding service from their bank. Advertising may be useful for bolstering corporate image, but its effect on sales is unclear or slight (Hay and Morris, *Industrial Economics, Theory and Evidence*, Oxford University Press, 1979), especially as all institutions advertise heavily. In a US survey, only 20.9 per cent of respondents rated financial institutions' advertisements as informative.

What do customers look for in a retail bank?

(The information in this section is drawn from 'Customer Service Strategies in Financial Retailing' by Su Mon Wong and Chad Perry, *International Journal of Bank Marketing, Vol.* 9, No. 3, 1991).

The factors customers consider important in the decision to choose a bank account have changed in recent years. In the 1970s, convenience of access to a branch was the single most important factor for selecting a bank (Meidan, 1984 *Bank Marketing Management*, Macmillan, London). Although still important to customers, the competitive advantage of location has now largely been lost with the expansion of the branch networks of most major UK banks.

Retail banking is a market where the development of new products does not appear to play a significant role at present. Competitive advantage from new products usually only lasts no more than six months. For example, the Bank of Melbourne introduced a cheque book for left handed individuals. This type of new product is very easy to copy, and the competitive advantage is rapidly eroded.

The key to marketing in the financial services industry now is 'customer service' (Lewis, 'Service quality in the financial sector', *International Journal of Bank Marketing*, Vol. 7, No. 5, 1989). One US survey of 1,500 customers found that:

(i)   44 per cent rated 'ease of doing business' as the principal factor in choosing a financial institution.
(ii) 28 per cent rated 'quality of personal service' as the principal factor.

These two service-related factors clearly were more important than other factors such as location (Skern and Gould, 'The consumer as financial leader', *Journal of Retail Banking*, Vol. x, No. 2, 1988).

Why do customers change the banks they do business with?

Two-thirds of customers who stop doing business with an particular organisation do so because they have received poor service (LeBoeuf, *How to Win Customers and Keep Them for Life*, Piatkus books, 1990).

An Australian study of factors influencing the decision to switch financial institutions provides an interesting insight into the requirements of customers. The five principal factors affecting the decision to switch were:

(i)   convenience of branch location;
(ii)   poor counter service;
(iii) disrespectful staff attitudes;
(iv)   excessive questioning and hassles by staff; and
(v)   niggling penalties and charges.

Customers are now increasingly looking for a high quality of service from their bank. The core qualities of a high quality banking service are detailed in Table 9.6.

What are the implications of this to retail banks?

Attracting a new customer to replace a lost one takes five times as much effort, time and money as it would have taken to keep an existing one (Seller, *Getting Customers to Love You*, Fortune, 13 March, 1989).

One dissatisfied customer will tell 25 other people. Thus 25 dissatisfied customers per month will tell as many as 7,500 other people a year about the poor service they received (Gattorna, 'Customer Service, cliche or clincher? *Marketing*, Feb/March, 1987). These comments may discourage the listeners from becoming customers. They may even encourage existing customers to seek a new bank if the comments

Core value	Operational response
1. Be responsive	• Identify customer requirements and take account of them when developing new services or improving existing services.
	• Reply to requests for new services, such as loans, sympathetically and promptly. If it is not possible to grant a loan or overdraft extension then ensure the customer is not given the impression it will be granted until a firm decision has been taken.
2. Be accessible	• Incoming calls should be routed directly to the appropriate employee who has responsibility for handling the enquiry.
	• Incoming calls should be answered promptly, perhaps by the fourth ring;
	• If a customer leaves a message, this should be answered on the same working day.
3. Be credible	• Do not promise more than you can deliver.
4. Be courteous	• Do not keep customers waiting for meetings; for delivery of services (eg for replies to requests for a loan, a new cheque book, or for bank statements); at the counter; or at Automatic Teller Machines.
	• The bank premises should be kept clean and tidy.
	• Employees should always look neat and be considerate to customers and fellow employees.
5. Be competent	• Employees should know your products.
	• Employees should be trained so they are able to deal with customer enquiries effectively and promptly.
6. Understand your customers	• Employees should take time to learn your customers' requirements.
	• Services should be developed which respond to customer requirements.
7. Be reliable	• Do every job right first time
8. Be reasonable	• Consider the overall business with each customer when assessing charges for facilities such as very short term overdrafts of a few days.
9. Communicate	• Be able to explain services to different customers in language they can understand.
	• Do not overburden customers with details of services they are not interested in when sending letters to them. Consider sending a brief guide to the range of services you offer. Customers can then request details of services they are interested in.

Table 9.6 Core qualities of a high-quality banking service

(Details adapted from 'A cultural approach to developing service quality' by R. Eric Reidenbach and M. Ray Grubbs; Reprinted from *Bankers Magazine*, New York: Warren Gorham and Lamont. © 1989 Research Institute of America, Inc. Used with permission).

reinforce a poor impression already held by the listener.

Good customer service will foster growth because each satisfied customer will tell at least five other people about the business, some of whom will become customers (Seller, *Getting Customers to Love You*, Fortune, 13 March, 1989).

The opinion of customers is likely to be influenced most by the service which offers the poorest performance.

How can banks achieve a high level of service

A business will only achieve outstanding customer service if there is demonstrable commitment to this objective throughout the organisation, starting from the top.

Although driven from the top, a high quality of service can only be achieved if all employees are involved: the key employees are those who are in day-to-day contact with customers.

> Banks that develop satisfied customers get new employees off to the right start with an effective orientation programme and then coach them through the learning curve. Supervisors stay in touch with the day-to-day problems of their employees and help to solve them; they give regular and positive feedback, and hold people accountable for results.
>
> Senior managers take customer service seriously and empower employees to do whatever it takes to resolve customer problems and to provide prompt service. They eliminate bureaucratic obstacles to good service and solicit employees' viewpoints on service delivery. They are highly visible, not just vocal, in their leadership on customer service issues.
>
> These banks are pleasant and efficient places to work. Crises are kept to a minimum and people are treated with respect. Employees serve internal customers as well as they serve external ones.

The authors of this article stress that although their findings do not indicate a causal link between satisfied customers and satisfied employees, such things as positive supervisory relationships, competitive pay and benefits, and a work environment relatively free of excessive pressures are not inconsistent with good customer service.

(from 'In search of excellent customer service', Jeffrey W. Jones, *Bank Management*, February 1991).

Where can banks obtain information about the requirements of their customers?

(i) An independent customer survey in the UK

In October, 1991, *Which* magazine published the results of a survey of 5,000 of their members on bank and building society current accounts. The responses, from the 2,786 who replied, make interesting reading in the increasingly competitive retail banking sector. Perhaps the key finding was that more than 10 per cent of customers were not happy with the level of service. This is more than twice the level in the 1990 survey.

This finding represents a tremendous opportunity for the banks and building societies which are best able to satisfy their customers. It also represents a critical threat to those businesses which are perceived as providing the worst service.

The main areas of complaint for most customers are as follows:

(i)   Errors in carrying out instructions, or instructions not followed. Almost 20 per cent of replies to the *Which* survey reported errors in standing orders or direct debits.
(ii) High charges which appear on bank statements without warning or explanation.
(iii) Bounced cheques.
(iv) Queues at the bank.
(v)   Empty or inoperative cash dispensing machines.
(vi) Not sending out bank statements sufficiently frequently.

(ii) The annual report of the Office of the Banking Ombudsman

The Report by the Office of the Banking Ombudsman also provides valuable information to help enable retail banks to understand the problems faced by customers. The report provides details of the complaints received during the year. These are divided into two categories:

(i) 'Mature' complaints are those for which the bank's complaint procedures have been exhausted. In this case, the bank and the customer have reached a deadlock and the case is taken up by the Office of the Banking Ombudsman.
(ii) 'Immature' complaints are those for which the bank's internal complaint procedures have not been exhausted. The Bank Ombudsman is not permitted to consider these issues under the terms of the Banking Ombudsman scheme.

	Number	%
ATMs (Automatic Teller Machines)	286	38.4
Negligence	72	9.7
Lending	45	6.0
Charges and interest	34	4.6
Dormant accounts and destroyed records	32	4.3
Cash dispute not ATM	31	4.2
Account errors	29	3.9
Cheque guarantee cards	28	3.8
Mortgages	28	3.8
Credit/debit cards	24	3.2
Direct debits/standing orders	21	2.8
Unauthorised debits not ATM	16	2.1
References	12	1.6
Dishonour, unwarranted	11	1.5
Confidentiality	10	1.3
Foreign currency and travel	10	1.3
Securities for advances	9	1.2
Investment	8	1.1
Multiple complaints	5	0.7
Miscellaneous	35	4.6
	746	100.0

Table 9.7 (a) 'Mature' complaints received in the year to 30th September 1991

What are the factors which banks should consider measuring and monitoring?

Having identified the key service requirements of their customers, it is necessary for banks to measure their performance against key service criteria. The following are examples of measurements which can readily be introduced by retail banking businesses to assess their existing performance. Banks may then determine targets for performance. Improvements can be measured against these objective criteria.

(i)   The time spent by customers in queues at the counter:

   ● at peak business times;
   ● on average.

(ii)   The time spent by customers queuing at ATMs:

   ● at peak business times;

- on average.

(iii)   The convenience of access to ATMs:

- on wet days;
- room to form a queue without inconveniencing other pavement users, or other nearby businesses;
- near to shopping centres.

(iv)   The time taken to respond to letters from customers.

	Number	%
Charges and interest	1,004	15.9
Lending	883	14.0
ATMs (Automatic Teller Machines)	667	10.5
Account errors	435	6.9
Negligence	429	6.8
Credit/debit cards	398	6.3
Cheque guarantee cards	306	4.8
Mortgages	299	4.7
Direct debits/standing orders	190	3.0
Miscellaneous	182	2.8
Unauthorised debits not ATM	158	2.5
Investment	146	2.3
Opening/closing of account	135	2.1
Foreign currency and travel	112	1.8
Securities for advances	111	1.8
Insurance	107	1.7
Registrar business	106	1.7
Discourtesy/delay	104	1.6
Dishonour, unwarranted	95	1.5
Dormant accounts/destroyed records	93	1.5
Cash dispute not ATM	84	1.3
Confidentiality	83	1.3
Executor/trustee and tax	64	1.0
Multiple complaints	61	1.0
References	30	0.5
Defamation	18	0.3
Safe deposit/custody	17	0.3
Fraudulent misrepresentation	10	0.2
	6,327	100.0

Table 9.7 (b) Types of 'Immature' complaint received in the year to 30th September 1991

(v)   The time taken to respond to telephone requests from customers. This requires the use of procedures to ensure customer requests are recorded and actioned. A letter should normally be issued to confirm arrangements.

(vi)   The number of errors made whilst processing cheques.

(vii)   The number of accounts closed at each branch each week or month.

(viii) The number of customer complaints received each month.

(ix)   The number of customer complaints satisfactorily resolved each month.

(x)   A comparison between the true cost of temporary overdrafts taken by customers and the charges levied on them. This will help to identify niggling bank charges.

What are banks doing to improve the quality of the service they provide to customers?

In order to retain their existing customers banks are putting considerable efforts into improving the quality of their service. This section explores the steps taken by two UK retail banks, and illustrates the type of service which may be available in the future under a service guarantee scheme.

National Westminster Bank PLC

The National Westminster Bank embarked upon a programme of quality improvement in 1987 which built on the success of an earlier campaign launched in 1983. The aim of this programme was to retain its leading position in the market by differentiating itself from the competition as a result of service excellence.

In 1988, NatWest estimated that up to 25 per cent of its operating costs were the result of not completing activities right first time. This included the cost of having to repeat activities, and correct errors. For example, replying to a letter of complaint may involve a number of people. The circumstances giving rise to the problem must be researched, and then the problem has to be resolved. This activity would not be necessary if the error had not been made in the first place.

NatWest is working towards identifying the cost of quality at the branch/unit level. This provides a base level from which improvements in efficiency can be made, and actions can be prioritised so that services can be improved, and unnecessary costs eliminated.

The overriding objective is to achieve direct improvements in performance by focusing on reducing failure costs.

The quality improvement process is driven by answering the following three questions:

(i)   Are we doing the right thing?
(ii) Are we doing things right?
(iii) What actions can we take to continue to seek improvement?

NatWest involves all management and staff in the quality improvement process. Whilst recognising the need for central solutions, local flexibility allows employees to gain increased ownership of the quality issue

This illustrates the spiral of continuous quality improvement.

(i)   First, identify your customers' requirements through market research and customer surveys;
(ii) Determine your present performance through customer surveys.
(iii) Compare your performance to that of your competitors using competitor analysis.
(iv) Establish world class performance targets as a result of benchmarking. This enables a business to set new performance standards.

(The information for this illustration was drawn from 'The case for costing quality', published by the Department of Trade and Industry as part of their programme 'Managing into the 1990s').

TSB – Retail Banking and Insurance
Background
TSB Retail Banking and Insurance employs approximately 28,000 people, many of whom are professional staff, in 1,400 branches throughout the country. The division is responsible for personal banking activities and banking for small and medium sized companies. It operates a comprehensive branch network ranging from small village branches to large city branches together with a central support function.

In the year ended 31 October 1990, the TSB Group made a profit of £353 million. At that time the Retail Banking Division contributed £258 million (73.1 per cent) of this profit.

The Decision
The retail banking division came into being towards the end of 1989 as

part of the re-structuring of the group. Following initial restructuring, the division's chief executive, Peter Ellwood decided to investigate the benefits which could result from implementing a Quality Improvement Programme. The three key objectives for the programme are:

1. To improve customer satisfaction. This would benefit the division by:

   - helping to retain existing customers;
   - attracting new business from existing customers; and
   - attracting new customers to the bank;

2. To save money as a result of eliminating errors; and
3. To improve the morale and motivation of employees. This would help by improving productivity and reducing staff turnover.

The Human Resources Director, David Owen, was appointed to investigate and implement a continuous Quality Improvement process.

The Mission

The Mission statement of the Retail Banking Division sums up its attitude to Quality, its ambitions and its determination to succeed:

> To be the UK's leading financial retailer through understanding and meeting customer needs and by being more professional and innovative than our competitors.

Planning

In view of the importance attached by management to the success of the programme, the planning process took a year to complete. This demonstrates the importance management places on getting the framework right before embarking on the road toward the continuous improvement of quality. Adequate planning at the outset of a programme of quality improvement is essential if an organisation is to succeed. At the TSB, this process has involved the following principal activities:

1. Investigating the whole field of Quality; the philosophy, the techniques available, organisations which have succeeded and how they have done it.
2. Understanding the culture of the company and how the philosophy could be adapted so everyone would feel comfortable with the methodology and follow it.
3. Understanding the methodologies available, their strengths and

weaknesses; and which could be best adapted to work within the organisation.

4. Investigating customer requirements so that the Programme implemented would strengthen the customer offering. This was done by surveying the requirements and perceptions of over 9,000 customers and monitoring how they subsequently managed their accounts; taking particular notice of reasons for opening and closing bank accounts. In this way the bank was able to identify the key requirements and perceptions which encouraged customers to make increased use of the services from the bank. These findings were built into the Improvement Programme.

5. Carrying out competitor analysis to determine the performance of the TSB against the competition in key areas.

6. Carrying out a cost of non-conformance survey to identify the potential gains which could be made through the implementation of TQM.

7. Carrying out a staff survey to determine attitudes to Quality, what they felt about current performance and how well they felt the bank met customer needs.

8. Pulling together all the market information available on recruiting and retaining customers, reasons for customer loyalty and reasons for account closures.

Having made an in-depth study of Quality, how it could be implemented within the TSB and the benefits it could bring in terms of retaining and recruiting customers, reducing operating costs and improving job satisfaction, the project was presented to the Board of Directors and given the go-ahead to continue.

Implementing Total Quality Management
The TSB decided to implement its own Improvement Programme drawing on established methodologies and adapting these to fit the TSB culture. A project plan was developed to control the implementation of each step. The first step was to train the Directors and introduce a structure and plan for implementation. The step which required the most effort was the measurement step. The key objective here was to identify key measurements which would have a direct impact on customer satisfaction.

In order to ensure the branches would hit the ground running instead of gradually building up momentum, a great deal of effort was spent before the Programme was launched stirring things up and generating enthusiasm for the Programme. This was achieved by a carefully selected combination of approaches: newsletters, videos, press cuttings, and presentations.

Once training began to be rolled out through the branches people were ready and waiting for it; this created a dynamic start to the process which fed on itself and was backed up as quickly as possible with successes. Generating interest beforehand and subsequently publicising successes was felt to be an essential part of giving the process momentum so that it would begin to perpetuate itself.

Since the end of June 1991, 4,000 people have been trained, with a plan to complete the training of existing staff by April 1993. Although still in the early stages, the TSB is already beginning to see some significant improvements in its ability to meet customer requirements and in the way it runs its business.

Service guaranteed – a new approach to banking service

In December 1990, there were more than 20 banks worldwide that either offered guarantee programmes or were committed to providing perfect service. Although many banks do not offer guarantees for their services – perhaps because they do not believe a service can be guaranteed – the provision of a guarantee may force a bank to confront the problems resulting in poor service, and produce outstanding service for customers.

In February 1990, First Interstate Bank of California sent out roughly 40,000 bank statements that were missing the figure for accrued interest. At that time, First Interstate was four months into a service guarantee that, among other things, promised customers perfect service. Every customer who received a statement which did not show the accrued interest could now claim US$5 for the bank's mistake. The error represented a US$200,000 potential liability.

The bank sent a letter to all affected customers, apologising and notifying them of the mistake. The bank paid all the customers who requested their US$5. However, very few people actually made the claim – perhaps because the bank notified them and they were not significantly inconvenienced by the error. The Vice President for sales and service is reported as saying: 'People want us to deliver the level of service that we promise, not the $5 that comes when we make a mistake. The payout is something they deserve if we don't deliver the level of service they expect from us.'

Features of a successful guarantee

In order for a service guarantee to be attractive to customers, it should be:

(i) Unconditional – or conditions should be simple. A five minute waiting pledge might require that customers wait inside the bank building during normal business hours.

(ii) Easy to understand – the guarantee should be specific and clear so that both employees and customers know what to expect. A promise that service will be provided in five minutes can be monitored. A promise of prompt service can not.

(iii) Meaningful – Maryland National Bank's 'Performance Guarantee' gives an example of the sort of terms customers expect from a bank which cares about its customers. This guarantee provides that if the bank makes a mistake in a customer's account it will give the customer $10; absorb any overdraft charges; apologise in writing to the customer; and apologise in writing to any third party affected by the mistake.

(iv) Easily invoked – if a customer has suffered from poor service then complex complaint procedures will only exacerbate the problem, and may result in the loss of the customer.

(v) Easily fulfilled – if a customer invokes a guarantee, then immediate corrective action may produce a satisfied customer.

A guarantee that is severely limited in scope and difficult to use is unlikely to be effective. Guarantees that offer recompense only if the customer closes their account do nothing to:

(i) improve the bank's service;

(ii) retain the customer's business; or

(iii) minimise damage to the reputation of the bank in the event of an error. An unsatisfactory, complicated procedure is likely to lead the aggrieved customer to complain to friends and colleagues.

Banks that promise perfect service do not appear to have been excessively hard hit by guarantee payouts.

The provision of service guarantees is not very widespread at present. However, they do represent an effective means of demonstrating to customers and employees the commitment by the bank to service quality.

Offering this type of guarantee is unlikely to be expensive for a bank which already achieves a high level of service quality. However, such a guarantee may be costly for a bank which only offers a poor service to customers at present. The principal benefits of a service guarantee include:

(i)   It demonstrates a commitment to customers that the bank will strive to provide a service which meets certain pre-determined criteria. If these criteria are not met, then the bank will make some form of restitution to the customer.

(ii) It focuses the attention of all employees on the continuous improvement of service quality.

(iii) It encourages management to identify the key service requirements of their customers. Performance against these criteria is likely to be the most effective means of satisfying customers.

The prospect of offering a service guarantee may be daunting for banks. However, they may provide a clear competitive advantage if employed effectively. They can also provide a focus for a strategy directed towards providing outstanding customer service.

(Based on information from 'An objective look at unconditional service guarantees', Christopher W. L. Hart. Reprinted from *Bankers Magazine* (New York: Warren Gorham and Lamont). © 1990 Research Institute of America Inc. Used with permission.

10 WHAT CAN WE LEARN FROM THE QUALITY GURUS?

INTRODUCTION

'Total Quality' is a systematic approach to quality planning and the management of activities. The underlying concepts were first conceived in the US in the late 1940s, by quality practitioners, such as W. E. Deming and J. Juran. After the Second World War, these principles were rapidly embraced by the Japanese during the rebuilding of its industry. At this time a number of American quality 'gurus' spent a considerable amount of time in Japan teaching the philosophy and techniques of quality control.

During this period, consumer demand in the West was so great that product quality did not seem particularly important, and so it was not clearly addressed by industry. However, in the 1960s and 1970s, US industry increasingly began to focus attention on quality issues. The drive for this quality revolution stemmed, primarily, from the demands of the military and related customers. Only later did the principles percolate through to consumer products.

In the UK, the drive towards increased quality has been late in starting. The Department of Trade and Industry took a lead in raising awareness within industry in the early 1980s with the following important initiatives:

- 1982 White Paper on standards, quality and international competitiveness.
- 1983 national quality campaign directed towards BS5750.
- 1989 'Managing into the 1990s' campaign, focusing on the understanding and implementation of Total Quality.

THE WORK OF THE QUALITY GURUS

A relatively small group of American and Japanese quality experts have developed a number of concepts and methodologies which have had a profound impact on how companies approach and manage quality. These experts are frequently referred to as quality 'gurus'. In addition to developing their own quality philosophy, many of the gurus are charismatic individuals who generate excitement and enthusiasm for quality.

Each expert has a different perspective and approach to quality, which depends in part on their business or professional background. Although there are differences in approach, there is also much common ground between the approaches of all the gurus. The common commitments of all the gurus include the following:

(i)   Quality is the key to a successful business. Inadequate attention to quality will lead to the failure of the business in the long run.
(ii) Quality improvements require the full commitment of management to succeed. This commitment to quality must be continuous. Once made, it will quickly be seen to be worthless if, for example, product is shipped although it does not conform to requirements.
(iii) Quality improvement is hard work. There are no short cuts or quick fixes. Successful quality improvement frequently requires a change in culture for the whole organisation.
(iv) Quality improvement always requires extensive training.
(v)   Successful quality improvement requires the active involvement of all employees, and absolute commitment from senior management.

The methodologies of most of the gurus focus on a basic underlying philosophy together with tools and actions to effect quality improvement. Some of the experts focus on particular tools for quality improvement in specific areas, while others consider the business as a whole.

Each of the gurus can provide an important insight into the way to tackle problems and implement quality improvement in practice. Some of the philosophies are more accessible than others. Perhaps the most accessible guru, world-wide, is Philip Crosby. Philip Crosby has written a number of books on quality management. He has also founded Crosby Associates, which is now a worldwide quality consultancy specialising in the practical implementation of quality improvement methods. Although Crosby Associates follows the Crosby methodology, it tailors the implementation of quality improvement programmes to ensure its clients take ownership of them.

Other gurus, such as Deming, have written extensively on quality issues, and give talks and lead training seminars. However, Deming does not have an associated consultancy with a standard methodology to implement. The Deming approach appears to be that there is no methodology to 'install'; the only way to succeed is for the company to work out an approach that fits the organisation's own culture and language.

For most companies the most appropriate approach is to take account of the ideas of the gurus and adapt these to suit the culture of the organisation. Companies frequently find it helpful to take advice from external quality consultants during the implementation process. However, a business can only obtain a long-term benefit if it takes ownership of the Quality Improvement Programme. This approach may take longer, and require greater perseverance and experimentation to implement successfully, than to rely on the approach put forward by any one of the gurus in isolation.

The remainder of this chapter describes briefly the key ideas of the principal gurus, and how they may be applied in practice. It is not possible to give a full description of the contributions and thinking of the gurus in one short chapter. There are a number of books available on each of the gurus which provide in-depth information.

PHILIP CROSBY

Crosby's quality experience was gained through working on a number of American missile projects and from 14 years' experience as corporate vice president, responsible for quality, within ITT.

His philosophy is underpinned by the four 'absolutes of quality' which answer the following fundamental questions:

1. What is Quality?
2. What system is needed to cause Quality?
3. What performance standard should be used?
4. What measurement system is required?

The Four Absolutes are:

1. Quality has to be defined as conformance to requirements, not as goodness nor excellence.
2. The system for causing Quality is Prevention, not appraisal.
3. The performance standard must be Zero Defects, not 'that's close enough'.

4. The measurement of Quality is the price of non-conformance, not indices.

These concepts have a wide range of supporters, although many people have difficulty accepting the concept of Zero Defects. It is sometimes portrayed as simplistic and unrealistic to expect individuals to perform every activity perfectly. It just will not happen. Crosby's explanation of Zero Defects is that it is not an exhortation to the work-force to do better but it is a management performance target. It is not meant to imply that errors will never happen, but that they should not be expected to happen. When errors do occur, they should not be accepted as inevitable. Prevention activities should be introduced to ensure errors do not occur.

Crosby believes that management is the cause of at least 80 per cent of the quality problems within an organisation. The only way to improve is through the leadership of management. To eliminate the many non-conformances which exist in an organisation, Crosby recommends administering a Quality Vaccine.

The Quality Vaccine

This consists of the following components, administered in equal measure:

(i)   Determination: management recognises that its action is the only tool that will change the profile of the organisation.
(ii) Education: helping all employees develop a common language of quality and understand their individual roles in the quality improvement process.
(iii) Implementation: guiding the improvement programme.

Building on the philosophy of the four absolutes and the components of the Quality Vaccine, Crosby recommends fourteen steps which any organisation can follow to achieve continuous quality improvement:

The Crosby fourteen steps to Quality Improvement

1. Management commitment
2. Quality improvement team to pilot the improvement process
3. Measurement of Quality throughout the organisation
4. Cost of Quality analysis throughout the organisation
5. Quality awareness of all employees
6. Corrective action implementation

7. Zero Defects programme planning to plan the commitment to Zero Defects
8. Employee education
9. Zero Defects day to make the Zero Defects commitment
10. Goal setting to target improvements
11. Error-cause removal to highlight and fix problems causing non-conformances
12. Recognition of those who make an outstanding contribution
13. Quality councils to co-ordinate improvement and share ideas across sites/divisions
14. Do it all over again

W. EDWARDS DEMING

Dr Deming is perhaps the most widely known of all the quality gurus. After graduating as a doctor of physics, he spent his early years as a US government employee. He spent most of this time with the Department of Agriculture and the Bureau of Census, where he specialised in statistical techniques.

Following World War Two, the US government played a significant role in rebuilding Japanese industry. It was in this role that Dr Deming first became involved in Japanese quality. Following his introduction of the concept of statistical quality control into Japan, the Japanese Union of Scientists and Engineers held a number of seminars to spread this knowledge throughout Japanese industry. Dr Deming was invited to participate in this lecture tour. This led to his long-term involvement in the development of Japanese management thinking on Quality.

Statistical quality control methods have been widely adopted throughout Japan and taken up with great enthusiasm by the work-force. In the early days Deming focused on statistical quality control methods. In later years he developed the concept of quality as a management activity.

Dr Deming has been recognised by the Japanese as making an outstanding contribution to quality in Japan. In 1960, he was awarded Japan's highest Imperial honour, the Second Order of the Sacred Treasure. Even today, Dr Deming's contribution is recognised in the annual awards made for outstanding application of statistical quality control throughout industry, the Deming Prizes.

Deming's major philosophy is that quality improvement is achieved through the statistical control of all processes (not just those involved with the product) and the reduction in variability of these processes. He emphasises that this can only happen if management allows it to happen by encouraging employee participation, and if employees are able to contribute through understanding processes and how they can be improved.

This management requirement is embodied in Deming's fourteen points for management.

Deming's fourteen points

1. Create constancy of purpose to improve product and service.
2. Adopt new philosophy. Management must accept responsibility and lead the change process.
3. Cease dependence on inspection; build quality into the product.
4. End the awarding of business on price. Instead minimise total cost of ownership.
5. Improve constantly and forever the system of production and service.
6. Institute training on the job.
7. Institute leadership and supervision of workers.
8. Drive out fear to improve the effectiveness of all employees.
9. Break down barriers between departments; all departments must work together to achieve results.
10. Eliminate slogans, exhortations and numerical targets.
11. Eliminate quotas or work standards, and management by objectives or numerical goals.
12. Remove barriers that rob people of their right to pride of workmanship.
13. Institute a vigorous education and self-improvement programme.
14. Put everyone in the company to work to accomplish the change in how the company works.

These fourteen steps summarise the management goals. Dr Deming has been highly critical of Western managers, viewing the way they work as totally counter-productive to quality improvement through employee involvement. He terms the key weaknesses in Western management style as the 'Deadly Diseases'. These include:

1. a lack of constancy of purpose;
2. emphasis on short-term goals (especially profits);
3. evaluation of performance, merit rating or annual review;
4. mobility of management; and

5. management only by the use of visible figures with no consideration for unknown figures.

In order to overcome the Deadly Diseases, Dr Deming proposed an action plan for management:

1. Management must understand and accept the fourteen points and the undesirability of the Deadly Diseases. They must then formulate an action plan for change.
2. Management takes pride in having taken this decision and develops courage to follow the new direction.
3. Management explains to everyone in the company why change is required.
4. Every activity within the company is divided into stages. The customers and suppliers of each stage are identified. Each stage should be improved continually and each stage should work together.
5. An organisation should be put together to guide quality improvement. Deming advocates the Plan, Do, Check, Action cycle when introducing any improvement.
6. Every employee can take part in a team to improve.
7. An organisation for quality is required (this requires the participation of statisticians to guide process improvement).

Dr Deming has written a number of books which provide information on his philosophy and methods. The British Deming Association (BDA) exists to help companies and individuals understand the Deming philosophies and how they can be applied in practice. They also co-ordinate the visits of Dr Deming to the UK. The only way to decide whether Dr Deming's philosophy has something to offer a company is to invest time to really investigate and understand his philosophy and how it can be applied.

JOSEPH JURAN

Joseph Juran is another guru of long standing. Like Deming, Juran was part of the early quality movement in Japan and participated in the lecture tours organised by JUSE. Unlike Deming, Juran's focus was on the management of quality. He believed that quality control was an integral part of management control. His view in the early 1950s was that the technical control of quality was well developed but there was no knowledge of how quality should be managed. The Juran approach was, therefore, focused on top and middle managers. He believes that the vast majority of quality problems are caused by management, and the only way to improve quality is through the participation of management.

Juran, like Deming, made an important contribution to the development of quality in Japan. This was recognised by the award of the Second Order of the Sacred Treasure by the Emperor of Japan.

In 1951 Juran drew together many of his ideas on the management of quality, together with information on the technical control of quality, into what is probably the best known quality book so far published: *The Quality Control Handbook*. New editions of this book are still regularly published and for many years it was regarded by many practitioners as the 'Quality Bible'. Later publications have focused on the planning and management of quality, rather than technical quality control. This reflects Juran's ever increasing commitment to the view that quality is an essential management discipline and that quality does not just happen, it must be planned. Quality control is important but it is only part of total quality improvement. Juran puts forward his 'quality trilogy' for total quality improvement:

1. Quality planning.
2. Quality control.
3. Quality improvement.

Overall improvement requires the implementation of each part of the trilogy. Juran proposes key activities for each part of the trilogy, particularly in the areas of quality planning and quality improvement.

His proposals for quality planning are:

1. Identify customers and their needs. This includes internal and external customers.
2. Translate the customer needs into the language of the company.
3. Set quality goals based on these needs.
4. Develop and optimise the product/service to meet those needs.
5. Develop and optimise the process which produces the product/service.

Having understood its customers' requirements, the organisation must continuously improve its ability to meet their current and future needs. In order to achieve this Juran recommends ten steps to quality improvement:

Juran's ten steps to quality improvement
1. Ensure all employees are aware of the need for quality improvement. This requires management leadership.
2. Set specific goals for the continuous improvement of quality in all activities.
3. Establish an organisation to ensure goals are set and a process for achieving them is established.
4. Ensure all employees are trained to understand their role in quality improvement. This must include upper management since they are the cause of most of the quality problems.
5. Ensure problems preventing quality improvement are eliminated by setting up problem-solving project teams.
6. Ensure quality improvement progress is monitored.
7. Ensure outstanding contributions to quality improvement are recognised.
8. Ensure progress and outstanding contributions are publicised.
9. Measure all processes and improvements
10. Make sure the continuous improvement of quality and the setting of new quality goals is incorporated into the management systems of the company. Make sure rewards are based on the results achieved.

This summary illustrates that the three principal Total Quality gurus have many ideas in common. However, they do have differences in approach, and so each guru has something to offer. Every company needs to identify the most appropriate approach for them. Each company is unique and so each improvement programme needs to be individually tailored. There is no one right way to succeed with continuous quality improvement.

THE JAPANESE QUALITY GURUS

Three Japanese gurus have made a significant contribution to quality improvement in Japan. Certain of their ideas have also spread to the Western world and are applied in specific areas. These gurus have developed techniques which can be used to effect quality improvements in specific applications. They have not generally developed a comprehensive programme of continuous quality improvement.

Shigeo Shingo

A graduate mechanical engineer, born in 1909, Shingo has spent time in industry, including the Taipei railway factory, Toyota and Mitsubishi shipbuilding.

Shingo has focused on the control of production quality, rather than the management of quality. Initially he concentrated on the concept of statistical process control. Later he developed the Zero Defects or Poka-Yoke concept. This concept is based on the theory that each process'may be continuously monitored at the point where potential errors could occur. Once an error has been identified, the process is stopped until the source of the error is identified and corrected. In this way, Shingo claims that errors can be prevented from becoming defects, and so defect free processes can be developed. The difference between poka-yoke and statistical process control is that the process parameters are monitored rather than the output of the process. In a poka-yoke system instrumentation, not humans, is generally used to monitor the potential sources of error, since it is less fallible than humans. The skill of the human is used to identify the potential sources of error and determine the best instrumentation to use to monitor these sources.

Kaoru Ishikawa

Born in 1915, Ishikawa is a graduate in applied chemistry and a doctor of engineering. He has spent his working life as an academic at Tokyo university, much of this time writing and working with Japanese industry on the introduction of quality control techniques.

The main focus of Ishikawa's work has been to make available statistical techniques for improving quality to grassroot workers within Japanese industry. Perhaps his greatest achievement was the successful introduction of quality circles into Japan. The success of the quality circle movement in Japan was greatly influenced by the user-friendly problem solving techniques which Ishikawa introduced. These enabled quality circles effectively to investigate problems, collect good data to identify their cause, and implement solutions to eliminate them and lead to improved quality. He also developed the cause-and-effect (or Ishikawa) diagram for use by quality circles. This is a diagram used to identify, sort and document the potential causes of a problem so that relationships between the causes can be identified.

Genichi Taguchi

Born in 1924, Taguchi gained his early experience in the Ministry of Health, Ministry of Education and the Institute of Statistical Mathematics. He later joined Nippon Telephone and Telegraph Corporation where he began to apply statistical techniques to improve the productivity of the R&D process. The publication of a number of books, the support of a number of well-respected American statisticians and visits to the United States have led to the application of Taguchi methods in American companies such as Ford, Xerox, ITT and Bell Laboratories. To date, his methods have made little impact in Europe. The UK Taguchi club, set up in 1987, exists to publicise and assist in the application of Taguchi methods in the UK.

Taguchi has developed three key ideas, which have proven controversial in the West:

1. The quadratic loss function.
2. Parameter design.
3. Statistically planned experiments.

Quadratic loss function
Taguchi has developed a unique definition of quality which underpins the rest of his philosophy. He defines quality as 'the loss imparted to society from the time a product is shipped'. This includes the loss to the company and the total loss to society caused by the product. This loss is defined mathematically as a quadratic loss function around the target value for the characteristic concerned. The minimum loss occurs at the target value, and the loss increases quadratically with variation from this target. This loss is minimised, and quality is optimised, when variation is minimised and the product is manufactured to the target value. Any item which varies from the target value may cause some problems and loss to the customer or society.

This differs from the traditional concept underlying quality management in the West, which holds that anything within the specification limits is equally acceptable to the customer whereas anything outside the limits is unacceptable. Taguchi has realised that, in reality, the further away the product is from the target value, the less acceptable it is. The specification limit is just the cut-off point at which the product becomes totally unacceptable.

This philosophy produces the same results as an SPC environment in which the objective is to reduce variability in output, as a result of controlling all processes.

Parameter design

Taguchi considers that the reduction in variability of output is best achieved by optimising product and process specifications during the design stage rather than through quality control methods such as inspection or SPC.

Careful design of the product, the parts used to produce the product, the processes, the equipment and settings used to produce the product, and the tolerances of both the parts and the process settings should ensure a robust product and process which is little affected by changes in external conditions. This is achieved by assessing the susceptibility of each parameter to external factors: its signal-to-noise ratio. The signal represents the required output from the process, and the noise represents how much the output is affected by external factors. Parameters and processes with the highest signal-to-noise ratio should then be selected as they produce the most robust designs.

Statistically planned experiments

A process which produces a part often has many parameters which can be varied. Changing any of the settings will affect the product. Experimentation to determine the correct setting for each parameter to optimise output can be an expensive and time-consuming task because many combinations may need to be considered. The Taguchi methodology, 'Orthogonal Arrays', is a mathematical technique which minimises the number of combinations, and consequently the number of experiments, which have to be carried out.

Although the Japanese gurus have a number of ideas to offer companies in specific areas of quality improvement, they are not so accessible as the ideas of their western counterparts. Companies should consider the ideas of the Japanese gurus, but only those techniques which fit the organisation and which have the potential for significant benefits should be adopted.

Footnote
    The authors wish to thank Professor Tony Bendell, East Midlands Electricity Professor of Quality Management and Director of the Quality Unit at Nottingham Polytechnic for permission to quote from 'The Quality Gurus; what can they do for your company?'; a booklet prepared by him for the Department of Trade and Industry's 'Managing into the 90's' programme on behalf of Services Ltd., Nottingham.
    The DTI publications are freely available in small quantities from DTI c/o Mediascene Ltd. (Tel 0443 821877).

INDEX